CYCLING IN THE FRENCH ALPS

By
Paul Henderson

2 POLICE SQUARE, MILNTHORPE, CUMBRIA LA7 7PY
www.cicerone.co.uk

ISBN-10 1-85284-445-0
ISBN-13 978-1-85284-445-5

A catalogue record for this book is available from the British Library.
All photographs, maps and route profiles by the author

Acknowledgements

This book would not have been possible without the support and enthusiasm of my wife, Alice.

Thank you to Claude, Marie-Christine, Simon, Richard, Jo and all my other friends who accompanied me on exploratory bike trips, stopping whenever asked to set up photos and take notes. I would also like to thank Jacques Leleu, journalist with the *Dauphiné Libéré*, for his help in checking facts and anecdotes in the newspaper archives.

A special mention must go to Tom Payne for his advice and proofreading skills, which have made this a better book than it otherwise would have been. Sandrine Rutigliano's research on the facilities available around Vinadio was also invaluable.

Finally, I would like to thank Pierre Lortet for his encouragement and for all the work he has done for cyclists in Savoie and around France.

Advice to Readers

Readers are advised that while every effort is taken by the author to ensure the accuracy of this guidebook, changes can occur which may affect the contents. It is advisable to check locally on roads, transport, accommodation and shops.

Please advise the publishers of any changes.

Front cover: Cycling up the Col de la Croix de Fer (Tour of the Ecrins and Grands Rousses)

CONTENTS

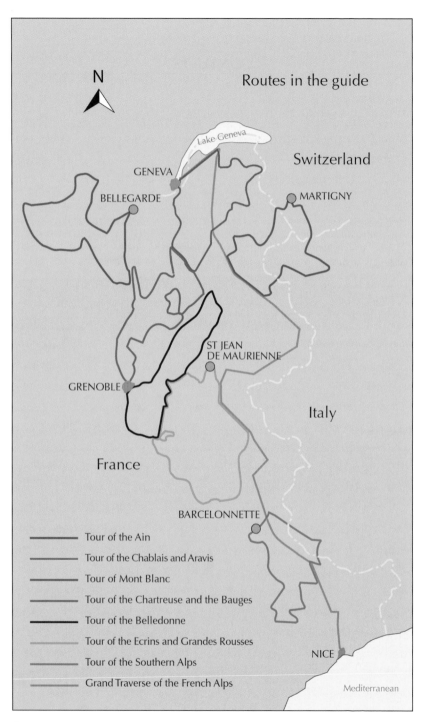

Routes in the guide

N

Lake Geneva

Switzerland

GENEVA

MARTIGNY

BELLEGARDE

ST JEAN
DE MAURIENNE

GRENOBLE

Italy

France

BARCELONNETTE

——— Tour of the Ain
——— Tour of the Chablais and Aravis
——— Tour of Mont Blanc
——— Tour of the Chartreuse and the Bauges
——— Tour of the Belledonne
——— Tour of the Ecrins and Grandes Rousses
——— Tour of the Southern Alps
——— Grand Traverse of the French Alps

NICE

Mediterranean

CYCLING IN THE FRENCH ALPS

About the Author

Paul Henderson was born in Durham in 1963. Despite a lifetime's passion for outdoor sports, he was a relative latecomer to cycling, buying his first bike at the age of 32. It was his wife, Alice, who talked him into this rash expenditure when they moved to Chambéry and he had to give up his company car. Since then, he has cycled tens of thousands of kilometres and enjoyed numerous cycle touring trips around the French Alps and Provence.

This guidebook is the result of his wish to share with others his enthusiasm for cycling and for the wonderful area in which he is fortunate enough to live.

He earns his living as a freelance translator.

INTRODUCTION

For most cyclists the French Alps conjure up images of the great champions of the Tour de France racing up legendary passes such as the Galibier, Izoard or Madeleine. Many dream of following in their tracks, but most are realistic enough to know that if they do so it will be at much more modest speeds. No matter how long the ascent takes, cycling over the summit of a mountain pass is a marvellous experience that never pales. The feeling of achievement is immense and there is a wonderful sensation of being both alive and at peace. As though this were not compensation enough for all the hard work of getting to the top, most high passes also offer outstanding views and an exhilarating descent as a final reward.

Of course, mountains do not have to be snow-capped giants to provide worthwhile cycling. Many lower areas are criss-crossed by quiet roads that meander through varied landscapes of open pastures, dark forests, deep gorges and unspoilt villages. The scenery is often just as beautiful as in the high mountains, but this beauty tends to be quieter and less ostentatious.

ABOUT THIS BOOK

Cycle Touring in the French Alps describes eight cycling routes through south-east France, between Lake Geneva and the Mediterranean. Seven of the routes are circular tours that start and finish at the same place; the final route is the Grand Traverse of the Alps from Geneva to Nice. As well as exploring the 'true' Alps, the routes cover the southern tip of the Jura and the northern pre-Alps. With the exception of the Tour of the Ain, which would be a good introduction to cycle touring in the mountains, all of the routes are difficult and aimed at fit and experienced cyclists.

When cycling in the mountains, the amount of vertical height gain is a much better indication of the difficulty of a route than the distance covered. The circuits were planned with this in mind and most stages include an average of between 1000 metres and 1500 metres of height gain, with an absolute maximum of 2000 metres for any single day (the stage from Bourg St Maurice to Bessans in Route 8 is the one exception to this rule). Most

River Rhone, Lac du Lit du Roi (Route 1, day 1)

Entremont-le-Vieux and Mont Granier (Route 4, day 6)

of the stages are between 50km and 80km long. Of course, some people will want to do longer stages than others. With this in mind, the facilities chart for each day (see below) shows all of the places along the route where accommodation can be found.

Anyone with basic map-reading skills can plan a cycling trip, so why would they need a guidebook? The answer is very simple: there are a lot of things that a map will not tell you – where you will find accommodation, shops, water and banks; what there is to see along the way; where the quietest roads are (the colour-coding systems used by maps for major and minor roads do not always tell the whole story); the best ways to cycle through larger towns and cities; the ins and outs of using public transport in a foreign country, and so on. This book provides all of this information and more in order to help you get the most from a cycling holiday in the French Alps.

The routes were chosen to include the areas I have most enjoyed cycling around during the nine years that I have lived in the Alps. In some areas, the choice of itinerary was easy as there are only a very small number of options. In other areas, the choice was more difficult and some wonderful places and spectacular passes had to be omitted. Even my adopted home (Chambéry) has not made it into the guide, despite being a beautiful city

and superbly situated for cycling. With the exception of the Grand Traverse, which will take most cyclists two weeks, the routes were designed so they can be completed within one week. If you would like to do a longer tour, why not combine two of the routes. The two combinations I would recommend the most highly would be the Tour of the Ain plus the Chartreuse-Bauges and the Tour of the Ecrins and Grandes Rousses plus the Tour of the Southern Alps (linked via the Col de Vars and the Col de Pontis).

HOW TO GET THERE

By car

The distances and approximate driving times from the ferry terminal at Calais to the start/finish point of the tours are given in the introduction to each tour. These distances are based on RAC or AA recommended routes, avoiding Paris, which adds about 20 to 25km to your journey, but reduces the risk of getting caught up in heavy traffic. French motorways are toll roads and are quite expensive, but it is rare for them to be congested, with the notable exception being roads to the south of France on Saturdays during the summer holidays. Useful route planning information can be obtained from **www.theaa.com** and **www.rac.co.uk**.

By rail and coach

It is always easier to use public transport if your bike is stowed in a bike-box or bike bag. Most hotels and B&Bs will look after bike-boxes/bags if you stay with them for at least one night at the beginning and one night at the end of the tour, however you should check this when you book.

France has an excellent train service (when it is not on strike!), but there is no national coach network.

There are regular coach and rail services from Britain to most of the start points, but, with the advent of low-cost airlines, overland travel is not always the cheapest option. Bicycles will only be allowed on long-distance coaches and high-speed trains if they are packed in a bike-box/bag. Coaches often have very strict limits on the amount of luggage they will accept. Check with the coach operator before leaving. There is no luggage limit on trains.

Timetable and pricing information can be found on the International Coach Services website: **www.eurolines.com**; and Eurostar train services: **www.eurostar.com** or **www.sncf.com**.

By air

Generally the quickest way to arrive at your destination when using public transport is to fly to a nearby airport, generally Geneva or Lyon, and then use local train or bus services. There are also regular flights from London Stansted and Luton to Grenoble. At present flights from Southampton, Birmingham and Norwich to Chambery only run during the ski season.

The **Tour of the Chablais–Aravis** starts and finishes at Geneva airport. **The Grand Traverse of the Alps** starts at Geneva airport and finishes at Nice airport.

If you are thinking of flying to France and then renting a car, it is better to organise the rental before leaving home. Car rental in France is expensive and many companies impose a mileage rate as well as the daily rental charge.

Lyon St Exupéry Airport Unfortunately, the only trains that stop at Lyon St Exupéry are high-speed TGVs; the service is very limited

Naves-Parmelan and the Dents de Lanfon (Route 2, day 7)

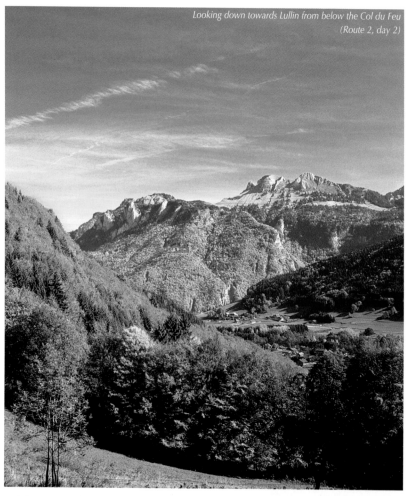

Looking down towards Lullin from below the Col du Feu (Route 2, day 2)

and the trains will only carry bikes that are packed in bike-boxes. There are regular shuttle bus services to most of the major towns around the airport (Lyon, Grenoble, Annecy, Chambéry, etc). These buses will accept bikes that are not in bike-boxes or bags 'if there is room' and the decision is left to the driver's discretion. If your bike is in a box or bag, there should be no problem putting it on the bus. If the shuttle bus will not take your bike, the only alternative is to cycle to a railway station and take the train.

It is much easier to cycle to one of the stations outside Lyon than to go into the city centre. Depending on your final destination,

you can either cycle to Meximieux (for destinations north and north-east of Lyon) or La Verpillière (for destinations south or south-east of Lyon). For destinations that are more or less due east of Lyon, such as St Jean-de-Maurienne (**Tour of the Ecrins and Grandes Rousses**), the best station to cycle to will depend on the times of the trains to your final destination. Details of how to cycle from the airport to these stations are given in Appendix 1. **The Tour of the Ain** can be started directly from Lyon airport by cycling to Meximieux.

For more information about Lyon airport shuttle buses, go to **www.satobus.com** or **www.lyon.aeroport.fr.**

For more information about train services, go to **www.sncf.com**.

Geneva–Cointrin Airport Geneva airport has its own railway station with regular services to Bellegarde (**Tour of the Ain**) and to Martigny (**Tour of Mont Blanc**). Rail services from Geneva to Grenoble and to St Jean-de-Maurienne (**Tours of the Chartreuse–Bauges, Belledonne** and **Ecrins and Grandes Rousses**) are limited so check that there is a suitable connection before booking your flight. It is theoretically possible to travel by public transport from Geneva to Barcelonnette (**Tour of the Southern Alps**), but the journey Geneva–Grenoble–Gap, by train, and then Gap–Barcelonnette, by bus, will take at least a day!

For the **Tour of the Chablais–Aravis** and the **Grand Traverse of the Alps** directions from and to the airport are given in Appendix 1.

For more information about Geneva airport, go to **www.gva.ch**. For more information about train services, go to **www.sncf.com** or **www.cff.ch**.

Grenoble – St Geoirs Airport There are now regular services to Grenoble airport from London–Stansted and London–Luton. Grenoble airport is ideally situated for starting the Tour of the Chartreuse-Bauges and the Tour of the Belledonne. The route between the airport and Grenoble city centre (a distance of 48km) is described in Appendix 1. It is a very pleasant ride along quiet roads and the excellent cycleway beside the River Isère.

For the Tour of the Chartreuse-Bauges, I would recommend cycling straight from the airport to Lake Aiguebelette, via Le Grand-Lemps, Chirens and St Geoire-en-Valdaine, a distance of approximately 60km. If you don't have time to get all the way to Lake Aiguebelette, there is a full range of accommodation in Charavines (4km west of Chirens, on the shores of Lake Paladru).

If you would prefer to take the train into the centre of Grenoble, go to the railway station at Rives (14km from the airport – the nearest railway station is actually at Le Grand-Lemps, but there are far fewer services from here). There is at least one train every hour and the journey takes approximately 30 minutes.

Chambéry Airport Flybe operates direct flights to Chambéry from Southampton,

*The spectacular view of Entrevaux from below the Col des Félines
(Route 7, day 4)*

Birmingham and (starting in autumn 2005) Norwich; but, currently, services only run until the middle of March. Chambéry is a convenient starting point for the Tours of the Ain and the Chartreuse-Bauges. There are also excellent rail services from Chambéry to Grenoble (Tour of the Belledonne) and St Jean de Maurienne (Tour of the Grandes Rousses and Ecrins). The railway station is in Chambéry city centre, 10km south of the airport. See Appendix 1 for airport access details.

GETTING AROUND BY TRAIN

French railways (SNCF) French trains are usually quite reliable, but the French railway company, SNCF, has a reputation for not being particularly accommodating to cyclists. However, in all the years I have transported my bike around France (at least half a dozen journeys per year), I have never had any problems. The following pointers should help you avoid major problems when using the trains.

For timetable and ticket price information, including connections to Switzerland, go to **www.sncf.com**.

TIPS FOR TAKING BIKES ON FRENCH TRAINS

1. High speed (TGV) and most long-distance express (Corail) trains will only carry bikes if they are packed in a bike-box/bag.
2. All regional trains (TER) in the Rhone–Alps Region (Tours of the Ain, Chablais–Aravis, Mont Blanc, Chartreuse–Bauges, Belledonne and northern parts of the Ecrins and Grandes Rousses route and Grand Traverse) accept bikes. All TER trains in the Provence–Alps–Cote d'Azur Region (southern parts of Ecrins and Grandes Rousses tour, Southern Alps and Grand Traverse) accept bikes except for services between 7am and 9am. Bikes are carried free of charge.
3. Passengers are responsible for loading their own bikes onto the train.
4. Bikes should be put in the goods wagon, if the train has one. These generally have hooks to hang bikes from and are usually the first or last carriage of the train.
5. Modern 'commuter' trains have one or two cars with hooks for bikes. There is a bike symbol on the door of these carriages.
6. If the train does not have a goods wagon or any specific place to put bikes, you will usually be allowed to put your bike in the spaces at the end of each carriage.
7. SNCF's website gives timetable and ticket price information in several languages, including English. A bicycle symbol is used to indicate which trains accept bikes, but the absence of the symbol does not necessarily mean that bikes are not accepted!

NB On most trains there is a limited amount of space for bikes, and you may not be the only cyclists on the train. Many trains only have space for up to six bikes. (This is not always the case; a ticket inspector once told me about a group of German cyclists that had taken the train from Chambéry to Bourg St Maurice – there were 18 of them! Fortunately, the train had a goods wagon).

Swiss railways (CFF) As you would expect, Swiss trains are extremely punctual. Most, but not all, will accept bicycles, although advance booking is obligatory on some trains and there is a supplement for bikes. Details, in English, French and German, are given on the Swiss railways website.

For timetable and ticket price information, including connections to France, go to **www.cff.ch**.

WHEN TO GO

The cycling season in the Alps runs from the middle of April to the middle of October for areas below 1500 metres, and from the middle of May to the end of September for higher areas. The winter months, from November to March, are usually too cold for enjoyable cycling in the mountains.

Access to mountain passes

Many mountain passes are closed during the winter. As a general rule, passes that are lower than 2000 metres are closed from early November to early May, passes at altitudes of between 2000 metres and 2500 metres are closed from late October to late May/early June, and passes above 2500 metres are closed from mid October to early/mid June. Actual closure dates vary according to the height of the pass and the harshness of the winter. Information about which passes are open and which are closed can be obtained at **www.bison-fute.equipement.gouv.fr** in the section 'accés aux cols'. The following websites provide detailed information for Savoie and Isère.

Savoie: **www.savoie.equipement. gouv.fr/html/EtatRout.htm**

Isère: **www.isere.equipement.gouv.fr/ enneigement_des_cols/index.htm**

If you need more precise information, contact the tourist office nearest to the pass you are interested in.

Weather

Another major consideration when planning a cycling trip is the weather. Though mountain weather is very variable, both from day to day and from year to year, it is still possible to make a few general comments.

a) In most areas, the driest months of the year are July and August.

b) Rainfall during the summer is often in the form of violent but short-lived afternoon storms. A typical summer day starts with clear blue skies, but cloud starts to build up towards the end of the morning. Generally, the weather does not become too threatening until the middle of the afternoon. Storms usually do not break until at least 3pm and only last a few hours.

c) September is often an excellent month for cycling, although the temperatures are a little cooler, especially at altitude.

d) Changes in the weather can be very sudden and quite brusque. Temperature variations of up to 10°C from one day to the next are not uncommon.

Average temperature and rainfall statistics for five towns at different latitudes and altitudes are given in Appendix 2.

The average adiabatic lapse rate is 6.5°C per 1000 metres, so for every 1000 metres increase in altitude, the temperature falls by 6.5°C. The lapse rate is often greater than this and there can be a much bigger difference in temperature between the valleys and the high passes than expected. For example, if it is 30°C in the shade at Bourg St Maurice (800

Arriving at the Col de Larche (Route 7, day 1)

Col de Larche
Alt. 1991 m

Mount Obiou as seen from the Col de l'Holme (Route 6, day 5)

metres), it might only be 10°C at the Col de l'Iseran (2770 metres), not the 17°C you would expect. If there is a breeze, wind chill will also add to the feeling of cold. Above 2000 metres snow is not uncommon, even in July and August, although it generally won't last for long. Be prepared.

Weather forecasts There are numerous websites that give weather forecasts for the Alps. Sites that I have used include: **www.meteo.fr**, **www.meteoconsult.com** and **www.met-office.gov.uk**. Many tourist office websites also give weather forecasts. The Chamonix site gives a particularly good mountain forecast: **www.chamonix.com**. When you are in France, weather forecasts can be obtained from most tourist offices.

Traffic

When planning your trip, another factor to consider is traffic. The Alps are a very popular holiday destination and the busiest time of year is from the beginning of the second week in July to the end of the third week in August. Although the tours avoid busy roads wherever possible, there is always a certain amount of traffic on the roads up to the highest and most famous passes. The best time to do the tours of the Chablais–Aravis, Mont Blanc, Ecrins and Grandes Rousses and the Grand Traverse is before the middle of July or after the middle of August. In the less touristy areas, such as the Ain and the Chartreuse–Bauges, you are unlikely to encounter heavy traffic even in the middle of the summer holidays.

CYCLING IN FRANCE

Language

Most hotels, restaurants and shops in resort towns will have staff who speak at least a little English. In quieter areas, there is no guarantee that this will be the case. Wherever you are, people will always appreciate it if you try to speak French, even if you are limited to a few simple words and feel as if you are massacring the language. A common complaint from shop staff is that many English visitors do not even say *bonjour* when they enter a shop. Being able to use a few basic French sentences in bakeries, cafés and hotels can radically change the degree of friendliness with which you are welcomed.

A short glossary of French cycling terms and some useful French phrases for getting your bike repaired are given in Appendix 3.

Local government

As when visiting any foreign country, you will notice that things are done differently in France compared to your home country. The sometimes perplexing place names or the way the French road-numbering system works, may seem confusing and frustrating. However, once it is understood that many of these things are related to the country's complex system of local government, you may find them easier to tolerate.

There are three basic levels of local government in France: the *region*, the *département* and the *commune*. The regional council is responsible for, amongst other things, large-scale infrastructure, such as new railway lines. *Départemental* councils are responsible for most of the road network and for the development of tourism within the *département*. The tours in this guide go through two regions (Rhone-Alps and Provence-Alps-Cote d'Azur – usually abbreviated to PACA) and seven *départe-* ments (Ain, Haute-Savoie, Savoie, Isère, Hautes-Alpes, Alpes-de-Haute-Provence and Alpes-Maritimes). Each *département* is sub-divided into a number of district councils or *communes*, which are responsible for very minor roads (C-roads) and local tourism development. Each level of government jealously guards its own prerogatives and responsibilities, and there is often quite a lot of competition between neighbouring authorities, whether it be on the regional, *départementale* or *communale* level.

The main practical repercussions of this for the cycle-tourist (or tourist in general) are as follows:

TIPS FOR CYCLING IN FRANCE

1. If a road number changes without any apparent reason, you have probably crossed the border between two *départements*.
2. A *commune* may include several villages and cover several square kilometres. The sign at the entrance to each of these villages will give the name of the *commune* first, with the name of the village below. The *Chef-lieu* is the main town/village in the *commune*. Addresses on internet sites and in brochures will sometimes give the name of the *commune*, but not the exact location. Be careful when booking accommodation as you may find yourself several kilometres away from where you wanted to be.
3. Occasionally, the boundary between two *départements* will go through the middle of what appears to be one village. Sometimes the two villages will have the same name and sometimes they will have different names. For example, during the Tour of the Chartreuse–Bauges you will go through St Pierre d'Entremont (Savoie) and St Pierre d'Entremont (Isère). Later the same day you will get to Entre-Deux-Guiers (Isère) which is contiguous with Les Echelles (Savoie).
4. Most local tourist offices are run by the *commune* and will only have information about that commune and its immediate surroundings. Fortunately, many *communes* are starting to work together to provide tourist services for wider areas. Tourist offices in larger towns will usually have some information for other parts of the *département*, but very rarely for neighbouring *départements*, however close the border may be.

Public Holidays
France has several public holidays during the spring and summer, although the government is trying to reduce the number. With the exception of Easter Monday and Ascension, the holidays are on a fixed date regardless of which day of the week they fall.

French public holidays in spring and summer are: Easter Monday (NB Good Friday is not a holiday), 1st May, 8th May, Ascension, 14th July (not called Bastille Day in France) and 15th August.

Swiss public holidays are: Good Friday, Easter Monday, 1st May, Ascension, Pentecost and 1st August.

Italian public holidays are: Easter Monday, 25th April, 1st May, 2nd June and 15th August.

Money
The cost of living in France is generally considered to be about 20% less than in the UK, but whether or not life appears to be cheaper depends on the exchange rate. Since the

St Hugues and the Grand Som (Route 4, day 7)

introduction of the Euro on 1st January 2002 the exchange rate has varied between 1.3 and 1.6 Euros to the pound.

If you are on a tight budget it is possible to live for as little as 25 Euros per day, by camping and cooking for yourself, but this won't include very many luxuries. A more reasonable budget would be around 35 to 40 Euros per day.

There are a lot of quite cheap but pleasant hotels and *gîtes d'étapes* in France, so it is possible to travel light at a reasonable cost, especially if there are two of you to share a room. Two people travelling together should expect to spend a minimum of around 50 Euros per person per day. Of course, the amount you spend will depend on the quality of the hotels you choose and how much you spend on meals.

Most restaurants offer a choice of set-price menus, which are usually very good value for money. Expect to pay between 15 and 25 Euros per person, not including drinks. If a set menu costs more than 25 Euros, the quality should be exceptional. Naturally, eating *à la carte* will be more expensive.

Cycling on French roads

As well as the difficulty (for British cyclists) of cycling on the right-hand side of the road,

there are a number of other particularities of the French Highway Code and French driving habits that should be noted.

1. Where there is no give-way sign or line, vehicles approaching from your right have right of way, even when they are on a minor road that joins a major one. When they know they have right of way, many drivers don't even look to see if another vehicle is coming as they expect oncoming traffic to give way to them. When you don't know the roads, it is not always easy to see if there is a give-way sign, so be careful whenever a road joins from the right. A white diamond-shaped road sign with a yellow diamond in the middle indicates a stretch of road where you have right of way over vehicles coming from the right. A similar sign with a black line through the yellow diamond indicates the end of this section of road.

2. At roundabouts, traffic should give way to vehicles that are already on the roundabout. The rule is simple, but drivers often try to force their way onto the roundabout and will not even slow down unless a collision is imminent. Cyclists are not always considered an 'obstacle' worth braking for! Some people, especially older drivers, will stop to let another car join the roundabout – be careful not to run into the back of somebody who brakes unexpectedly.

3. Very few drivers indicate at round-abouts and lane discipline is a completely alien concept. Just because a vehicle is in the right-hand lane does not mean that it will be turning right, or even going straight on.

4. Most drivers will move over a reasonable distance when overtaking cyclists, although not many respect the legal minima of 1 metre in towns and 1.5 metres elsewhere. On average, 250 cyclists are killed on French roads every year.

5. Drivers often cut corners on winding mountain roads, even if they can't see what is coming towards them! Be extremely careful, especially when speeding downhill.

6. Road numbers change surprisingly frequently and the numbers that you see on maps do not always correspond to the numbers on road signs.

7. Other changes to the road system can occur through urban development or natural events such as landslides. Temporary road closures due to landslides or rock fall are quite common: for example, in 2003 the main trunk road from Ugine to Megève was closed for a total of 212 days because of a succession of landslides. Road works may also lead to road closures.

8. Specific rules for cyclists include:

a) Bicycles must be fitted with a bell (a law that is never enforced).

b) The use of cycle lanes or cycleways is not mandatory.

c) Lights are mandatory at night, but not during the day or in tunnels. However, it is a good idea to have a light on your bike as many mountain roads go through unlit or poorly lit tunnels.

d) Wearing a helmet is not mandatory, but it is highly recommended.

Le Mourre Froid from Siguret (Route 6, day 3)

Cycling in the mountains

When cycling in the mountains, your average speed will be much lower than on the flat as the time 'gained' during the descents will not compensate for the time 'lost' going uphill. Hills can be very long so the golden rule is to start gently, find a comfortable speed, and then relax and enjoy the scenery. Remember, the only imperative is to get to a place where you can eat and sleep before nightfall.

Few Alpine roads are as steep as those in the English Pennines or Lake District, but the climbs are very much longer. Gradients rarely exceed 10% and average gradients tend to be around 6 to 7%. To gain 1000 metres of altitude at a gradient of 6% means covering a distance of 17km. To be able to cycle uphill for such long distances, without exhausting muscles or damaging tendons, it is essential to have a bike with suitable gear ratios (see the 'What to take: Bikes and luggage' section below).

WHAT TO TAKE

Insurance, health, accidents and emergencies

Visitors to France from the European Union should have a completed E111 form (available from post offices in the UK). Any health care you need should be free, but it is a good idea to take out some general travel insurance in case there are incidental expenses, such as repatriation, to be covered.

According to the World Health Organisation, France has the best health service in the world. It is not perfect, but the treatment you get is both good and quick. If you have a specific medical condition, it is a good idea to carry a letter from your doctor, translated into French, giving details. If you need to carry any medicines with you, keep the prescription with them, especially if the medicine is in the form of pills packaged loose in a jar. I once spent a very uncomfortable few hours with French customs accused of drug smuggling because the ibuprofen I had with me tested positive for amphetamines!

All major UK mobile phone services work in France and coverage in the mountains is now very good, although there are some areas were there is still no service. Even if you cannot make a standard call, you should be able to contact the emergency services. **In case of an accident call 112** (the number for the emergency services in any country within the EU). You should be connected with an operator who speaks your language. French emergency services (*sapeurs-pompiers*) can be contacted by calling 18. The police can be contacted by calling 17.

If you are stranded due to a mechanical failure and need a taxi to pick you up, you can ask via directory enquiries for the number of a taxi firm – dial 12. If you do not feel your French is good enough for that and you have booked your accommodation in advance, call your next port of call and ask them to organise a taxi for you.

Bikes and luggage

This is not the place for a detailed review of different types of cycle-touring gear. Every cyclist will have his/her own preferences and ideas about what to take and how much they are prepared to carry. However, I would like to make a few comments that are specifically related to cycling in mountain areas.

Weight is a much more important factor when cycling in the mountains than on the flat. As a rule of thumb, for every 1kg increase in the weight of the bike, you will use 1% more energy. A heavy bike is also less manoeuvrable and will have a much greater braking distance. How much weight there is on the bike will depend on whether you are camping or using hotels, but when packing 'keep it light' should be the constant watchword.

A road bike or standard cycle-touring bike is perfectly adequate for all of the tours. Only two of the circuits (Chablais–Aravis and Ecrins and Grandes Rousses tours) involve off road sections (4km and 2km respectively) and both of these sections are at least 75% cycle-able with a road bike. There is no advantage to be gained from using a mountain bike apart from the very low gear ratios such a bike offers.

Having the right gear ratios is extremely important when cycling in the mountains. On long hills, even if the gradient is not extreme,

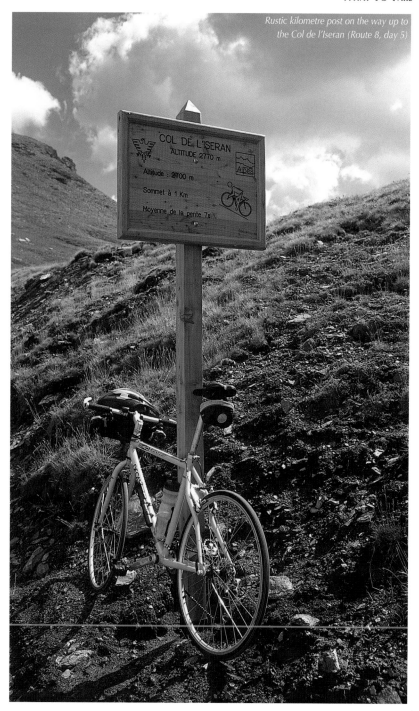

Rustic kilometre post on the way up to the Col de l'Iseran (Route 8, day 5)

it is much more comfortable to maintain a relatively high cadence with a short development than a low cadence with a long development. (The development is the distance the bike moves forward for each rotation of the pedals, calculated by multiplying the diameter of the wheel by the ratio of the number of teeth on the chain-ring and the number of teeth on the sprocket). Most of the cyclists I know in the Alps use a triple chain-ring (30/42/52 or 30/40/50) and a nine or ten-speed sprocket (12–23 or 13–26).

Given the scarcity of bike shops, it is a good idea to carry a full repair kit, including spare inner tubes, tyre levers, puncture repair kit, spanner(s), screwdriver(s) chain tool, spoke tool and spare brake/derailleur cable. In nine years of cycling in the Alps, I have never had to do more than repair a chain or unbuckle a wheel. The most frustrating incident was having to push my bike for 11km in 35°C heat after multiple punctures irreparably destroyed three inner tubes. Of course, the most important thing is to make sure that your bike is in excellent condition before setting off.

A bike lock is essential, even if many hotels, B&Bs and *gîtes* have garages where you can leave your bike. In one hotel, we had to leave our bikes in the bar – no one minded, but it was reassuring to be able to lock the bikes to the water pipes.

Tents

Storms in the Alps can be violent, so, as well as being lightweight and compact, any tent used for cycle touring must be sturdy and completely waterproof.

Clothing

Most of the time while cycling, a light T-shirt or cycling jersey, combined with a windproof jacket for long descents, is sufficient. However, in the high mountains you need to be prepared for very variable conditions: temperatures can reach 40°C in the valleys or fall to zero at the top of the high passes. A layered system, consisting of a light base layer, warm middle layer and waterproof outer layer, should be sufficient to cope with all eventualities. Leggings may be very welcome early or late in the season. It is highly advisable to

wear a helmet, especially during descents.

Most evenings will be spent at relatively low altitude, but it can still get chilly enough to require long trousers and a light sweater or fleece jacket. During the summer months, any clothes that you wash at the end of the day will usually dry over night, so you do not have to take too many clothes.

Food and drink

Always carry at least one or two cereal/energy bars and 1 litre of water (2 litres is a good idea if it is hot), as shops and water fountains can be few and far between. Remember, the human body loses moisture more quickly at altitude than at sea level. Dehydration can become a major problem if you don't drink regularly: aim for a minimum of 1 litre per hour. While you are cycling it is almost impossible to drink enough to replace all the water your body is losing, so try and re-hydrate at the end of the day (preferably before ordering that long anticipated cold beer).

Maps

The route descriptions have been designed to give all necessary navigational information and can be followed without recourse to a map. However, I would not advise anyone to set off on a cycle-tour without the relevant map(s) as you may need to change your itinerary due to unforeseen circumstances – accident, bad weather, road closures, etc.

I use a combination of Michelin and French Geographical Survey (IGN) maps. The new series of 1:150,000 Michelin 'Local' maps are ideal for cycle-touring and usually only one map is needed for each circuit. The Michelin 1:200,000 'Regional' maps give a good overview of an area and are generally detailed enough for day-to-day navigation. The IGN 'TOP 100' series of 1:100,000 scale maps give more detail than the Michelin maps, but they are not as easy to read. There is also a series of 1:250,000 scale maps ('TOP 250'), but they do not always give enough detail, especially around towns.

I have given the reference numbers of the relevant Michelin 1:150,000 and 1:200,000 and IGN 1:100,000 scale maps in the introductory section of each tour.

The vineyards of Jongieux, home to some of Savoie's best white wines (Route 4, day 2)

HOW TO USE THIS GUIDE

Each chapter begins with a chart showing the distance covered and height gained on each day, followed by an outline map and description of the route. These travelogues give an overview of the area through which you will be cycling, pointing out places to visit, things to see, local traditions and interesting snippets of history. This is followed by detailed navigational information, in the form of a route card, a facilities chart and a route profile. A list of accommodation for the recommended overnight stops and the telephone numbers and internet addresses of local tourist offices are given at the end of each chapter. The spellings of place names can vary in France; here they conform to those on the Michelin maps except in cases where a sign post is being quoted when the exact spelling used on the sign is given.

Route cards

The route descriptions are presented in the form of daily route cards, which contain all necessary navigational information. It would be impossible to note every junction along the route, so directions are only given for when a decision needs to be made. If no directions are given, continue straight on.

Local authorities seem to enjoy building new roundabouts, so do not be surprised if a junction marked on the route card has metamorphosed into a roundabout.

The summits of passes are also shown on the route cards, as are the lengths and AVERAGE gradients of all the significant climbs. To be regarded as significant, an uphill section must be at least 2km long and/or involve at least 100 metres of height gain. Note that uphill sections do not always neatly start and finish at junctions or significant landmarks (nor are passes always the highest point of the road) so the distance given in conjunction with a gradient does not necessarily correspond to the distance between two points on the route card.

Distances were measured with a computer on a bike and are quoted to the nearest 100m. Even assuming that the computer is perfectly calibrated, it is very difficult to measure distances with pinpoint accuracy. Errors can be caused by differences in tyre pressure, stopping and starting and not cycling in a straight line, for instance. Comparisons with other bike computers, road signs and distances marked on maps indicate that the distances quoted are accurate to within 2%.

Each stage starts and finishes at an easily recognisable and easy to find point in the town or village. This is usually the tourist

ABBREVIATIONS USED

So that the information can be presented in a precise and easy to read form, the following abbreviations have been used:

L = left
R = right
jtn = junction (either a crossroads or a T-junction)
(Grenoble) = follow road signs for Grenoble
[Grenoble] = follow cycling or pedestrian signs for Grenoble
TO = tourist office
station = railway station
D911/D912 = junction between D911 and D912
D201–D154 = road number changes other than at a junction, for example, at the border between *départements*.
Turn L – D81 (Albanne) = Turn left onto the D81 and follow signs to Albanne

office, railway station or *mairie/hotel de ville* (town hall). The description for the start of each stage is given assuming that you are coming out of this building.

Route profile

More information about the nature of the terrain is given in the form of a route profile. There is one profile for each day of the tour. The same vertical and horizontal scales have been used throughout the guide so that individual stages can be compared at a glance.

Facilities chart

A facilities chart is provided for each stage, showing where essential/useful services can be found along the route. These services are:

Water: unless marked with a sign reading *eau non-potable*, the water from fountains is drinkable. As drinking water has to be regularly tested by the local council, more and more fountains are marked *eau non-controlée* (not tested) or are being turned into flowerbeds! You drink *eau non-controlée* at your own risk. All the water points marked in the facilities chart provide tested drinking water. The list does not contain cemeteries; by law, all cemeteries in France must have a source of drinking water.

Shops: at least a *boulangerie* or an *épicerie* where you can buy food. Opening hours tend to be 9am to 12 noon and 2pm to 7pm. Bakeries open at 7 or 7.30am. The lunchtime break will sometimes start at 12.30

(especially for bakeries) and may last longer than two hours. Most food shops are open from Monday to Saturday. Bakeries and shops in resorts may be open on Sundays. Many shops in small villages are closed on Mondays.

Cafés: includes cafés, bars and restaurants.

Campsites: the chart shows all of the campsites along the route, but some are only open in July and August.

B&Bs: this list includes standard bed-and-breakfast style accommodation (*chambres d'hôtes*), as well as youth hostels (*auberges de jeunesse*) and *gîtes d'étapes*. Bed and breakfast accommodation is becoming very popular in France and the number of establishments is growing rapidly. The price range for this type of accommodation is enormous: from 25 to 100 Euros per person. *Auberges de jeunesse* are very similar to UK youth hostels. *Gîtes d'étapes* provide excellent value for money; most are small, family run hostels with a combination of individual rooms and small dormitories that sleep four to eight people. You will need to have your own towels and toiletries. Blankets or duvets are supplied but some *gîtes* require you to use a sheet sleeping bag or hire a sheet for the night. Half-board rates are usually between 30 and 40 Euros per night and this often includes wine with the evening meal. They are designed for 'outdoor' people, so the breakfasts are generally copious. Many have accommodation-only rates (from 10 to 15 Euros per person) and provide cooking facilities for people who want to go self-catering. *Gîtes d'étape* should not be confused with *gîtes rural*, which are holiday cottages.

Hotels: Hotels in France are much cheaper than in Britain. Room rates for two people sharing in a two-star hotel are between 30 Euros and 60 Euros a night. Room rates for three-star hotels are around 40 to 75 Euros per night. Breakfast is not included. Half-board rates are sometimes available, but they can be limited to guests who stay for two or more nights, especially during the summer holidays. Outside the main holiday season, some hotels close for one night of the week, often the Monday night. Outside the main towns and major resorts there are surprisingly few three-star hotels and virtually no four-star establishments. Many good hotels in rural areas have a relatively low star rating simply because they lack a specific facility, such as televisions in the rooms. Other hotels have

simply opted out of the star-rating system, preferring to be classified as *hôtels du charme*, although this label gives no more than a very general indication of the quality of the establishment.

Banks (and post offices with ATMs)**:** banks are open from Tuesday to Friday from 8.30am to 12 noon, and from 2pm to 6 or 7pm. They are also open on Saturdays from 8.30am to 12 noon. Banks in small villages may only be open one or two days per week. Most ATMs accept Visa and Mastercard, but not all accept American Express. Most shops and hotels will accept credit cards, but you may need your passport to prove your identity.

Bike shops: outside the main towns, true bike shops are few and far between. Many of the bike shops in resorts deal mostly with mountain bikes and only have a very limited range of spare parts for road bikes. If there is no bike shop at one of the recommended

Bonneval-en-Tarentaise (Route 5, day 3)

Kilometre post, Col de la Cayolle (Route 7, day 5)

overnight stops, I have shown where the most easily accessible bike shop is. In some areas, especially in the Southern Alps, the nearest bike shop can be more than 60km away.

Accommodation list
The accommodation list gives the names and telephone numbers of the campsites, B&Bs/hostels and hotels at all of the recommended overnight stops. For campsites, the opening dates are also given. Other than during the main summer holiday period, or where there is only a very limited choice of accommodation, it is not usually necessary to book in advance. In a book of this size, it would be impossible to list all the options in the larger towns/resorts (there are more than 100 hotels in Geneva alone), so where there are more than eight campsites, B&Bs or hotels, the reader is referred to the local tourist office. Phone numbers and internet addresses for both *départementale* and local tourist offices are given at the end of the accommodation section.

ROUTE ONE

TOUR OF THE AIN

Day	Route	Distance	Height Gain
1	Bellegarde to Yenne	63.4km	898m
2	Yenne to St Rambert-en-Bugey	64.3km	912m
3	St Rambert-en-Bugey to Chatillon-sur-Chalaronne	77.2km	500m
4	Chatillon-sur-Chalaronne to Thoirette	74.4km	615m
5	Thoirette to Hauteville-Lompnes	66.9km	1197m
6	Hauteville-Lompnes to Bellegarde	46.1km	535m
	Totals	**392.3km**	**4657m**

The Tour of the Ain explores a very accessible but poorly known *département* of south-east France. Despite its proximity to both Lyon and Geneva, the Ain has remained relatively unspoilt: an authentic corner of *La France profonde*, dotted with sleepy villages, rambling farms and dense forests. The geography of the area is dominated by three large rivers: the Saone, which marks the *département's* western border; the Rhone, which marks its eastern and southern borders; and the Ain, which runs through the middle. The countryside to the west of the River Ain is almost completely flat and dotted with hundreds of lakes and marshes, whereas to the east the landscape is much more rugged: this is the southern end of the Jura Mountains. The area's unspoilt countryside and picturesque villages, combined with a very well developed network of virtually traffic-free roads, make it a fabulous place for cyclists. One of the reasons why the roads are so quiet, even during the summer holidays, is that the Ain is very much a tourist backwater. Therefore, most towns and villages have very few hotels and restaurants and the overnight-stops noted here had to be chosen as much for the range of facilities they offer as for their historical, cultural or scenic interest.

This circuit focuses on the southern part of the *département*, and takes you through the mountains of the Haut-Bugey and the wetlands of the Dombes. Although the route includes some quite long climbs, the Tour of the Ain is the least mountainous circuit in this guide and therefore provides an ideal introduction to cycle touring in the mountains. The tour can easily be extended by combining it with the Tour of the Chartreuse-Bauges, or by incorporating one or more of the 25 signposted circuits described in a guide published by the Ain Tourist Board (available from **www.ain-tourisme.com**).

Bellegarde-sur-Valserine, a small town on the banks of the Rhone, was chosen as the start and finish point for the tour because it is within easy reach of Geneva airport. There is a regular train service from Geneva and the journey takes around 25 mins. Despite being only 40km from Geneva, cycling to Bellegarde is not recommended, as it is impossible to avoid the very busy and dangerous main roads. If you are flying into Lyon, it would be better to start at Meximieux.

Bellegarde offers little to retain even the most open-minded visitor – perhaps its greatest claim to fame is that it was the first town in France to install electric streetlights, in 1883. However, the town is quickly left behind as you head south-east into the Bugey, via the Col de Richemont. Although long (around 15km), the climb is never too steep and you will soon be at the top with the satisfaction of having the hardest part of the day's cycling behind you. Once over the Col de Richemont, the road emerges from the forest to give spectacular views of the idyllic Séran Valley and

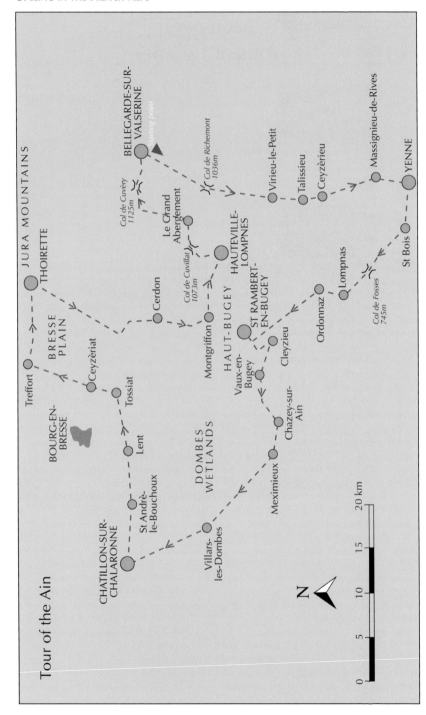

Tour of the Ain

JURA MOUNTAINS

BELLEGARDE-SUR-
VALSERINE

Starting point

*Col de Cuvéry
1125m*

*Col de Richemont
1036m*

Virieu-le-Petit

Talissieu

Ceyzérieu

Massignieu-de-Rives

YENNE

Le Grand
Abergement

*Col de Cuvillat
1073m*

HAUTEVILLE-
LOMPNES

St Bois

THOIRETTE

Cerdon

HAUT-BUGEY

Lompnas

Treffort

BRESSE
PLAIN

Ceyzériat

Montgriffon

ST RAMBERT-
EN-BUGEY

Ordonnaz

*Col de Fosses
745m*

BOURG-EN-
BRESSE

Tossiat

Vaux-en-
Bugey

Cleyzieu

Lent

Chazey-sur-
Ain

St André-
le-Bouchoux

DOMBES
WETLANDS

Meximieux

CHATILLON-SUR-
CHALARONNE

Villars-
les-Dombes

N

20 km

0   5   10   15

26

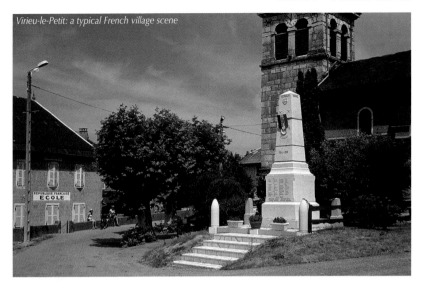
Virieu-le-Petit: a typical French village scene

the rolling hills of the Haut-Bugey. The next 20km wind gently downhill, across the western flanks of the Grand Colombier, to the village of Talissieu. If you found the climb to the Col de Richemont easy, you may like to make a detour over the Grand Colombier. There are several roads to the top of this mountain; the steepest starts in Virieu-le-Petit and rises 865 metres in a little under 9km with gradients of up to 19%. As you would expect from the highest mountain in the area, the views from the top are superb. The standard route from Talissieu to Ceyzérieu crosses the northern edge of the Lavours Marsh, one of the last remaining, large continental marshes in western Europe and now a nature reserve. It is also one of the few places in France where you can see highland cattle! The reserve's visitor centre, a very pleasant café and the start of a 2.4km long nature trail are in Aignoz, 1.5km east of Ceyzérieu. The countryside to the south, with its unspoilt villages and vineyards, set against a backdrop of spectacular mountains, is picture-postcard France at its very best. The area also has its little surprises, such as the sculptures at the Lac de Barterand, the largest of which depicts a local legend of the giant Gargantua breaking open the mountainside to free the mermaid of the vines who had been trapped inside (no one seems to know why she had been imprisoned). From the lake,

a short descent takes you back down into the Rhone Valley at a point where there are two branches to the river. The first branch is quickly crossed, but you won't cross the second until you reach the small market town of Yenne, 9km further along the road.

From Yenne, the route heads due west along the *route nationale*, through the Gorges de la Balme. After about 5km, in the village of Virignin, you leave the traffic behind, and the rest of the day follows quiet country lanes through forests, fields and open moorland. This is perfect cycling country where other vehicles are rarely seen – you can consider yourself unlucky if you are passed by more than a handful of cars in the 50km that separate Virignin from St Rambert. However, there are also very few opportunities to buy any sort of refreshments so, unless you want to rely on one of the cafés in Lompnas or Ordonnaz being open, take a packed lunch with you. The wooded banks of Lake Ambléon, just before the Col de Fosses, provide an ideal picnic site. Other than the superb scenery, there are few tourist attractions along the route (one being the Palaeoecology Museum in Cerin). St Rambert is the only village in a 20km radius to have hotels (both 1.5km east of the village), a B&B (in Serrières, 1km west of the village) and a campsite (1km east of the village). It is a former industrial village that is now making strenuous efforts to raise its tourist profile, having recently opened both a local heritage museum and an art gallery.

The third leg of the tour starts with a final incursion into the Bugey, past the village of Cleyzieu to Vaux-en-Bugey, before turning its back on the hills to cross the floodplain of the River Ain. Of all the picturesque villages in the Ain, the most spectacular is undoubtedly the mediaeval citadel of Pérouges. The village was probably founded in Roman times, but most of the buildings that you can see today date from the 15th century. Wandering through the cobbled streets is like walking back through time, an impression that is enhanced by little details, such as the bakery that leaves its bread to rise in the sun of an open window. Pérouges is also the gateway to the wetlands of the Dombes, a huge expanse of lakes and marshes that boasts extremely rich flora and fauna. Although most of these lakes (there are more than a thousand of them) have existed for centuries, they are nearly all man-made – fish farming is not a recent development. They provide an excellent habitat for many different species of sedentary and migratory birds, including kestrels, grey herons and storks. An even greater variety of birds, from all around the world, can be seen at the Villars-les-Dombes Bird Garden, 20km northwest of Pérouges.

The day ends at Chatillon-sur-Chalaronne, a very pretty town of half-timbered houses that prides itself on its gastronomy. There is no better place to try frog's legs, a local speciality, followed by local freshwater fish or wildfowl. For the inquisitive visitor there are also several interesting museums and historical buildings to visit, including the castle ruins and the 17th-century market hall, which still houses the local market every Saturday morning.

Day four picks up where day three left off, crossing the northern part of the Dombes and skirting round Bourg-en-Bresse, the capital of the Ain. Cycling through such peaceful countryside is always enjoyable, but the pleasure is even greater early in the morning when the air smells freshest and the mist still hovers above the lakes. Once across the wetlands, the itinerary turns north and follows the eastern edge of the Bresse Plain to Treffort. This is an excellent place for a short break before leaving the flat plains behind and heading back into the mountains. The cafés are in the main square at the bottom of the hill, however the prettiest corner of the village, with its 14th-century church and castle, is at the top of the very steep Rue Ferrachat. The view across the Bresse Plain to the hills west of Macon is well worth the climb. From Treffort the route runs more or less due east across the foothills of the Jura to Thoirette on the banks of the Ain. Thoirette has little to offer the cultural tourist, but its superb riverside location and very welcoming hotels and campsite make it an ideal stopping-off point.

On leaving Thoirette, the route turns right to follow the banks of the Ain southwards for about 20km. The strenuous cycling starts just before the village of Merpuis, where a steep, but short climb leads through Challes, over an unnamed pass and down to Cerdon. Cerdon has three claims to fame: its show caves, its working coppersmith's and an eponymous sparkling rosé wine. Unfortunately, getting to the show caves involves a detour of about 6km (turn right from D85A onto D11, then D11H and N84), but the coppersmith's and wine museum are in the village itself. Many local wineries are also open to the public: a map in the village gives details. Once past Cerdon, the road rises again to go over the Col de Montratier and onto the central plateau of the Haut-Bugey. From here it is possible to head straight to Hauteville-Lompnes, but the most picturesque route branches off the main road at Châtillon-sur-Corneille to explore the hidden valleys to the south. This is deepest rural France and certainly not the sort of place you would expect to find an Australian restaurant (in the tiny hamlet of Pezières – 18km from Cerdon). Hauteville-Lompnes, the next port of call, is the capital of the Haut-Bugey. For a small town of less than 4000 inhabitants it can be quite a lively place with music, dance and arts festivals all through the summer.

The final leg of the tour is quite short, although there are several ways in which it could be extended (eg. via Brénod, Col de Belleroche, Le Poizat and Col de Bérentin). The most direct route takes you over the Col de Cuvillat and through Les Abergements to

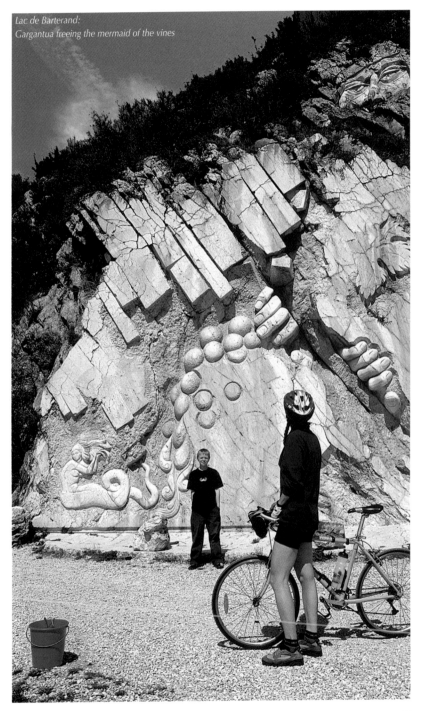

Lac de Barterand:
Gargantua freeing the mermaid of the vines

Chatillon-sur-Chalaronne
(Day 3)

the Plateau de Retord, home to one of the area's largest cross-country skiing centres. The journey truly ends on a high, as the pass that marks the eastern edge of the plateau, the Col de Cuvéry, is the highest point on the circuit and the14km descent back to Bellegarde is great fun. If you are not in a rush, why not celebrate the end of the tour with lunch at the excellent Auberge de la Fontaine in Ochiaz, just outside Bellegarde?

GETTING THERE

By car
Bellegarde-sur-Valserine is 775km from Calais.

By plane
Via Geneva: Take the train from the airport to Geneva central station (Cornavin). The number of trains from Geneva–Cornavin to Bellegarde varies from one train every two hours to three trains per hour, depending on the time of day. The journey takes around 25 mins.

Via Lyon: If you fly into Lyon St Exupéry, you can start the tour by cycling from the airport to Meximieux. Directions are given in Appendix 1.

Via Chambéry: If you fly into Chambéry, you can join the tour at Yenne (end of Day One). Directions from the airport to Yenne are given in Appendix 1. A better option for the final day of the tour would then be to follow Day Six as described to Le Grand Abergement. From here take the D39 to Hotonnes, and then follow the D9 for about 4.5km to join Day One of the standard route at the D9/D30 junction, just below the Col de Richemont.

WHEN TO GO

Due to its modest altitude, this tour is feasible from April to October. The roads are always quiet, even during the peak holiday months of July and August. Given the limited number of hotels and campsites, it is advisable to book accommodation in advance.

MAPS

Michelin: Local – Sheet 328, Ain, Haute-Savoie

Michelin: Regional – Sheet 244, Rhône-Alpes

IGN: Top 100 – Sheet 44: Lyon, Genève and Sheet 51: Lyon, Grenoble

The River Rhone near Yenne (Day 1)

Day 1 – Bellegarde-sur-Valserine to Yenne

Within the next few years, it should become possible to cycle from Geneva to Bellegarde without having to brave the busy main roads. A European cycleway project, called Du Léman à la Mer, has been set up to build a cycle path along the River Rhone, from Lake Geneva to the Mediterranean. To date, progress has been slow due to the reluctance of certain local authorities to get involved and to the difficulties of reconciling the interests of others. More information and progress reports can be found at **www.dulemanalamer.com**.

Distance	Location	Directions
0.0	Bellegarde station	Come out of the station and turn R onto Rue Joseph Bertola (Centre Ville)
0.1	Traffic lights	Turn R – Rue Lafayette
0.6	Jtn	Turn R (Genève) and go under railway line
1.0	Roundabout	Turn L 3rd exit D25 (Billiat)
7.7	Billiat: D25/D991	Turn R – D991 (Génissiat)
9.1	D991/D30	Turn L – D30 (Injoux): 9.7km at 6%
18.8	Col de Richemont	Go straight on
22.6	D30/D9	Turn L – D30 (Brénaz)
28.0	Brénaz: D30/D69	Turn L – D69 (Virieu-le-Petit). Go through Virieu-le-Petit to Munet.
34.8	Munet: D69/D105	Turn L – D105 (Talissieu)
37.0	Jtn	Turn R (Artemare)
37.5	Jtn	Turn L (Talissieu)
40.3	Talissieu: D105/D904	Turn L – D904
41.1	D904/D105	Turn R – D105 (Ceyzérieu)
43.8	D105/D37	Turn R – D37
44.9	Ceyzérieu: D105/D37	Go straight on along D37 and go through Vongnes
50.4	D37/D37A	Turn L onto D37A (Cressin)
52.8	Jtn	Turn R (Belley)
53.9	D37A/D992	Turn R – D992 (Belley)
54.6	D992/D37	Turn L – D37 (Massignieu)
56.8	D37/D37A	Turn R – D37 (Yenne)
62.9	D37/N504	Turn L – N504 (Yenne), and then immediately R to go into the village
63.4	Yenne: *mairie*	The *mairie* is on the L

Wheat fields and the Rhone Valley near Cressin

FACILITIES AND SERVICES								
Location	Distance (km)	Water	Shops	Café	Campsite	B&B	Hotel	Bank	Bike Shop
Bellegarde	0.0	x	x	x	x	—	x	x	x
Billiat	7.7	x	x	x	—	—	—	—	—
Brénaz	28.0	x	—	—	—	—	—	—	—
Virieu-le-Petit	33.3	x	—	—	—	—	—	—	—
Ceyzérieu	44.9	x	x	x	—	x	—	—	—
Massignieu	56.8	x	x	x	x	—	—	—	—
Yenne	63.4	x	x	x	x	x	x	x	(1)

(1) Nearest bike shop is in Belley, 12km northwest of Yenne

River Rhone
233m

Yenne
230m

St Bois
300m

Ambléon
400m

Col des Fosses
745m

Day 2

(km)   60   70   80   90   100

Day 2 – Yenne to St Rambert-en-Bugey

In 2003, France was hit by the worst heatwave in living memory. At least 15,000 people died as temperatures peaked at more than 40°C after three long months of exceptional heat and drought. Forest fires ravaged the countryside, coming uncomfortably close to many towns and villages. To give just one small example, the blackened stumps of trees around St Bois (still visible in 2005) show how close the village came to being destroyed. Water levels in major rivers, such as the Rhone and the Ain, fell to record lows and many power stations had to be run at reduced capacity because the water was too hot to cool them. Fish stocks in the rivers were devastated and even the water that emerged from underground springs was warm.

Distance	Location	Directions
0.0	Yenne *mairie*	Turn R in front of the *marie* and go to N504
0.5	N504	Turn L – N504 (Lyon)
2.6	N504/N516	Turn R – N504 (Belley)
4.5	Virignin: N504/D31A	Turn L – D31A (Peyrieu) and cross the Rhone Canal: road turns sharp L and becomes D31B
6.2	D31B/D24A	Turn R along D31B (Champtel)
8.0	D31B/D992	Turn R – D992 (Belley)
9.6	D992/D10	Turn L – D10 and go through (Peyzieu)
12.8	D10/D24	Turn R – D24 (St Bois)
22.7	D24/D41	Turn L – D41 (Innimont): 6.3km at 5.5%
29.0	Col des Fosses	Go straight on
30.3	D41/D87	Turn R – D87 (Lompnaz)
32.0	D87/D87D	Turn R along D87 and go through Cerin
37.4	Lompnas: D87/D94	Turn R – D94 (Ordonnaz): 3.6km at 6.5%
43.5	Ordonnaz: D94/D32	Turn L – D32 (Col de Portes)
47.4	D32/D99	Turn R – D99 (Col de Portes)
48.0	D99/D73	Turn R – D73 (St Rambert-en-Bugey)
60.0	D73/D104	Go straight on along D73
63.1	Roundabout: D73/N504	Turn R – N504 (St Rambert-en-Bugey)
64.3	St Rambert-en-Bugey	TO is on the R

Ordonnaz: fountain decorated for Tour de France 2003

FACILITIES AND SERVICES

Location	Distance (km)	Water	Shops	Café	Campsite	B&B	Hotel	Bank	Bike Shop
Yenne	0.0	x	x	x	x	x	x	x	(1)
Virignin	4.5	—	x	—	—	—	—	—	—
Ambléon	20.9	x	—	—	—	—	—	—	—
Cerin	32.4	x	—	x	—	—	—	—	—
Lompnas	37.4	—	—	x	—	—	—	—	—
Ordonnaz	43.5	—	—	x	—	x	—	—	—
Conand	56.4	x	—	—	—	—	—	—	—
St Rambert	64.3	x	x	x	x	x	x	x	(2)

(1) Nearest bike shop is in Belley, 12km northwest of Yenne

(2) Nearest bike shop is in Ambérieu-en-Bugey, 10km west of St Rambert

Ordonnaz 856m

St Rambert-en-Bugey 281m

Cleyzieu 590m

Day 2

Day 3

110   120   130   140   150

km)

35

Day 3 – Rambert-en-Bugey to Chatillon-sur-Chalaronne

Periodically, the fish-producing lakes of the Dombes are drained and planted with wheat, oats or maize. After the harvest, the lakes are re-filled and re-stocked with fish.

Distance	Location	Directions
0.0	St Rambert-en-Bugey TO	Come out of TO and turn L – N504
1.2	Roundabout: N504/D73	Turn R – D73 (Le Chauchay)
3.2	Le Chauchay	Turn L – D60 and cross N504 (Cleyzieu)
8.5	Cleyzieu	Bear R past fountain (Vaux-en-Bugey)
14.2	D60/D60A	Turn R – D60A (Vaux-en-Bugey)
20.2	Vaux-en-Bugey	Go straight on – D77A (Leyment)
25.4	Leyment: D77B/D77	Turn L – D77 (Ste Julie)
27.4	D77/D77C	Turn R – D77C (Chazey-sur-Ain)
30.1	Chazey-sur-Ain	Turn R onto Grande Rue (D40)
31.7	D40/N84	Turn L – N84 (Meximieux)
35.2	2nd roundabout	Turn R (Meximieux)
35.4	Meximieux: jtn	Turn L and follow railway line past station
36.2	Roundabout	Turn L (Pérouges)
36.5	Jtn	Turn R onto D4 (Pérouges)
42.3	Roundabout: D4/D22	Go straight on along D4 (Le Montellier)
42.6	Jtn	Turn R (Joyeux)
47.7	Jtn	Turn R onto D61 and go through Joyeux
50.0	D61/D904	Turn L onto D904 (Villars-les-Dombes)
55.6	Villars-les-Dombes: lights	Go straight on – D904 (Chatillon-sur-Ch.).
56.5	D904/D70	Turn R – D70 (Ste Olive)
64.2	Ste Olive: D70/D82	Turn R – D82 (Chatillon-sur-Ch.) Follow D82 to Chatillon
75.8	Chatillon-sur-Chalaronne	Turn R onto Boulevard de la Resistance. Go into village and follow one way system to jtn with D2
76.7	Jtn	Turn L – D2 (Bourg-en-Bresse)
76.9	Roundabout	Go straight on (Centre Ville)
77.2	Main Square	Mairie is on the L (set back from the road)

36

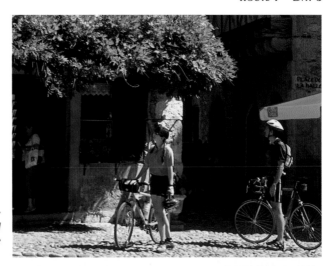

*Pérouges: a superbly
well-preserved
mediaeval village*

FACILITIES AND SERVICES								
Location	Distance (km)	Water	Shops	Café	Campsite	B&B	Hotel	Bank	Bike Shop
St Rambert	0.0	x	x	x	x	x	x	x	(1)
Cléyzieu	8.5	x	—	—	—	—	—	—	—
Vaux-en-Bugey	20.2	x	x	x	—	—	—	—	—
Leyment	25.4	—	x	x	—	—	—	—	—
Chazey-sur-Ain	30.1	—	x	x	—	—	x	—	—
Meximieux/Pérouges	36.2	x	x	x	x	—	x	x	x
Joyeux	42.5	—	—	x	—	x	—	—	—
Villars-les-Dombes	55.6	x	x	x	x	x	x	x	—
Ste Olive	64.2	—	—	x	—	—	x	—	—
Chatillon-sur-Chalaronne	77.2	x	x	x	x	x	x	x	x

(1) Nearest bike shop is in Ambérieu-en-Bugey – 10km west of St Rambert

Villars-les-Dombes
282m

Chatillon-sur-
Chalaronne
240m

Day 4

180   190   200   210   220

(km)

Day 4 – Chantillon-sur-Chalaronne to Thoirette

Distance	Location	Directions
0.0	Chatillon *mairie*	Come out of the *mairie*, turn R then R again
0.3	Roundabout	Turn L – D7 (Chalamont)
1.5	Jtn	Turn L (Montaplan)
2.1	Jtn	Turn R (no sign)
3.9	Jtn	Turn R – hiking sign (St Georges-sur-Renon)
6.7	St Georges-sur-Renon	Go straight on – D67 (St André-le-Bouchoux)
10.7	D67/D26	Turn L – D26 into St André-le-Bouchoux
10.9	D26/D17	Turn R – D17 – then L – D67 (St André/Vieux Jonc)
15.1	Jtn	Turn R (no sign) onto minor road. The jtn is just after a lake on L of road and before a house on R.
16.3	Le Buttoir: jtn	Go straight on
18.6	Jtn	Turn R – D64 and go through Servas to (Lent)
21.5	Lent D64/D22	Turn R – D22 (Meximieux)
21.9	D22/D23	Turn L – D23 (Certines)
22.5	D23/D64	Turn R – D64 (Certines) then (Tossiat)
32.4	Tossiat: D64/D52	Turn R – D52 (Ceyzériat)
37.3	Ceyzériat	Turn R (Centre Village)
37.5	Jtn	Turn L (Observatoire)
37.8	Jtn	Turn R – D52 (Treffort)
41.7	Jasseron: D52/D936	Turn R – D936 and then L – D52 (Treffort)
49.1	Jtn	Turn R to go into Treffort
49.4	Treffort	Turn R – D3 (Corveissiat): 2.7km at 6.5%
54.0	D3/D936	Turn L – D936 (Corveissiat)
56.3	D936/D3	Turn L – D3 (Chavannes-sur-Suran)
58.0	Chavannes: D3/D42	Turn L – D42 then R – D3 (Arnans): 5.2km at 5%
63.9	Arnans	Go straight on (Aromas)
67.0	C7/D86	Go straight on (Ceffia)
68.8	D59/D200	Go straight on – D59 (Thoirette)
73.6	D59/D936	Turn L – D936 (Thoirette)
74.4	Thoirette campsite	Campsite entrance is on the R

Church near St Georges-sur-Renon

FACILITIES AND SERVICES

Location	Distance (km)	Water	Shops	Café	Campsite	B&B	Hotel	Bank	Bike Shop
Chatillon-sur-Chalaronne	0	x	x	x	x	x	x	x	x
St André-le-Bouchoux	10.7	—	—	x	—	—	—	—	—
Lent	21.5	—	x	x	—	—	x	—	—
Certines	28.7	—	x	x	—	—	—	—	—
Ceyzériat	37.3	x	x	x	x	—	—	x	—
Treffort	49.4	x	x	x	x	x	x	x	—
Chavannes-sur-Suran	58.0	—	x	x	x	—	—	—	—
Arnans	63.9	x	—	—	—	—	—	—	—
Thoirette	74.4	x	x	x	x	x	x	x	(1)

(1) Nearest bike shop is in Oyonnax, 16km east of Thoirette

High Point
450m
Treffort
280m
Amans
569m
Thoirette
291m
Day 5

260   270   280   290   300

e (km)

39

On the left-hand side of the road just before entering Hauteville, you cannot fail to notice a rather modest-looking quarry. This is the home of Hauteville marble, an orangey-yellow limestone that has been used in the construction of some of the world's most famous buildings, including the White House, the elevator halls of the Empire State Building and the plinth supporting the Statue of Liberty.

Distance	Location	Directions
0.0	Thoirette campsite: D936	Turn R – D936. Go through village and over river.
0.6	D936/D91	Turn R – D91 (Granges)
11.6	D91/D91A	Bear R – D91 (Poncin)
22.7	Jtn	Turn L (just before Merpuis) (Route du Bugey): 2.5km at 7%
26.5	Jtn	Turn R and go into Challes la Montagne
26.8	Challes	Turn L (Route du Bugey): 1.9km at 5.5%
30.0	C1/D85A	Turn L (no sign)
30.6	D85A/D11	Turn R – D11 (Cerdon)
35.3	D11/N84	Go straight on – D11 (Corlier): 6.1km at 4.5%
39.3	D11/D11J	Turn L – D11 (Hauteville-Lompnes)
40.1	D11/D12	Turn L – D12 (Hauteville-Lompnes)
41.4	D12/D12C	Turn R – D12C (Boyeux-St Jérôme)
43.5	Boyeux: D12/D12C	Turn L – D12C (St Jérôme)
43.6	Jtn	Turn L (Montgriffon): 2km at 11%
46.6	D12B/D11	Turn R – D11 (Montgriffon)
48.3	Montgriffon: D11/D63A	Turn L – D63A (Resinand): 2.8km descent then 6.7km at 5%
52.4	Resinand: D63A/D34	Turn L – D34 (Aranc)
55.9	Aranc: D34/D102	Turn L onto D102 and then R back onto D34 (Rougemeont)
59.9	D34/D8	Turn R – D8 (Hauteville-Lompnes)
64.7	Roundabout	Go straight on (Hauteville-Lompnes)
66.5	Roundabout	Go straight on (Centre Ville)
66.7	Hauteville-Lompnes	Bear R onto Rue Jean Miguet
66.9	Centre of Hauteville	Stop in front of Bistrot de la Fontaine

Tour of the Ain Day 5

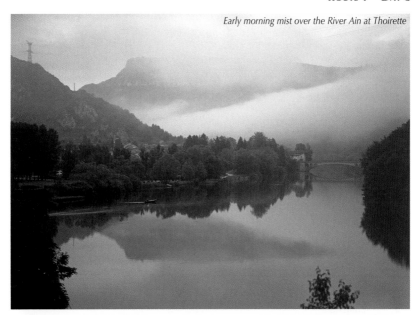

Early morning mist over the River Ain at Thoirette

FACILITIES AND SERVICES

Location	Distance (km)	Water	Shops	Café	Campsite	B&B	Hotel	Bank	Bike Shop
Thoirette	0.0	x	x	x	x	x	x	x	(1)
Granges	5.9	x	—	—	—	—	—	—	—
Cerdon	33.8	x	x	x	—	x	x	—	—
Montgriffon	48.3	x	—	—	—	—	—	—	—
Pezières/Resinand	52.0	x	—	x	—	—	—	—	—
Hauteville-Lompnes	66.9	x	x	x	x	x	x	x	x

(1) Nearest bike shop is in Oyonnax, 16km east of Thoirette

41

Extra day: At Thoirette, you already have one foot in the Jura, so why not explore the *département* a little further? The village of Orgelet, reached via Arinthod, provides a picturesque objective for a day trip. The return leg takes you past the Lac de Vouglans, a lake on the River Ain formed by a hydroelectricity dam, and then through Cernon and Condes. There are no big hills along the route, but cycling through such rolling countryside can be just as tiring as going over a high pass.

Distance	Location	Directions
0.0	Hauteville-Lompnes: Bistrot de la Fontaine	Go past the public toilets and up to a T-jtn in front of MMA Assurances
0.1	Jtn	Turn L
0.5	Roundabout	Turn R – D21 (Champdor)
5.5	Champdor: D21/D57A	Turn R – D57A (Le Petit Abergement): 4.6km at 5.5%
9.4	Col de Cuvillat	Go straight on
13.8	D57A/D31	Turn R – D31 (Le Petit Abergement)
14.3	Le Petit Abergement: D31/D39C	Turn L – D39C (Le Grand Abergement): short descent then 11.2km at 3.5%
15.9	Le Grand Abergement: D39C/D39	Turn L – D39 (Les Plans d'Hotonnes)
18.2	D39/D39A	Go straight on – D39 (Le Poizat)
19.5	D39/D55	Turn R – D55 (Bellegarde)
26.0	D55/D101	Turn R – D101 (Bellegarde)
30.4	Col de Cuvéry	Go straight on
39.7	D101/D101B	Turn R – D101B (Ochiaz)
40.5	Ochiaz: D101B/D991	Turn L – D991 then first R onto Route de Mussel. Keep going downhill to jtn with D25.
44.0	Jtn	Turn L – D25 – Rue de l'Avenir
44.9	Roundabout	Turn R – filter lane (Annecy)
45.2	Traffic lights	Turn L (Centre Ville)
45.8	Jtn	Turn L onto Rue Joseph Bertola – next to the *hotel de ville*
46.1	Bellegarde station	

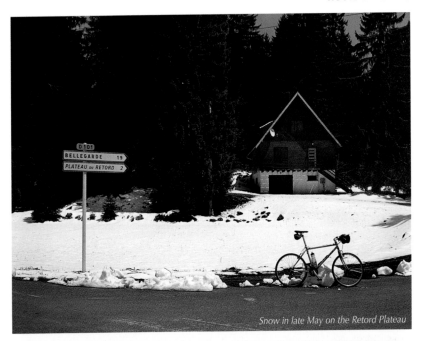

Snow in late May on the Retord Plateau

FACILITIES AND SERVICES

Location	Distance (km)	Water	Shops	Café	Campsite	B&B	Hotel	Bank	Bike Shop
Hauteville-Lompnes	0.0	x	x	x	x	x	x	x	x
Champdor	5.5	x	x	x	—	—	—	—	—
Les Abergements	15.0	x	—	x	—	—	x	—	—
Col de Cuvéry	30.4	—	—	x	—	—	—	—	—
Ochiaz	40.5	x	—	x	—	x	x	—	—
Bellegarde	46.1	x	x	x	x	—	x	x	x

Col de Cuvillat 1073m
Le Petit Abergement 770m
Col de Cuvéry 1125m
Bellegarde-sur-Valserine 380m

Day 6

360 370 380 390 400
(km)

ACCOMMODATION

Bellegarde-sur-Valserine

Campsites

Le Crêt d'Eau (all year), Tel. 04 50 56 60 81

Bed & Breakfast

There are no bed & breakfasts in Bellegarde

Hotels

La Belle Epoque (***), Tel. 04 50 48 14 46

La Colonne (**), Tel. 04 50 48 10 45

Hotel Gril Adria (**), Tel. 04 50 48 14 10

Touring Hôtel (**), Tel. 04 50 56 08 08

Hotel 1ere Classe, Tel. 04 50 56 62 53

Yenne

Campsites

Camping du Flon (mid-June to end August), Tel. 04 79 36 82 70

Les Soudans (early May to end September), Tel. 04 79 36 73 19

Bed & Breakfast

Au Tote Sayon (in Nattages, 4km north of Yenne), Tel. 04 79 44 40 69

Hotels

Le Fer à Cheval (**), Tel. 04 79 36 70 33

St Rambert-en-Bugey

Campsites

Le Domelin (1.5km east of St Rambert; June to end Sept), Tel. 04 79 38 33 88

Bed & Breakfast

There are no bed & breakfasts in St Rambert.

Hotels

Le Calypso, Tel. 04 74 36 36 80

Auberge de l'Adret, Tel. 04 74 36 27 44

Villars-les-Dombes

Campsites

Les Autières (early April to end Sept), Tel. 04 74 98 00 21

Le Large (early April to end Sept), Tel. 04 74 98 15 66

Bed & Breakfast

Mr and Mrs Back, Tel. 04 74 98 17 74

Mr and Mrs George, Tel. 04 74 98 05 44

Hotels

Ribotel Le Parc, Tel. 04 74 98 08 03

Thoirette

Campsites

Les Vernes (dates not known), Tel. 04 74 76 80 71

Bed & Breakfast

Gite "La Cabotte", Tel. 04 74 76 88 97

Hotels

L'Auberge du Pont, Tel. 04 74 76 80 46

Hotel de la Source (*), Tel. 04 74 76 80 42

Hauteville-Lompnes

Campsites

Camping Municipal (all year), Tel. 04 74 35 36 73

Bed & Breakfast

La Praille, Tel. 04 74 35 29 81

Hotels

Hotel des Tilleuls, Tel. 04 74 35 30 25

Le Provençal (**), Tel. 04 74 35 30 43

Hotel de Lyon, Tel. 04 74 35 30 18

TOURIST INFORMATION

Regional Information

	Telephone	Website
Ain	04 74 32 31 30	www.ain-tourisme.com

Tourist Information Offices

Location	Telephone	Website
Bellegarde	04 50 48 48 68	www.pays-de-gex.org
Yenne	04 79 36 71 54	www.avant-pays-savoyard.com
Ordonnaz	04 74 39 80 92	http://perso.wanadoo.fr/pierre.bonny
St Rambert-en-Bugey	04 74 36 32 86	www.tourisme-albarine.com
Villars-les-Dombes	04 74 98 06 29	www.tourisme.fr/villarslesdombes
Thoirette (Oyonnax)	04 74 77 94 46	www.tourisme-oyonnax.com
Hauteville-Lompnes	04 74 35 39 73	www.plateau-hauteville.com

Half-timbered house in Chatillon-sur-Chalaronne (Day 3)

ROUTE TWO

TOUR OF THE CHABLAIS–ARAVIS

Day	Route	Distance	Height Gain
1	Geneva to Thonon-les-Bains	51.1km	200m
2	Thonon-les-Bains to Chatel	61.6km	1390m
3	Chatel to Samoëns	52.8km	1480m
4	Samoëns to La Clusaz	56.4km	1390m
5	La Clusaz to Annecy	61.3km	680m
6	Annecy to Geneva	74.9km	1300m
	Totals	**358.3km**	**6440m**

Chablais is a name that everyone in the *département* of Haute-Savoie uses to describe the northernmost part of the Pre-Alps, but no two people seem to agree on exactly where the boundaries of this region lie. Here, I have used the broadest possible definition of the term to encompass the whole area between Lake Geneva and the Arve Valley. On the other hand, the Aravis Range is much easier to define, as it is a single chain of mountains that runs south-east from the Arve Valley to the town of Faverges, just south of Lake Annecy. The tour of the Chablais–Aravis also includes the out-lying mass of Mont Salève, generally considered to be Geneva's own mountain.

Quite understandably, the French are extremely proud of their country's culinary reputation and if you talk to any French person for long enough, the conversation will inevitably turn to food and, more particularly, to local gastronomy. Every region of the country has its own specialities and the Chablais and the Aravis are no exceptions. Being so close to Lakes Geneva and Annecy, it is not surprising that many restaurants in the area specialise in locally caught fish. At higher altitudes, lush alpine pastures provide ideal grazing for the dairy cows which produce the milk used to make the area's cheeses, three of which – Abondance from the Chablais, and Reblochon and Chevrotin from the Aravis – have been awarded Appellation d'Origine Contrôlée (AOC) status. Many local dishes

(raclette, tartiflette, reblochonade, etc) are simple variations on the theme of meat, potatoes and cheese, the only differences between them being the type of cheese and the way they are cooked. These are good, hearty farmhouse dishes – just what you need after a long day's cycling, especially if the evenings are cool.

Geneva was chosen as the start point for the tour as it is both easy to get to by public transport and easy to cycle through. Geneva City Council has made strenuous efforts to promote cycling, developing an extensive network of cycleways and cycle lanes, providing free bicycle hire and producing a free map of cycle routes around the city. (To obtain this map, contact Mr Claude Morel at Geneva City Council: **claude.morel@voi.ville-ge.ch**).

Despite its long and colourful past, Geneva is a thoroughly modern and forward-looking city, best known as the home of international organisations such as the United Nations and the Red Cross. More interestingly for the visiting tourist, Geneva also boasts a wide range of excellent museums that deal with subjects as diverse as art, archaeology and automobiles. The Swiss are famous for their common sense and pragmatism, so it is perhaps unsurprising that Geneva's most famous landmark, the water jet of 140m, was originally created as a simple pressure relief valve for the city's water pumps. The first jet, created in 1886, was only a few metres high; it wasn't until 1891 that it was moved to

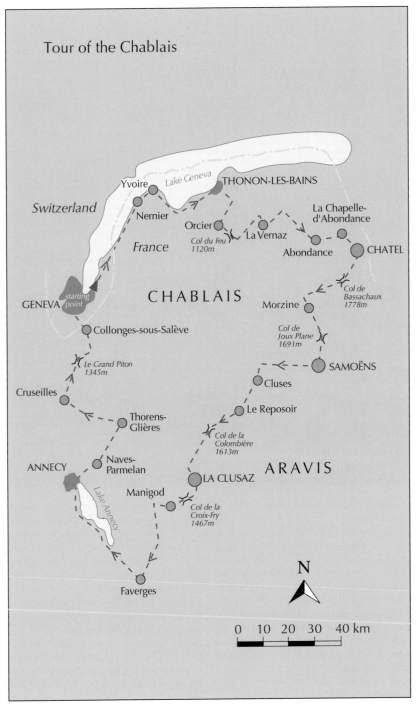

Tour of the Chablais

Switzerland

Lake Geneva

Yvoire
Nernier
THONON-LES-BAINS
Orcier
Col du feu
1120m
La Vernaz
La Chapelle-
d'Abondance
Abondance
CHATEL

France

GENEVA
starting
point
CHABLAIS
Morzine
Col de
Bassachaux
1778m

Collonges-sous-Salève

Col de
Joux Plane
1691m

Le Grand Piton
1345m

SAMOËNS

Cruseilles

Cluses

Thorens-
Glières

Le Reposoir

Col de la
Colombière
1613m

ANNECY
Naves-
Parmelan
ARAVIS
LA CLUSAZ

Manigod

Lake Annecy

Col de la
Croix-fry
1467m

N

Faverges

0 10 20 30 40 km

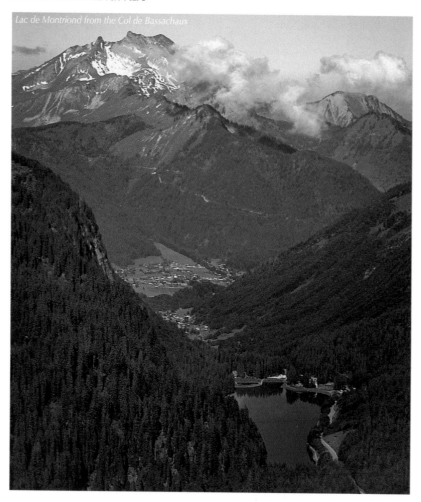

Lac de Montriond from the Col de Bassachaux

its present position and turned into a decorative fountain.

As Thonon-les-Bains is only 51km from Geneva, it may be possible to do this first leg of the tour the day you arrive, although it would be a shame to be in too much of a rush to make the minor detours necessary to visit the lakeside villages of Nernier and/or Yvoire. Nernier, the smaller and quieter of the two ports, is a charming hamlet of stone-built houses on the edge of the lake. Yvoire's beautifully preserved mediaeval streets and castle have made it one of the most popular tourist attractions on the southern shore of Lake Geneva. The village is renowned for its flowers and gardens and is

regularly awarded the highest distinctions by the Conseil National des Villes et Villages Fleuris (France in Bloom) organisation. A more peaceful side to Yvoire can be seen in the early morning or late evening, when the daytime hustle and bustle gives way to a much more contemplative atmosphere.

From Yvoire, the route turns south to briefly join the main RN5, and then heads back to the lakeshore near Séchex. The road into Thonon is very easy to follow, as it is part of the well signposted Tour de Bas Chablais cycling itinerary. Haute-Savoie and Savoie councils have set up 90 of these one-day cycling circuits and a guidebook is available, free of charge, from most large tourist offices.

Although Thonon's pedestrianised town centre is quite pleasant, most visitors make a beeline for the lakefront and the fisherman's harbour. Over 50 fishermen still make a living from the lake, supplying fresh fish to local restaurants. The most popular fish is perch, but other local specialities include fera (lake whitefish), lotte (burbot) and omble-chevalier (char). One of the best views of the harbour is from the gardens surrounding the Chateau de Sonnaz (home to the Chablais Museum), from where a steep path leads down to the shore. From the harbour it is a very pleasant stroll to the 15th-century Chateau de Ripaille, a luxurious castle built by Marie of Burgundy, wife of Amadeus VIII, the First Duke of Savoie. When Marie died Amadeus retreated into a more spiritual existence and founded the Order of Saint Maurice. He later became Pope taking the name Felix V.

From Thonon the route heads into the foothills of the Chablais and up to the first pass of the tour, the Col du Feu. The last 6km below the col are quite steep, but the panorama of the lake and the Jura Mountains beyond provides ample reward for your hard work. A short, but steep descent leads to Lullin and then to Vailly, where the route turns right to reach the junction of the Gorges de la Dranse and the Abondance Valley. The village of Abondance, with its traditional wooden houses and magnificent 11th-century abbey, is one of the most beautiful in the Chablais. Its two main attractions, other than the simple pleasure of ambling through such a lovely place, are the abbey cloisters, which house some exceptional 15th-century frescoes, and the Maison du Val d'Abondance, a local heritage museum, where pride of place is given to the valley's eponymous cheese.

Chatel was chosen as the overnight stopping point at the end of this first stage of the tour because of the range of accommodation it offers and because it is conveniently situated at the foot of the Col de Bassachaux. The village is pleasant and has some magnificent alpine chalets, but it does not have the same charm as Abondance. Chatel is first and foremost an outdoor-sports resort and one of its more unusual

summer attractions is the 'Fantasticable', a giant zip-wire ride that will quicken the pulse of even the most hardened 'adrenaline junky'. During the 3km 'flight', you swoosh across the valley at 100kph, suspended from a cable up to 240 metres above the ground. At 32 Euros, the thrills do not come cheap, but it is an unforgettable experience.

At 1783m, the Col de Bassachaux is one of the highest road passes in the Chablais. Despite being a challenging climb up a very quiet road, it is much less well known to cyclists than the neighbouring Col de Joux Plane: probably because the paved road ends at the summit and to traverse the pass to Morzine you have to cycle along a forest track for about 4km. Even with slick tyres, it is possible to cycle at least 75% of this off-road section and the beauty of the surroundings, especially the view down onto the Lac de Montriond, more than compensates for having to push your bike for a few minutes.

Where the forest track rejoins the paved road you can either turn left to go over the Col de Joux Verte, or turn right, as described here, to go down the Montriond Valley. If the café at the Col de Bassachaux was not open and you are looking for refreshments, there are plenty of cafés and restaurants at Les Lindarets, the first village you pass on the descent to Montriond and Morzine. Les Lindarets is also known as the 'village of the goats' for reasons that will quickly become clear as you near the first houses – be careful, goats never look before crossing the road!

Morzine, like Chatel, is primarily a ski resort and part of the Portes du Soleil ski area, although for cyclists it is better known as a regular host town for both the Tour de France and the Critérium de Dauphiné Libéré. The most famous pass accessible from Morzine is the Col de Joux Plane, but to get to it you first have to go over the Col de Ranfolly: an 8km climb at an average gradient of 8.5%. Fortunately, the last 2.5km from the Ranfolly to the Joux Plane are easy so you can relax and soak up the magnificent views of Mont Blanc before enjoying the sinuous and technical descent to Samoëns.

Samoëns is the only outdoor-sports resort in France to be listed as an historic monument by the National Historic Monuments Commission. The village square, with its ancient lime tree and 12th-century gothic church, is surrounded by delightful streets of wood and stone-built houses. In 1906, Marie-Louise Cognacq-Jaÿ created a botanical garden amongst the streams and waterfalls that tumble down the slopes on the northern edge of the village. These gardens, which now contain more than 8000 species of plant from all over the world, are undoubtedly the jewel in Samoëns' crown.

Day four starts peacefully beside the River Giffre, but after around 11km the route is forced to join the busy road that goes over the Col de Chatillon and down to Cluses. Cluses is the biggest town in the Arve Valley, Haute-Savoie's industrial heartland and a major centre for precision engineering. Fortunately, the valley is soon left behind as the road climbs into the Aravis Mountains over the Col de la Colombière. The first part of the ascent, to Le Reposoir, is a mere warm-up for the serious work ahead: over the last 8km to the summit the average gradient is almost 9%! The descent to Le Grand Bornand is one of the most enjoyable in the area: a 'mere' 12km, but the road surface is excellent and there are few tight bends. From here, another 5km, most of which is gently uphill, takes you through St Jean-de-Sixt to La Clusaz.

La Clusaz, surrounded by lush pastures and encircled by precipitous limestone peaks, lies at the heart of the Aravis Mountains. As well as being the perfect gradient for skiing in winter, the surrounding slopes provide excellent grazing land in summer and the valley produces several different cheeses. The most famous is Reblochon, an AOC cheese that is one of the main ingredients of tartiflette, the traditional Savoie dish par excellence. Other cheeses, such as Tomme Blanche, Chevrotin and Persillée des Aravis, are produced in smaller quantities and are worth looking out for.

When travelling south from La Clusaz, most cyclists head for the famous Col des Aravis (see Route 8), but the route described here goes over the less well known Col de la Croix-Fry (pronounced 'croix-free') in order to avoid the main road between Flumet and Ugine. It cannot be said that the Croix-Fry is a difficult pass to cycle over, but the road is steep in places, especially at the beginning. The last part of the climb is through dense forest and it is not until you get over the pass that the view opens out to reveal the picturesque Fier Valley and the imposing mass of the Tournette. After a winding descent through a traditional landscape of pastures, chalets and craggy peaks, the route turns left towards the Col du Marais. During

Le Reposoir and the Aravis Mountains

this second climb of the day, the gradient is never too severe and you are soon on your way down to St Ferréol and the Annecy Basin. If you are looking for a stiffer challenge, turn right at Vesonne and cycle up to the Col de la Forclaz above the eastern shore of Lake Annecy. The climb is hard, averaging 9% for 8km, but the view of the lake from the top is stunning.

Annecy is not only one of the most beautiful cities in the Alps, it is also one of the oldest: recent archaeological work has uncovered the remains of a village that dates back to at least 3100BC. The site was also occupied from Roman times through the Dark Ages, although very few buildings from that period have survived. The Annecy we know today first came to prominence in the 12th century when it became the seat of the Counts of Geneva, who had been forced out of their home city in a dispute with local bishops. Ironically, four centuries later, the Bishop of Geneva himself fled to Annecy to escape the turmoil of the Protestant Reformation. By this time, the Dukes of Savoie had succeeded the Counts of Geneva as lords of Annecy, and it was Amadeus VIII who rebuilt the city after it had been devastated by a series of fires in the middle of the 15th century. Of all the historic buildings to visit in Annecy, pride of place must go to the castle, perched on a low hill overlooking the old town. Even if you don't have the time or inclination to visit any of the city's many monuments, Annecy's old town is a fabulous place to explore.

The final leg of the tour follows the northwest edge of the Aravis to Thorens-Glières, and then heads west to Cruseilles and the foot of Mont Salève. The road to the top of the Salève climbs steadily through dense forest, which blocks the view but provides welcome shade on hot days. Near the first of the mountain's two summits the forest thins revealing the surrounding countryside, but the best views are from the second summit, 2.5km north of La Croisette. As the Salève stands apart from the neighbouring massifs, isolated between the Jura and the Aravis, the panorama from the top is truly exceptional. As usual, the mighty summit of Mont Blanc draws the eye, but even the highest summit in Europe cannot eclipse the spectacular view of Lake Annecy and the Tournette.

After a final café-break at La Croisette, it is time to head back to the big city bustle of Geneva. The first part of the descent is exceptionally steep, with gradients of up to 15%, so check your brakes before setting off. All too soon you are back at the Franco–Swiss border and at the end of this great circuit.

GETTING THERE

By car
Geneva is 760km from Calais.

By plane
Via Geneva: the tour starts directly from Geneva airport.

WHEN TO GO

The best months to do this tour are May and June, or September and early October.

The roads over the Col de Bassachaux, Col de Joux Plane and Col de la Colombière are closed from late November to early May (although at the beginning of May it is usually possible to get through on a bike even if the roads are officially still closed). Being so close to Geneva, Annecy and Mont Blanc, the Chablais and Aravis can be extremely busy during the summer holidays.

MAPS

Michelin: Local – Sheet 328, Ain, Haute-Savoie

Michelin: Regional – Sheet 244, Rhône-Alpes.

IGN: Top 100 – Sheet 45: Annecy, Lausanne; Sheet 53: Grenoble, Mont Blanc is also needed for the area to the south of Lake Annecy (Day 6)

Day 1 – Geneva to Thonon-les-Bains

Switzerland has a well-deserved reputation for being a very expensive country and Geneva is no exception: there cannot be many cities in the world with more four- and five-star hotels than one- and two-star establishments. If you are travelling on a tight budget, I would recommend Geneva City Hostel (listed as a one-star hotel, tel. (022) 901 1500). It is only a few minutes from the central railway station and offers accommodation for as little as 18 Euros per night. However limited your resources, the magnificent view of Mont Blanc, the lake and the Jura from the top of the towers of St Peter's Cathedral is well worth the 2 Euro entrance fee. Of course, many of the city's landmarks, such as the floral clock and the Reformation Wall, can be visited for free.

Distance	Location	Directions
0.0	Geneva airport	For directions from airport to Franco–Swiss border see Appendix 1
22.5	Hermance: Franco–Swiss border	Go straight on – D25
24.7	Chens-sur-Léman: D25/D20	Turn L – D25 (Thonon). Follow D25 through Messery, Yvoire and Excenevex to Sciez
39.5	Sciez: D25/N5	Turn L – N5 (Thonon)
41.0	N5/D325	Turn L – D325/Route du Port (Port de Sciez-Plage)
41.6	Roundabout	Turn R (Le Chatelet)
43.2	Roundabout	Turn R (Thonon)
43.6	Jtn	Turn R – D35/Route du Port de Sciez
43.9	Séchex: Jtn	Turn L – Rue Centrale/D35
45.8	Anthy-sur-Léman	Turn L in centre of village [Tour du Bas Chablais]. Follow these blue cycling signs to Thonon.
50.5	Thonon: roundabout	Go straight on (Office de Tourisme)
50.7	Jtn	Turn R onto Rue Vallon (Centre Ville–Rue Pietonnée). Follow road around to L and turn immediately R into square with large fountain. Go across square and then straight on along Rue St Sebastien.
51.0	Jtn	Turn R onto Place du Marché
51.1	Thonon TO	TO is on the L

52

Nernier, one of Lake Geneva's most picturesque villages

FACILITIES AND SERVICES

Location	Distance (km)	Water	Shops	Café	Campsite	B&B	Hotel	Bank	Bike Shop
Geneva	0.0	—	x	x	x	x	x	x	x
Vésenaz	13.7	—	x	x	—	—	x	x	x
Hermance	21.9	—	x	x	—	—	x	—	—
Chens-sur-Léman	25.7	x	x	x	x	—	x	—	—
Yvoire	32.2	x	x	x	x	—	x	—	—
Excenevex	35.5	—	x	x	x	x	x	—	—
Sciez (1)	39.2	—	x	x	x	x	x	x	(2)
Séchex	43.6	x	—	x	x	—	—	—	—
Thonon-les-Bains	50.8	x	x	x	x	—	x	x	x

(1) There are campsites, hotels and restaurants in several places between Sciez and Thonon

(2) The bike shop is actually in Bonnatrait, 1km from Sciez

es-Bains
◦m

Orcier
654m

Col du Feu
1117m

Vailly
785m

D902/D22
540m

Abondance
920m

Day 2

60   70   80   90   100

km)

It was whilst cycling up the Abondance Valley that I was first introduced to the world of Brévets. A 'Brévet' is a cycling challenge in which the objective is to cycle a set course within a fixed time. In theory, it is not a race and, as long as you arrive within the deadline, your exact time is unimportant. This approach ensures that the day is almost as much a social event as a sporting occasion and many of the participants are happy to chat to other cyclists to take their mind off how far their aching legs still have to go. In this way, I was able to glean a great deal of information about the most beautiful and quietest roads in the area. I also found out that, as friendly as the organisation is, the refreshment stands at strategic points along the route are only for registered participants!

Distance	Location	Directions
0.0	Thonon TO	Come out of the TO and turn R. After about 50 metres turn L onto Rue des Granges.
0.1	Roundabout	Go straight on (Chatel) and go over the level crossing
0.9	Roundabout: D902/D26	Take first exit – D26 (Armoy) 5.6km at 3.5%
6.9	Armoy: D26/D35	Turn R – D35 (Orcier)
11.9	Orcier D35/D36	Turn L – D36 (Col du Feu) 6.2km at 7.5%
13.3	D36/D36A	Turn R – D36A (Col du Feu)
14.1	D36A/D36	Go straight on – D36 (Lullin)
18.1	Col du Feu	Go straight on – D36 (Lullin)
21.1	Lullin: D36/D22	Turn L – D22 (Vailly)
23.9	Sous la Côte: D22/D26	Turn L – D26 (Vailly)
24.7	Vailly: D26/D22	Turn R – D22 (Chatel). Short descent, then 1.4km at 7%
30.3	La Vernaz: D22/D22A	Turn L – D22A (Thonon)
33.5	D22A/D902	Turn L – D902 (Thonon)
33.9	Roundabout: D902/D22	Turn R – D22 (Chatel). Follow D22 to Chatel
61.6	Chatel TO*	TO is on the L

* If you are camping, about 2km after La Chapelle d'Abondance turn R onto the D230. After 4.5km, turn L onto D228, and immediately L again just after the bridge. The campsite is about 300 metres on the L.

La Vailly: looking towards the Dent d'Oche

				FACILITIES AND SERVICES					
Location	Distance (km)	Water	Shops	Café	Campsite	B&B	Hotel	Bank	Bike Shop
Thonon-les-Bains	0.0	x	x	x	x	—	x	x	x
Armoy	6.9	—	x	x	—	—	x	—	—
Orcier	11.9	x	—	x	—	—	—	—	—
Col du Feu	18.1	—	—	x	—	—	—	—	—
Lullin	21.1	x	x	x	—	—	x	—	—
Vailly	24.7	x	—	x	—	x	—	—	—
Abondance	49.9	x	x	x	x	x	x	x	—
Chatel	61.6	x	x	x	x	x	x	x	x

Col de Bassachaux
1778m

Chatel
1180m

Abondance
920m

Day 3

(km)   100   110   120   130   140

Day 3 – Chatel to Samoëns

Although a recent addition to the Tour de France (first included in 1978), the Col de Joux-Plane has already featured in the race ten times. It is a pass that has frequently smiled on French riders, with six out of the ten winners of this stage being French, the most recent of whom was Richard Virenque in 2000. Other prestigious winners of Joux-Plane stages include Lance Armstrong in the 2002 Critérium du Dauphiné Libéré.

Distance	Location	Directions
0.0	Chatel TO	Come out of TO and turn R – D228 (Col de Bassachaux)* 9km at 7%
12.7	Col de Bassachaux	From end of tarmac, follow the track on the L, slightly uphill at first [Les Lindarets] – red and white waymarkers
14.5	Chairlift	Go under chairlift [Lac Vert]
14.9	Jtn	Turn R and follow mountain bike signs [Les Gets] (200 metres of path isn't suitable for cycling).
15.1	Jtn	Keep following the wide track downhill
17.1	Jtn with paved road	Turn R and follow D228 to Montriond
26.1	Montriond: roundabout	Turn L (Morzine)
26.3	D228/D229	Turn L – D229 (Morzine)
28.6	Morzine: jtn	Go straight on (Office de Tourisme)
28.7	'Semi' roundabout	Go straight on (Avoriaz)
29.1	Roundabout	Turn R (Cluses)
29.4	Roundabout	Turn R (Col de Joux Plane)
29.5	Jtn	Turn R – D354 (Col de Joux Plane) 8.1km at 8.5%
37.6	Col de Ranfolly	Go straight on
40.2	Col de Joux Plane	Go straight on
47.0	Jtn	Turn R (Poids Lourds et Bus)
52.5	Samoëns	Turn R
52.6	Jtn	Turn L (Centre Ville)
52.7	Roundabout	Turn L (Toutes Directions)
52.8	Samoëns TO	TO is on the L

* If you do not want to do any off-road cycling, go back through Abondance and over the Col du Corbier to follow the D902 back to Montriond

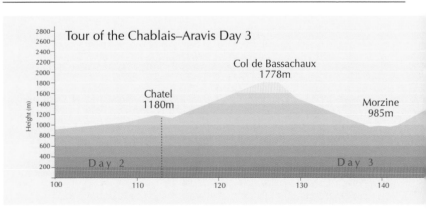

Tour of the Chablais–Aravis Day 3

Les Lindarets

FACILITIES AND SERVICES

Location	Distance (km)	Water	Shops	Café	Campsite	B&B	Hotel	Bank	Bike Shop
Chatel	0.0	x	x	x	x	x	x	x	x
Les Lindarets	17.5	x	—	x	—	—	—	—	—
Montriond	26.1	x	x	x	x	—	x	—	—
Morzine	28.6	x	x	x	—	x	x	x	x
Col de Joux Plane	40.2	—	x	—	—	—	—	—	—
Samoëns	52.8	x	x	x	x	x	x	x	(1)

(1) Nearest bike shop: Cluses, approx 18km south-west of Samoëns

If you have some energy to spare when you get to Samoëns, I strongly recommend the 25km round-trip to visit the Cirque du Fer à Cheval. The cycling is easy and the destination is one of the most spectacular corners of the Alps. Take a bike lock with you so you can stroll up the valley from the road head to get the best views of the spectacular cliffs, rock towers and waterfalls that make the cirque 'Un Grand Site de France'. For those who find even a small resort such as Samoëns too busy, there is a campsite at the entrance to the cirque and *gites d'étape* and hotels in the village of Sixt-Fer-à-Cheval. Go to **www.sixtferacheval.com** for details.

Distance	Location	Directions
0.0	Samoëns TO	Come out of the TO and turn L
0.1	Roundabout	Turn R – D4 (Cluses)
0.8	Roundabout	Turn R – D4 and follow (Cluses) through Morillon
10.9	D4/D902	Turn L – D902 (Cluses) 1.5km at 5%
12.4	Col du Chatillon	Go straight on
17.8	Cluses: roundabout	Go straight on (Centre Ville)
18.2	Traffic lights	Turn L (Centre Ville) and go through Cluses town centre
19.3	Roundabout	Turn R – N205 (Bonneville)
20.0	Roundabout	Turn L (Col de la Colombière)
21.1	Roundabout	Turn L – D4 (Col de la Colombière) 17.7km at 6.5%
38.8	Col de la Colombière	Go straight on
50.4	Jtn	Turn R (Annecy)
50.9	Le Grand Bornand: roundabout	Turn R (Annecy) and follow D4/D12 to St Jean de Sixt
53.4	St Jean de Sixt*: round-about: D12/D909	Turn L – D909 (La Clusaz)
56.1	La Clusaz: roundabout	Turn L and then take the first R (Centre village)
56.4	La Clusaz TO	TO is on the R

* If you are camping, you may want to spend the night at the campsite in Saint Jean de Sixt; the campsite at La Clusaz is 2km east of the village and 150 metres higher!

Col de la Colombière

FACILITIES AND SERVICES

Location	Distance (km)	Water	Shops	Café	Campsite	B&B	Hotel	Bank	Bike Shop
Samoëns	0.0	x	x	x	x	x	x	x	(1)
Morillon	4.5	x	x	x	x	x	x	—	—
Cluses	17.8	—	x	x	x	—	x	x	x
Le Reposoir	31.1	x	x	x	x	—	—	—	—
Le Chinaillon	43.2	—	x	x	—	—	x	—	—
Col de la Colombière	38.8	—	—	x	—	—	—	—	—
Le Grand Bornand	50.9	x	x	x	x	x	x	x	x
St Jean de Sixt	53.4	x	x	x	x	—	x	—	x
La Clusaz	56.4	x	x	x	x	x	x	x	x

(1) Nearest bike shop: Cluses, approx 18km south-west of Samoëns

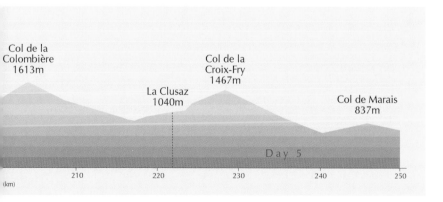

Col de la Colombière 1613m

Col de la Croix-Fry 1467m

La Clusaz 1040m

Col de Marais 837m

Day 5

210   220   230   240   250

(km)

If you would like to have a rest day in La Clusaz or Annecy, why not get a bird's-eye view of the Alps? The most luxurious way to fly is in a hot-air balloon, but this is also a very expensive option, with flights costing 250 Euros per person. For details of flights from Le Grand-Bornand go to **www.bapteme-montgolfiere.com**. A tandem flight in a paraglider is more reasonably priced at 80 to 120 Euros, but you will only be in the air for between 20 minutes and 1 hour. Several companies offer introductory flights at similar rates, for example **www.lespassagersduvent.com** and **www.aeroslide.com**. Pleasure flights in light aircraft provide the best value for money (around 200 Euros for a 1hr flight for three people), but the nearest airport to propose such excursions is Chambéry.

Distance	Location	Directions
0.0	La Clusaz TO	Come out of TO and turn R to go past police station
0.1	Jtn	Turn R onto Route de l'Etale and go past cinema
1.7	Jtn	Bear L onto Route de Sence (just after tiny chapel on R)
2.6	Jtn	Turn R – D16 (no sign)
6.6	Col de la Croix-Fry	Go straight on and follow D16 through Manigod to D12
18.5	D16/D12	Turn L – D12 (Faverges)
24.0	Col du MaraisGo	Straight on
34.3	St Ferréol: roundabout	Turn R – D12 (Faverges)
36.0	Roundabout	Turn R (Viuz)
36.7	Roundabout	Turn R [Tour de la Tournette]
37.0	Jtn	Go straight on (Rocher d'escalade). Continue through Vesonne to Jtn with D42.
39.6	Jtn	Turn L – D42 (no sign)
40.0	D42/N508	Go straight across N508 to join Annecy cycleway*
58.5	End of cycleway	Turn R – N508
60.7	Roundabout	Go straight on (Centre Ville)
61.3	Annecy TO	TO is on the L

* In spring 2004 work started on the extension of the cycleway to Faverges and Ugine. Work should be finished by summer 2005. However, following the minor road through Vesonne will still be a good option as this road sees very little traffic.

La Tournette from below the Col de la Croix-Fry

FACILITIES AND SERVICES

Location	Distance (km)	Water	Shops	Café	Campsite	B&B	Hotel	Bank	Bike Shop
La Clusaz	0.0	x	x	x	x	x	x	x	x
Col de la Croix-Fry	6.6	—	—	x	—	—	—	—	—
Manigod	13.8	x	x	x	—	—	x	—	—
Serraval	26.7	x	x	x	x	—	—	—	—
St Férreol	34.3	—	x	x	x	—	x	—	—
Faverges (1)	36.7	x	x	x	—	x	x	x	x
Doussard	42.3	—	x	—	x	x	x	x	—
Annecy	61.3	x	x	x	x	x	x	x	x

(1) The route goes around the edge of Faverges; all the facilities are in the town centre

Day 6 – Annecy to Geneva

Extra day: The easiest way to visit the Bauges Mountains is to traverse from Annecy to Chambéry via the Col de Leschaux, Lescheraines, and the Col de Plainpalais. There are trains back to Annecy every 30 to 60 minutes, depending on the time of day. If you are looking for a more challenging day out, turn right just after the Col de Plainpalais, go over Mont Revard (magnificent views) and head back to Annecy via Trévignin, Cusy and Gruffy.

Distance	Location	Directions
0.0	Annecy TO	Come out of TO and turn L
0.4	Jtn: Ave D'Albiny/Rue Louis Revon	Turn L onto Rue Louis Revon (Hôtel du Département) – start of intermittent cycle lane
0.6	Jtn	Turn R onto Ave de Parmelan. Follow (Annecy-le-Vieux)
1.7	Annecy-le-Vieux	Go straight on along Ave des Carrés. Continue straight on to pick up and follow (Thônes – Les Aravis).
2.7	Start of cycleway	Follow cycleway uphill – more or less parallel to road
5.1	Roundabout	Leave the cycleway and turn L at the roundabout (Thônes – Les Aravis)
5.8	Roundabout	Turn L onto D5 (Naves Parmelan). Follow D5 to Thorens-Glières.
20.8	Thorens-Glières: D5/D2	Go straight on – D2 (Groisy)
25.8	Groisy-Le Plot	Go under N203 and through Le Plot – D2D
26.1	D2D/D2	Turn R – D2 (Groisy)
28.7	Groisy: D2/D23	Turn R – D23 – 2nd of two Jtns (Cruseilles)
37.4	Cruseilles: T-Jtn	Turn R and then immediately L onto Rue de l'Arthaz
37.9	Crossroads	Go straight on – D41A (Le Salève)
50.2	High point	Go straight on
54.4	La Croisette: D41A/D45	Turn L – D45
59.0	Le Coin: D45/D145	Turn R – D145 and follow this road to Collonges-sous-Salève
61.7	Collonges	Turn L – one-way – then turn R onto Rue Lamartine
61.9	T-Jtn	Turn R and go over motorway and railway
62.3	Traffic lights	Go straight on to Franco–Swiss border
62.5	Franco-Swiss border	For directions to airport, see Appendix 1
74.9	Geneva airport	

Admiring Lake Annecy from one of the many pontoons along the edge of the lake

FACILITIES AND SERVICES

Location	Distance (km)	Water	Shops	Café	Campsite	B&B	Hotel	Bank	Bike Shop
Annecy	0.0	x	x	x	x	x	x	x	x
Naves Parmelan	10.0	x	—	x	x	x	x	—	—
Thorens-Glières	20.8	x	x	x	x	—	x	x	—
Groisy	28.7	—	x	x	—	—	—	x	—
Cruseilles	37.4	x	x	x	x	—	x	x	x
Le Salève (La Croisette)	54.4	—	—	x	—	—	—	—	—
Collonges-sous-Salève	61.7	x	x	x	x	—	—	x	—
Geneva	75.9	—	x	x	x	x	x	x	x

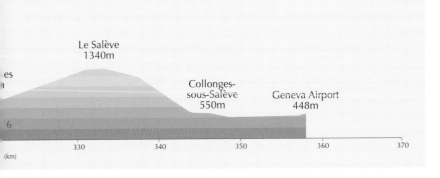

ACCOMMODATION

Geneva

Campsites

Pointe-à-la-Bise, in Vesenaz, 6km north-east of the city centre (early April to early Oct), Tel. (022) 752 12 96

Bois de Bay, in Satigny, 4km west of Geneva airport (all year), Tel. (022) 341 05 05

Val de l'Allondon, in Satigny, 4km west of Geneva airport (early April to end Oct), Tel. (022) 753 15 15

Bed & Breakfast

Geneva youth hostel, Tel. (022) 732 62 60

Hotels

There are more than 100 hotels in Geneva. Contact TO for details.

Thonon-les-Bains

Campsites

Le Lac Noir, 3km south of Thonon, on the D903 (June to Sept), Tel. 04 50 26 07 28

Le Morcy, 3km west of Thonon, at Morcy (Easter to mid-Sept), Tel. 04 50 70 44 87

Saint Disdille, 3km north of Thonon, near Port Ripaille (early April to end Sept), Tel. 04 50 71 14 11

Bed & Breakfast

La Clématite, Tel. 04 50 71 85 95

Centre International de Séjour (hostel, sleeps 200), Tel. 04 50 71 77 80

Hotels

There are 16 hotels in Thonon-les-Bains. Contact TO for details.

Chatel

Campsites

L'Oustalet (mid-June to end August), Tel. 04 50 73 21 97

Bed & Breakfast

Le P'tit Cornillon, Tel. 04 50 81 35 49

Chalet l'Etringa, Tel. 04 50 81 31 48

La Couqueille, Tel. 04 50 73 31 89

La Svoyarde, Tel. 04 50 73 23 17

Hotels

There are more than 25 hotels in Chatel. Contact TO for details.

Samoêns

Campsites

Le Giffre (all year), Tel. 04 50 34 41 92

Bed & Breakfast

Le Moulin du Bathieu, Verclaix, 2km south of Samoëns, Tel. 04 50 34 43 25

La Glière, Tel. 04 50 34 43 65

Les Moulins, Tel. 04 50 34 95 69

Les Couadzous, Tel. 04 50 34 41 62

M. Granger, Tel 04 50 34 41 62

Hotels

There are 14 hotels in Samoêns. Contact TO for details.

La Clusaz

Campsites

Le Plan du Fernuy (early June to early Sept), Tel. 04 50 02 44 75

At St Jean-de-Sixt:

Le Cret (mid-June to mid-Sept), Tel. 04 50 35 80 54

Bed & Breakfast

Youth hostel, Tel. 04 50 02 41 73

Mrs Suize, Tel. 04 50 02 42 81

La Ferme du Var, Tel. 04 50 02 26 56

La Trace, Tel. 04 50 02 46 76

Hotels

There are more than 20 hotels in La Clusaz. Contact TO for details.

Annecy

Campsites

Le Savoy (mid-April to end Sept), Tel. 04 50 23 62 92

Le Colovry (early June to mid-Sept), Tel. 04 50 23 13 29

Le Belvedere (end March to early Oct), Tel. 04 50 45 48 30

There are many other campsites along the lakeshore between Doussard and Annecy.

Bed & Breakfast

Youth hostel, Tel. 04 50 45 33 19

Mr Michel, Tel. 04 50 45 72 28

Hotels

There are more than 40 hotels in Annecy. Contact TO for details.

TOURIST INFORMATION

Regional Information

	Telephone	Website
Haute-Savoie	04 50 51 32 31	www.savoiehautesavoie.com

Tourist Information Offices

Location	Telephone	Website
Geneva	022 909 70 00	www.geneve-tourisme.ch
Yvoire	04 50 72 80 21	http://yvoire.free.fr/
Thonon-les-Bains	04 50 71 55 55	www.thononlesbains.com
Abondance/Chatel	04 50 73 02 90	www.valdabondance.com
Chatel	04 50 73 22 44	www.chatel.com
Morzine	04 50 74 72 72	www.morzine.com
Samoëns	04 50 34 40 28	www.samoens.com
Cluses	04 50 98 31 79	www.cluses.com
Le Grand Bornand	04 50 02 78 00	www.legrandbornand.com
La Clusaz	04 50 32 65 00	www.laclusaz.com
Manigod	04 50 44 92 44	www.manigod.com
Faverges	04 50 44 60 24	www.pays-de-faverges.com
Annecy	04 50 45 00 33	www.lac-annecy.com
Thorens-Glières	04 50 22 40 31	http://thorens-glieres.net
Cruseilles	04 50 44 81 69	no website

ROUTE THREE

TOUR OF MONT BLANC

Day	Route	Distance	Height Gain
1	Martigny to Chamonix	44.0km	1434m
2	Chamonix to Beaufort	82.5km	1526m
3	Beaufort to Bourg St Maurice	45.7km	1407m
4	Bourg St Maurice to Aosta	85.7km	1375m
5	Aosta to Martigny	83.7km	1889m
	Totals	**341.6km**	**7631**

As the highest mountain in western Europe, Mont Blanc attracts millions of visitors every year. Most come to just look at the Roof of Europe, a small minority actually climb to the top and an increasing number choose to do a circuit round the entire massif, either under their own steam (on foot or by bike) or by car, coach or motorbike. The classic circuit by road, via Martigny, Chamonix and Aosta, goes over some of the most famous passes in the Alps including the Grand St Bernard, the highest point on the circuit. Obviously, the roads around such a famous tourist honey-pot are not going to be deserted, especially during the holiday season. Where possible, the itinerary avoids the major tourist routes, but this is still a tour that is best enjoyed outside the main mid-July to mid-August holiday period.

The most obvious attraction of this area is the scenery, which is quite simply breathtaking, especially in the spring and the autumn, when the light is often at its sharpest. For a large part of the circuit it is Mont Blanc itself that dominates the horizon, a massive but shapely lump of rock and ice that dwarfs even the loftiest of its neighbours. On cloudless days, when deep blue skies hover over the pristine white of the summit snowfields and the vivid greens of the surrounding pastures, Mont Blanc is an invitation to climb towards the heavens. But seen in the lowering orange-grey light of an approaching storm, the mountain exudes a terrible menace that would discourage all but the (fool-) hardiest of climbers; local folklore long believed that only the damned were drawn towards the summit!

The tour is described starting from Martigny, as this is the easiest place to get to by public transport. (If you are driving to France, Sallanches would be a more convenient place to start). By travelling in a clockwise direction, the height of the passes that you go over gradually increases from day to day, and the tour finishes with a superbly enjoyable descent from the Grand St Bernard Pass.

Martigny may not be the most architecturally distinguished town in Switzerland, but it does boast an extremely impressive array of museums. Art lovers and historians could easily spend several days browsing through all the treasures the town has to offer. The most outstanding museum, for both the eclectic range of subjects that it covers (Roman history, fine art, classic cars) and the quality of its permanent and temporary exhibitions, is the Pierre Gianadda Foundation. Martigny is surrounded by vineyards, many of which cultivate Chasselas grapes, which are thought by many to be the first grape variety cultivated by man. The local wine is called Fendant, as, when ripe, the grapes split if pressed between finger and thumb (*fendre*: to split). Fendant is usually drunk as an aperitif or to accompany fish or cheese dishes, especially fondue.

Although the first stage of the tour is only 44km, it is worth making an early start as the lower slopes of the Col de la Forclaz offer no shade whatsoever: in the middle of summer the road can feel like a furnace. In marked contrast, the upper part of the road runs

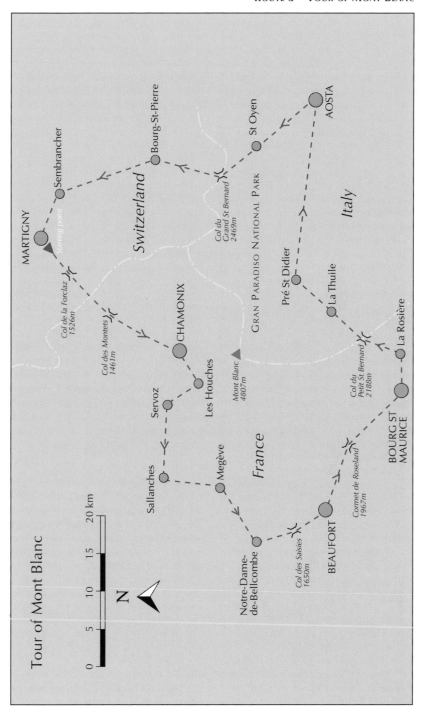

Tour of Mont Blanc

through dense forest, that cuts out the sun and blocks any view. Once over the pass, this corridor of trees opens out to reveal the spectacularly chaotic Glacier du Trient, a foretaste of the scenic delights to come. An all-too-brief descent through the steep-sided Trient Valley takes you to the Franco–Swiss border at Le Châtelard, an excellent place to stock up on chocolate!

Being the main route from Martigny to Chamonix, the road over the Forclaz Pass can be very busy, especially during the summer holidays. The only way to avoid the Forclaz is to go through the Trient Gorge. Unfortunately, a 5km section of this route is on an unpaved, but well maintained, forest track.

As long as your legs are not too tired after the Col de la Forclaz, the climb up to the Col des Montets should not feel too difficult and there is always the added incentive of knowing that from the pass it is downhill all the way to Chamonix and the end of this first stage. Needless to say, the scenery is magnificent: few valleys can boast such a spectacular mix of snowy domes, tortured glaciers and towering rock spires. Chamonix has used its position at the foot of Europe's highest mountain to transform itself from a tiny village into the undisputed mountaineering capital of the world. However, Mont Blanc does not 'belong' to Chamonix: the summit actually lies within the boundaries of St Gervais, and it is from here that most climbers start their ascent. Despite the cost (29 Euros in 2004) and the queues, every visitor to Chamonix should take the cable car to the top of the Aiguille du Midi. Rising 2800 metres above the town centre, the cable car itself is an engineering marvel and the panorama from the top is unbeatable.

Day two of the tour starts quite gently, following minor roads through Les Houches, from where the views of the Chamonix Aiguilles are arguably even better than those from Chamonix itself, to Sallanches, a bustling market town on the banks of the Arve. On leaving Sallanches, the tempo changes dramatically as the road climbs steeply (gradients of up to 15%) out of the valley. This road takes you through the village of Combloux, the holiday haunt of Jean-Pierre Raffarin, who was appointed Prime Minister of France in 2002.

Despite this excellent publicity, Combloux will probably never outshine nearby Megève in terms of chic and exclusivity. At the beginning of 2005, Megève became the first ski resort in the *département* of Haute-Savoie to be connected to a resort in Savoie. This fact is only particularly noteworthy when you consider that these neighbouring *départements* created links with Switzerland (Portes du Soleil) and Italy (La Rosière/La Thuile) many years ago, but have never before managed to overcome the intense rivalry between themselves.

From Megève, a 10km descent along the N212 leads to the foot of the Col des Saisies. This is the longest climb of the day, but the ascent is divided into two sections by a short descent, with the first section being longer and steeper than the second. For once, Mont Blanc cannot be seen, being hidden behind the Aiguille Croche, however the view of the Aravis Range to the north provides ample compensation. As every cycle ride in the mountains should, the day ends with a long and enjoyable descent to Beaufort, a truly authentic and unspoilt mountain village. Beaufort has given its name to the 'Prince of Gruyere Cheeses' and, like all traditional products, there is nowhere better to taste it than its place of origin – the village's co-operative dairy is open to visitors every day during the summer. Should you be tempted to buy some, go for the Beaufort d'alpage: it is by far the best. Beaufort also boasts a bakery that sells the best homemade ice cream you will find this side of Italy.

The third stage of the tour heads south to the village resort of Arèches, an excellent example of how to reap the benefits of tourism without destroying the landscape. From Arèches, the road rises very steeply, through picture-postcard alpine pastures and past traditional wooden chalets to the Col du Pré, which, rather unusually, is neither the geographical col nor the highest point of the road. During the descent from the pass, Mont Blanc once again comes into view, but it tends to be the extremely picturesque Roselend Reservoir that draws the eye. The road goes over the dam and around the northern end of the reservoir before once again striking uphill to the Cormet de Roselend. This area has one of the

The pleasant pedestrianised streets of Aosta

highest snowfalls in the French Alps, and it is not unusual to see two-metre-high walls of snow beside the road in the middle of May. As this stage is quite short, during the descent I recommend making a short detour to Les Chapieux, an excellent place to have lunch whilst admiring the majestic Aiguille des Glaciers, which reins over the northern end of the valley.

Day three ends at the busy little town of Bourg St Maurice. Being the gateway to several of the biggest ski resorts in Europe such as Tignes, Val d'Isère and Les Arcs, Bourg St Maurice's economy is very much dependent on tourism. However, it is not really a resort itself and has few tourist attractions of its own. The little minerals museum is quite interesting and, if you are still hungry for cheese, the town's co-operative dairy is open to visitors.

The Col du Petit St Bernard, which has been a point of passage between the Tarentaise and Aosta Valleys for at least three millennia, provides the objective for day four. Despite following a *route nationale*, traffic levels are rarely a problem as long as you are not on the road on the 20th August. This is Saint Bernard's Day, the occasion for a huge gather-

ing at the summit of the pass, during which pedestrian and vehicle traffic can be so dense that cycling becomes impossible! In around 25BC, the Romans built a temple and a column to the glory of Jupiter, naming the pass Columna Jovis. After the fall of the Roman Empire, cutthroats and brigands overran the area, curtailing the lucrative trans-alpine trade in wine and minerals. This sorry state of affairs was attributed to the evil powers exercised by the garnet carbuncle at the top of the Jupiter column, so, at the beginning of the 11th century, Bernard of Menthon, then Archdeacon of Aosta, was petitioned to exorcise the column. He quickly cast out the demons and toppled the malevolent stone. The base of the column and other archaeological remains can still be seen on either side of the road.

The pass is also the border between France and Italy, although there are few obvious signs that you have changed country. In fact, from 1032 until the unification of Italy in the second half of the 19th century, the Aosta Valley was governed by the house of Savoie, an historical connection to France that is still seen in many place names such as La Thuile and Pré St Didier. The valley retains a great deal of autonomy and French is still an official language alongside Italian. Aosta is an extremely pleasant city to explore with a great deal to see. There are too many places of interest to mention all of them here, but the Roman amphitheatre and the Sant'Orso cloisters should not be missed. The city's tourist

office provides an excellent free monument guide and map (in English).

All too soon, it is time to leave Aosta and head up to the second of the St Bernard Passes. Like it is smaller brother, the Grand St Bernard Pass has been used by travellers

Getting off the train in Bourg St Maurice

since pre-historic times. Julius Caesar is known to have crossed the pass in 57BC on his way to conquer the pagans of Martigny. The lawlessness into which the area descended towards the end of the first millennium AD was brought under control by King Canute of Denmark and Rudolph III of Burgundy, allowing Bernard of Menthon to build a hospice to provide shelter and a safe haven for merchants and pilgrims. Nearly a thousand years later the hospice still provides board and lodging for travellers all year round. In May 1800 Napoleon took his army across the pass into Italy, running up an enormous bill at the hospice, a debt that remained unsettled until it was symbolically repaid by President Mitterand in May 1984. You can learn more about the pass's fascinating history at the museum at the summit. Although no longer used for mountain rescue, the hospice still maintains a kennel for its famous Saint Bernard dogs. The kennel breeds about 15 pedigree puppies a year and sells them for around 1000 Euros each. This is not the only business carried out at the pass as the numerous souvenir stalls, shops and cafés testify.

The pass is also the border between Italy and Switzerland and, as Switzerland is not part of the European Union, the border is well policed. Once you have cleared customs, all that remains is the magnificent 40km descent to Martigny, 2000 metres below: a fitting finale to a spectacular tour.

GETTING THERE

By car
For cyclists driving from the UK, Sallanches is a more convenient town than Martigny from which to start the tour. If you start in Sallanches, the first day of the tour would be from Sallanches to Beaufort (52km), and the last day would be from Martigny to Sallanches (75km). Sallanches is 800km from Calais.

By plane
Via Geneva: There is a train every hour (that will accept bikes) from Geneva Airport to Martigny, via Lausanne. The journey takes around 2 hours.

Via Lyon: If you fly into Lyon Airport, the easiest place to start the tour from is Bourg St Maurice. However, even this 'easiest' of options can still be very time consuming.

Shuttle bus/train: If the shuttle bus will accept your bike, there is a direct service from Lyon airport to Bourg St Maurice, or you can take the bus to Chambéry and the train from Chambéry to Bourg St Maurice. (Chambéry coach station is next to the railway station.) For both of these routes, there are only two to five buses per day, depending on the exact time of year and the day of the week.

Cycle/Train: To take the train you have to cycle to Bourgoin Jallieu (see Appendix 1 for route details). There are only three or four trains per day and the journey takes three to four hours.

Via Turin: The tour could also be started from Aosta by flying to Turin. Contact Turin airport (**www.aeroportoditorino.it**) and/or Italian railways (**www.trenitalia.com**) for information about connections from Turin to Aosta.

WHEN TO GO

The ideal time to do this circuit is June or September as the roads over both of the St Bernard Passes are closed from late November to the end of May and some of the roads, especially those between Martigny and Chamonix, can be very busy during the summer holidays.

MAPS

No single map covers the entire area in enough detail for comfortable navigation. A combination of the Michelin Local Map, Sheet 328: Ain, Haute-Savoie, and the Italian Istituto Geografico Centrale 1:50,000 scale map for the *Massiccio del Monte Bianco*, which can be bought in Italy, works well.

Like most high mountains, Mont Blanc 'creates' its own weather and the summit is often battered by raging blizzards while the surrounding peaks bask under clear blue skies. However, according to local lore, the mountains can give you a good weather forecast: when there is a lenticular cloud covering Mont Blanc and the other summits are clear, it will stay fine; but if the Aiguille Verte is also shrouded in cloud, storms are brewing.

Distance	Location	Directions
0.0	Martigny station	Come out of the station and go straight ahead past 'Helvetia Patria'. Keep going straight on, first following (Centre Ville), and then (Forclaz).
3.0	Roundabout	Go straight on (Col de la Forclaz) 13.3km at 8%
16.3	Col de la Forclaz	Go straight on through Trient to the Franco–Swiss border
25.1	Le Châtelard: customs post	Go straight on – N506 6.7km at 4.5%
31.8	Col des Montets	Go straight on and down through Argentière (Chamonix)
41.1	Les Praz	Turn R (Les Praz)
43.6	Chamonix: jtn	Go straight on
43.8	Go straight on	Pedestrian sign for TO (Do not follow road signs to TO)
43.9	Jtn	Turn R – pedestrian sign for TO
44.0	Chamonix TO	TO is on your L

FACILITIES AND SERVICES

Location	Distance (km)	Water	Shops	Café	Campsite	B&B	Hotel	Bank	Bike Shop
Martigny	0.0	x	x	x	x	x	x	x	x
Col de la Forclaz	16.3	x	x	x	x	x	x	—	—
Trient	19.4	x	x	x	—	x	—	—	—
Le Châtelard	25.1	x	x	x	—	—	x	—	—
Vallorcine	27.5	x	x	x	x	x	x	—	—
Argentière	35.1	x	x	x	x	x	x	x	—
Chamonix	44.0	x	x	x	x	x	x	x	x

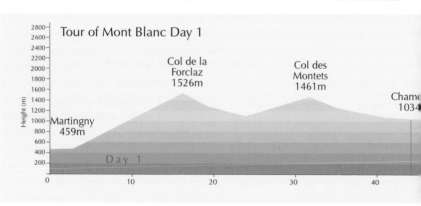

Tour of Mont Blanc Day 1

Chamonix and the statue commemorating Balmat and Saussure's ascent of Mont Blanc

Chamonix has become so synonymous with Mont Blanc that the town has officially changed its name to Chamonix-Mont Blanc. The highest mountain in Western Europe was first climbed by Michel-Gabriel Paccard and Jacques Balmat in 1786. Their ascent took two days, following a route from Chamonix (now called the Grands Mulets Route). Today, the most popular route to the summit starts in Saint Gervais (via the Nid d'Aigle mountain railway), but most mountaineers still take two days to get to the top. The current record for climbing Mont Blanc from the church in the centre of Chamonix was set in 1990. Pierre-André Gobet took 3hrs 38mins to reach the summit and 1hr 32mins to get back to Chamonix. In 2003, the record was attempted on skis by Stéphane Brosse and Pierre Gignoux. Carrying their skis over the bottom section, where there was no snow, they did the climb in 4hrs 04mins and completed the descent in 1hr 08mins.

Vaudagne
1110m

Servoz
814m

Salanches
549m

Combloux
980m

Megève
1100m

Day 2

6390   70   80   90   100

km)

Day 2 – Chamonix to Beaufort

Distance	Location	Directions
0.0	Chamonix TO	Come out of the TO and turn L
0.1	Roundabout	Turn L (Toutes Directions)
0.6	Jtn	Turn R – second of two parallel roads (Les Bossons)
4.9	Jtn (just before *route nationale*)	Turn L – Route de Taconnaz*
5.3	Jtn	Turn R – Rue de l'Ecole
5.5	Jtn	Go straight on along path (Chemin des Villages)
6.2	Jtn just after small chapel	Turn R
6.5	Hotel des S'nailles	Turn L
7.3	Mini-roundabout	Bear L onto Ave des Alpages
8.9	Jtn	Go straight on – Rue de Bellevue
9.8	Roundabout	Turn L – Route des Chavants
10.3	Jtn	Follow Route de Vaudagne through Vaudagne (Annecy)
16.0	Bridge over dual-carriageway	Go over dual-carriageway – D13 (Chamonix/ Servoz). Follow D13 to (Sallanches).
30.3	Sallanches: roundabout	Turn L (Centre Ville)
31.0	Traffic lights	Go straight on – Ave St Martin
31.2	Sallanches main square	Turn R at traffic lights, then take first L (Combloux)
31.4	Jtn	Turn L (Combloux)
31.5	Jtn	Turn R – D113 (Cordon) then immediately L (Combloux par ancienne route) 5.3km at 8%
36.8	Combloux: jtn	Turn R (La Cry-Cachet) 2.5km at 7%
37.8	Jtn	Turn L (Megéve)
41.5	Jtn N212	Turn R – N212 and go through Megéve and Praz-sur-Arly (Albertville)
51.1	N212/D218A	Turn L – D218A (Les Saisies) and go up to Les Saisies 8km at 6.5%, short descent, then 5km at 4%
65.1	Col des Saisies	Go straight on
72.1	D218/D218E	Turn L onto D218E (Hauteluce)
73.1	D218E/D70	Go straight on along D218E
73.9	Hauteluce	Turn R – D70 (Beaufort)
81.1	D70/D925	Turn R – D925

* The direct road into Les Houches was closed for major road works in 2004. The route described here is currently the recommended route for cyclists, however this may change when the road works are finished.

74

The fabulous view of the Chamonix Aiguilles from Les Houches

FACILITIES AND SERVICES

Location	Distance (km)	Water	Shops	Café	Campsite	B&B	Hotel	Bank	Bike Shop
Chamonix	0.0	x	x	x	x	x	x	x	x
Les Houches	8.2	x	x	x	x	x	x	x	—
Passy	26.8	x	x	x	x	x	x	x	—
Sallanches	31.2	x	x	x	x	x	x	x	x
Combloux	36.8	x	x	x	x	x	x	x	x
Megève	42.0	x	x	x	x	x	x	x	x
Praz-sur-Arly	46.5	x	x	x	—	x	x	—	—
Notre Dame de Bellecombe	54.0	x	x	x	—	x	x	—	x
Les Saisies	65.1	x	x	x	—	x	x	x	—
Hauteluce	73.9	x	x	x	—	x	x	x	—
Beaufort	82.5	x	x	x	x	x	x	x	(1)

(1) Nearest bike shop is in Albertville, 20km southwest of Beaufort

Col des Saisies 1650m

Col du Pré 1703m

Beaufort 755m

Day 2

Day 3

100   110   120   130   140

Day 3 – Beaufort to Bourg St Maurice

Extra day: Beaufort provides an excellent base from which to add an extra day (or days) to the tour. The village is at the centre of a superb network of cycling circuits, which were set up at the instigation of a group of local cyclists in order to develop cycling tourism in this wonderfully beautiful area. Thirteen different routes, of all levels of difficulty, have now been clearly signposted and a small descriptive brochure has been published (available from local tourist offices). The most challenging circuit is the 155km-long Grand Tour of the Beaufortain, which includes 3850 metres of height gain.

Distance	Location	Directions
0.0	Beaufort TO	Come out of TO and turn L – D218 (Arêches-Le Planay) 4km at 6.5%
5.0	Arêches: D218/D85	Go straight on – D218 (Col du Pré) 7.3km at 9%
12.3	Col du Pré	Go straight on
15.7	Low point	Go straight on
17.7	Col de Meraillet: D217/D925	Turn R – D217 (Bourg Saint Maurice) Short descent then 5.9km at 6.5%
25.9	Cormet de Roseland	Go straight on (D217 becomes D902)
45.6	Bourg St Maurice: roundabout: D902/N90	Turn R – N90 (Aime)
45.7	Bourg St Maurice TO	TO is on the R

FACILITIES AND SERVICES

Location	Distance (km)	Water	Shops	Café	Campsite	B&B	Hotel	Bank	Bike Shop
Beaufort	0.0	x	x	x	x	x	x	x	(1)
Arêches	5.0	x	x	x	x	x	x	—	—
Col du Pré	12.3	—	—	x	—	—	—	—	—
Col de Meraillet	17.7	—	—	x	—	—	—	—	—
Bourg St Maurice	45.7	x	x	x	x	—	x	x	x

(1) Nearest bike shop is in Albertville, 20km southwest of Beaufort

76

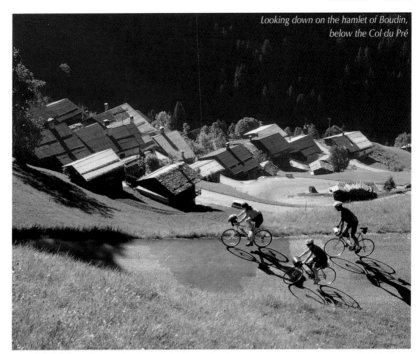

Looking down on the hamlet of Boudin, below the Col du Pré

Although 80% of France's electricity is produced by nuclear power stations, the country's hydropower plants are a key part of the electricity network. Unlike nuclear plants, hydropower stations can be switched on and off in minutes to respond to peaks and troughs in demand and they are very economical: hydro-electricity is 50% cheaper than nuclear electricity. Water from Roseland Reservoir is fed to a generating plant in the Tarentaise Valley via a 13km penstock. Due to the 1km height difference between the dam and the power plant, the water has enough power to produce more than 500MW of electricity. Positioning the gener-ating plant at the bottom of an industrial valley also helps to minimise the installation's impact on the mountain environment.

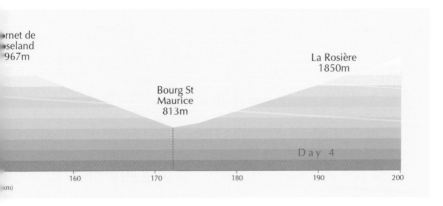

77

Day 4 – Bourg St Maurice to Aosta

Aosta is surrounded by four of Europe's highest and most famous mountains: Mont Blanc, Monte Rosa, the Matterhorn and the Gran Paradiso.

Distance	Location	Directions
0.0	Bourg St Maurice TO	Come out of the TO and turn R – N90
0.1	Roundabout	Go straight on – N90 (Italy) 31.2km at 4.5%
0.8	Roundabout	Go straight on – N90 (La Rosière)
2.9	Séez N90/D902	Bear L – N90 (Aosta)
22.4	La Rosière	Go straight on
31.3	Col du Petit St Bernard	Go straight on
54.4	Pré St Didier S26/S26D	Turn R – S26 (Aosta)
83.0	Entrance to Aosta	Bear R – Rue de Petit St Bernard (Aosta)
84.5	Aosta: roundabout	Turn R – Rue de Chambéry (Centre Ville)
85.4	Jtn Rue de Chambéry/Ave des Maquisards	Get into LH lane and turn L – Ave des Maquisards
85.5	Jtn Ave des Maquisards/Place de la République	Turn R – Place de la République (Hotel de Ville). Go through the pedestrian area to the Hotel de Ville and TO.
85.7	Aosta: Place Emilio Chanoux	TO is on the L

FACILITIES AND SERVICES									
Location	Distance (km)	Water	Shops	Café	Campsite	B&B	Hotel	Bank	Bike Shop
Bourg St Maurice	0.0	x	x	x	x	—	x	x	x
Séez	2.9	x	x	x	x	x	x	—	—
La Rosière	22.4	x	x	x	—	—	x	x	—
Col du Petit St Bernard	31.3	—	x	x	—	—	—	—	—
La Thuile	44.1	x	x	x	x	x	x	x	—
Pré St Didier	54.4	x	x	x	—	—	x	x	—
Aosta	85.7	x	x	x	x	x	x	x	x

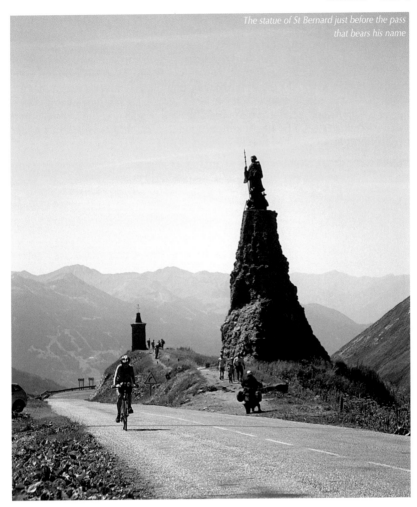

The statue of St Bernard just before the pass that bears his name

Pré St Didier
1030m

Aosta
580m

Day 5

230   240   250   260   270

km)

Cycling long distances burns enormous quantities of fuel, but huge midday meals are not a good idea. After a leisurely climb over the Grand Saint Bernard Pass, my wife and I were feeling strong, so we decided to keep going to Argentière. However, we needed to eat first and the open-air restaurants in Martigny were just too inviting. After a generous three-course lunch, we were back on the bikes grinding up to the Forclaz under the blazing afternoon sun. We made it over the pass – just – and checked into a hotel at Le Châtelard. Our laziness was punished by the weather gods and we woke to rain hammering against the bedroom window. We quickly covered the 10km to Argentière, but it was two very wet and very cold cyclists that rolled into the village.

Distance	Location	Directions
0.0	Aosta TO	Come out of the TO and turn L. Go to Rue Xavier Maistre and turn L, 4.4km at 4.5%
0.3	Traffic lights	Go straight on. Rue Xavier Maistre becomes Ave Pierre Laurent.
0.5	Traffic lights	Go straight on along Ave Pierre Laurent.
0.7	Ave Pierre Laurent/ Rue Roma	Go straight across Rue Roma (underpass for pedestrians and cyclists) and up the very steep Chemin des Capucins – no street name sign.
0.7	Chemin des Capucins/ Ave Grand St Bernard	Turn R onto Ave Grand St Bernard
4.4	Variney	Turn R (Valpelline)
7.7	Castello	Bear L (Allein) 8.5km at 4.5%
12.5	Jtn	Turn L (Allein)
14.3	Jtn	Turn R: no signs
16.2	Allein "chef-lieu"	Bear L (Etroubles)
20.8	Etroubles	Turn R – S27 18.1km at 6.5%
24.1	Jtn	Turn R (Martigny): the main road goes through the Grand St Bernard tunnel.
38.4	Italian border post	Go straight on
38.9	Col du Grand St Bernard	Go straight on and follow N21 to Martigny
80.7	Martigny: roundabout	Turn R (Martigny)
81.2	Roundabout	Go straight on (Centre Ville). Go straight through town centre to station.
83.7	Martigny station	Station is in front of you

In summer, the Col du Grand St Bernard is overrun with souvenir stalls

FACILITIES AND SERVICES								
Location	Distance (km)	Water	Shops	Café	Campsite	B&B	Hotel	Bank	Bike Shop
Aosta	0.0	x	x	x	x	x	x	x	x
St Oyen	22.0	x	x	x	x	x	—	—	—
Col du Grand St Bernard	38.9	—	x	x	—	—	—	—	—
Bourg St Pierre	51.5	x	x	x	x	x	x	—	—
Liddes	58.0	—	x	x	—	—	x	x	—
Orsières	65.4	—	x	x	—	x	x	x	—
Martigny	83.7	x	x	x	x	x	x	x	x

ACCOMMODATION

Martigny

Campsites

TCS (all year round), Tel. 02 77 22 45 44

Bed & Breakfast

Mrs Troillet, Tel. 02 77 22 72 16

Hotels

There are 13 hotels in Martigny. Contact TO for details.

Chamonix

Campsites

There are 15 campsites in Chamonix. Contact TO for details.

Bed & Breakfast

There are more than 20 bed & breakfasts/*gites d'étapes* in Chamonix. Contact TO for details.

Hotels

There are more than 60 hotels in Chamonix. Contact TO for details.

Beaufort

Campsites

Le Domelin (June to end Sept), Tel. 04 79 38 33 88

Bed & Breakfast

There are no bed & breakfasts/*gites d'étapes* in Beaufort

Hotels

Le Doron (**), Tel. 04 79 38 33 18

Hotel du Grand Mont (**), Tel. 04 79 38 33 36

La Cascade (**) 3km west of Beaufort on D925, Tel. 04 79 38 70 00

Hotel de la Roche (*), Tel. 04 79 38 33 31

Bourg St Maurice

Campsites

Le Versoyen (mid-May to end Oct), Tel. 04 79 07 03 45

Bed & Breakfast

There are no bed & breakfasts in Bourg St Maurice

Hotels

There are nine hotels in Bourg St Maurice. Contact TO for details.

Aosta

Campsites

Milleluci (all year round), Tel. (0165) 23 52 78

Ville d'Aoste (mid-May to mid-Sept – closed in 2004 for renovation), Tel. (0165) 36 13 60

Bed & Breakfast

Nabuisson, Tel. (0165) 36 30 06

Porta Praetoria, Tel. (mobile) 338 982 8440

Hotels

There are 27 hotels in Aosta. Contact TO for details.

TOURIST INFORMATION

Regional Information

	Telephone	Website
Haute-Savoie	04 50 51 32 31	**www.savoiehautesavoie.com**
Savoie	04 79 85 12 45	**www.savoiehautesavoie.com**
Aosta Valley	01 65 23 66 27	**www.regione.vda.it**

Tourist Information Offices

Location	Telephone	Website
Martigny	02 77 21 22 20	**www.martignytourism.ch**
Vallorcine	04 50 54 60 71	**www.vallorcine.com**
Chamonix	04 50 53 00 24	**www.chamonix.com**
Passy	04 50 58 80 52	**www.ot-passy.com**
Sallanches	04 50 58 04 25	**www.sallanches.com**
Combloux	04 50 58 60 49	**www.combloux.com**
Megève	04 50 21 27 28	**www.megeve.com**
Praz-sur-Arly	04 50 21 90 57	**www.prazsurarly.com**
Notre Dame de Bellecombe	04 79 31 61 40	**www.ot-ndb.com**
Les Saisies	04 79 38 90 30	**www.lessaisies.com**
Arêches-Beaufort	04 79 38 37 57	**www.areches-beaufort.com**
Bourg Saint Maurice	04 79 07 04 92	**www.lesarcs.com**
La Rosière	04 79 06 80 51	**www.larosiere.net**
La Thuile	0165 884150	**www.lathuile.net**
Bourg Saint Pierre/Liddes/Orsières	02 77 83 32 48	**www.saint-bernard.ch**

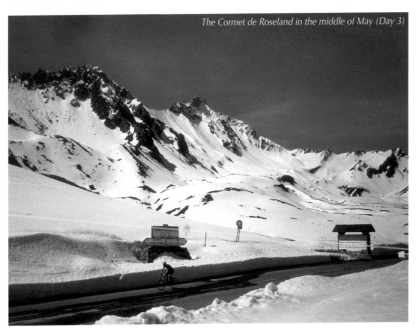

The Cormet de Roseland in the middle of May (Day 3)

ROUTE FOUR

TOUR OF THE CHARTREUSE–BAUGES

Day	Route	Distance	Height Gain
1	Grenoble to Aiguebelette-le-Lac	71.9km	1060m
2	Aiguebelette-le-Lac to Le Bourget-du-Lac	71.5km	740m
3	Le Bourget-du-Lac to Annecy	75.0km	1600m
4	Annecy to St Pierre d'Albigny	61.0km	640m
5	Bauges circuit from St Pierre d'Albigny	68.4km	1300m
6	St Pierre d'Albigny to Les Echelles	61.3km	1050m
7	Les Echelles to Grenoble	44.0km	1010m
	Totals	**453.1km**	**7400m**

The Chartreuse and Bauges Regional Parks lie between Grenoble and Annecy, with Chambéry, the former capital of the Dukes of Savoie, sandwiched between them. Despite the proximity of these three regional centres, the two parks have remained relatively quiet backwaters where tourism, although an important part of the local economy, has not completely superseded more traditional industries such as agriculture and forestry. The Regional Park authorities continue to promote these industries whilst also encouraging the growth of new economic activities compatible with the conservation of the environment. As in all areas of outstanding natural beauty, tourism is seen as an important element in the Parks' economic survival, with the emphasis being put on low-impact tourism. Visitor numbers are increasing but car traffic remains light, even in the height of summer.

Many people are familiar with the name Chartreuse, either through the monastic order that Saint Bruno founded here in 1084, or through the famous Chartreuse liqueur (the 'elixir of long-life') that was invented by the monks in 1737. When Saint Bruno founded his monastery, he was looking for a place where he could devote himself to a life of contemplation, undisturbed by the hustle and bustle of the outside world. It is easy to see why he chose the Chartreuse: the mountainous interior of the massif, protected by an almost unbroken ring of high cliffs and only accessible via steep mountain passes or through deep, dark gorges, would have been particularly forbidding to most 11th-century travellers. In many ways, little has changed since Saint Bruno's day; modern transport has made access much easier, but the roads are just as spectacular and the landscape just as rugged.

The Bauges is perhaps the least known of the Pre-Alpine massifs. Even in France, when you mention the 'Bauges' to people from outside the area, they often think that you have simply mispronounced 'Vosges'! Typically for a country where gastronomy is such an important part of everyday life, when people do think of the Bauges it is in terms of food or, to be more exact, cheese. Tome des Bauges (one M) is the pride of local cheese-makers and woe betide anyone who confuses it with the 'Tomme' (two Ms) cheeses from other areas. Whereas the Chartreuse is characterised by spectacular cliffs and dramatic gorges, the Bauges is characterised by a gentler landscape of verdant U-shaped valleys, dotted with tiny villages that don't seem to have changed for centuries. The whole area has a very peaceful, pastoral atmosphere: this is a place in which to relax and enjoy the simple things in life.

The tour starts in Grenoble, which though a city surrounded by mountains is also the flattest city in France, making it ideal for cycling. (Plans of the city's well-developed

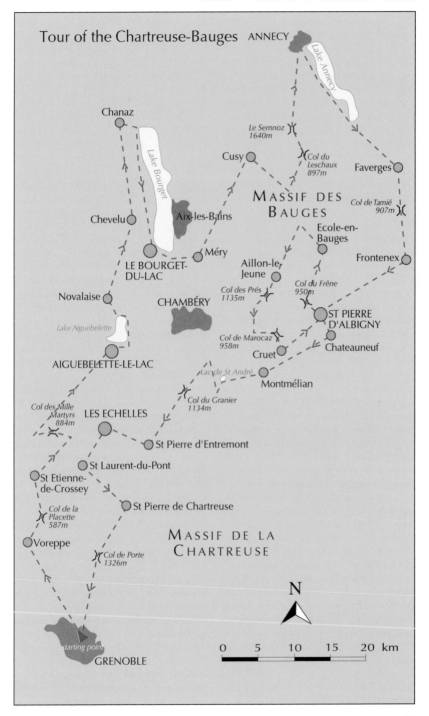

Tour of the Chartreuse-Bauges

ANNECY

Lake Annecy

Chanaz

Lake Bourget

Le Semnoz
1640m

Cusy

Col du
Leschaux
897m

Faverges

MASSIF DES
BAUGES

Col de Tamié
907m

Chevelu

Aix-les-Bains

Ecole-en-
Bauges

LE BOURGET-
DU-LAC

Méry

Aillon-le-
Jeune

Frontenex

Novalaise

CHAMBÉRY

Col des Prés
1135m

Col du Frêne
950m

ST PIERRE
D'ALBIGNY

Lake Aiguebelette

Col de Marocaz
958m

Chateauneuf

AIGUEBELETTE-LE-LAC

Cruet

Lac de St André

Montmélian

Col des Mille
Martyrs
884m

Col du Granier
1134m

LES ECHELLES

St Pierre d'Entremont

St Laurent-du-Pont

St Etienne-
de-Crossey

St Pierre de Chartreuse

Col de la
Placette
587m

MASSIF DE LA
CHARTREUSE

Voreppe

Col de Porte
1326m

N

0   5   10   15   20 km

starting point

GRENOBLE

network of cycleways and cycle lanes can be obtained from the tourist office.) Grenoble is a determinedly forward-looking city and has carved itself a niche as France's 'silicon valley'. The old town, which remains the vibrant heart of the city, reflects Grenoble's long and illustrious history and, as befits an important regional centre, is home to many interesting museums. These include the Musée de l'Ancien Eveché (local history), the Musée de la Résistance et de la Déportation (Grenoble was a very important centre for the Resistance during the Second World War), the Musée de Grenoble (considered one of the best fine arts museums outside Paris) and the Natural History Museum.

An easy 15km cycle along the flat roads between Grenoble and Voreppe leads to the Col de la Placette: the first pass of the day and the gateway to the western part of the Chartreuse Park. To the north of the pass the very pleasant, rolling countryside is dominated by the spectacular limestone cliffs that form the western ramparts of the Chartreuse mountains. There are few outstanding landmarks along these quiet roads, but a 360° loop in the road – Le Tourniquet – between St Etienne-de-Crossey and Meribel-les-Echelles is quite an unusual feature. Once over the highest point on the day's circuit, the Col de la Croix des Mille Martyrs, 30km of quite easy cycling takes you to the shores of Lake Aiguebelette, and the end of this first stage. Lake Aiguebelette is a wonderful place to go swimming as the water is exceptionally clean and warm.

Day two continues along the shores of the lake to the village of Novalaise and the southern edge of the Avant-Pays Savoyard. This is an area of traditional farms and rolling hills between the Pre-Alps and the River Rhone: truly *La France profonde* and a delightful area for cycling. Wine production is an increasingly important part of the local economy – unlike many areas of France, where the wine industry is in crisis – and vineyards are taking over larger and larger areas of the countryside. Wines from Jongieux are particularly worth looking out for. Chanaz, the next port of call, is a picturesque village on the banks of the Rhone and a favourite haunt for artists who come to paint the river, the boats and the waterside houses.

A few kilometres from the village you get your first glimpse of Lake Bourget, the largest natural lake in France and currently the subject of a huge development programme aimed at protecting the natural beauty of the area. The route follows the lakeshore from Portout to Conjux, before heading inland to St Pierre-de-Curtille. From just after Conjux, it is possible to make a 10km detour to visit Hautecombe Abbey, the traditional last resting place for members of the House of Savoie. Guided visits, which provide an interesting insight into the history of Savoie, are available in several languages. The steep hillsides that drop directly into the lake prevent the road following the water's edge, so to reach Le Bourget-du-Lac you have to leave the lakeshore and climb Mont de la Charvaz. As this is the most difficult ascent of the day, it is easy to justify a short break at the café at the highest point of the road to admire the bird's-eye view of the Abbey, the lake and the mountains to the east. The day ends at Le Bourget-du-Lac, a small lakeside village with an exceptional range of restaurants, from unpresuming family affairs to luxurious two-star Michelin establishments.

Day three starts by following the Chambéry-Aix-les-Bains cycleway around the southern end of Lake Bourget. The route then leaves the lakeshore, to avoid the busy roads through Aix-les-Bains (one of the aims of The Great Lake Project is to reduce traffic along the eastern shore of the lake), and climbs up into the Bauges across the foot of Mont Revard. The Revard was one of France's first purpose built ski resorts and the remains of the cable-car that serviced the resort from 1935 to 1969 can still be seen above the village of Mouxy. The route rejoins the main road just before Cusy, the last place to stock up on calories before the climb to the Col de Leschaux. It is possible to go straight down to Annecy from the col, but, if you have the strength in your legs, it is worth continuing up to the Semnoz, as the views from the top, especially of Mont Blanc, are magnificent. It is not often that you have the opportunity to cycle to the top of a mountain and enjoy a 360° panorama! The long descent into the centre of Annecy is also great fun.

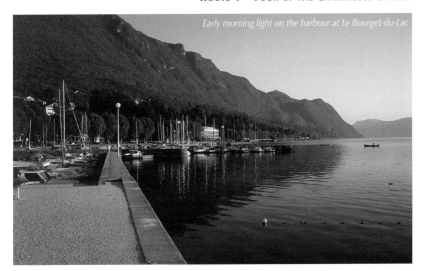
Early morning light on the harbour at Le Bourget-du-Lac

Annecy is generally considered the most beautiful city in the French Alps and is therefore a very popular tourist destination (book accommodation in advance for July and August!). During the summer months, the city entertains its visitors with a wide range of events, from ambulatory street theatre to the Fête du Lac firework display. Even without the added entertainment, just wandering through the narrow, cobbled streets of the old town is a delight. For more information about Annecy, see Route Two.

The route now heads south, along the Annecy cycleway – a much more pleasant alternative to the congested roads out of the city, especially in the morning before the cycleway itself becomes busy. At the moment, the cycleway ends at Doussard, but work to extend it to Faverges, Ugine and Albertville began in the spring of 2004. Interesting diversions along the lakeshore include the bell foundry and museum (Musée de la Cloche) at Sévrier and the village of Duingt with its *vieux château*. Faverges marks the start of the climb up to the Col de Tamié, the only pass on the day's itinerary. About 2km before the pass, you go past Tamié Abbey which, as well as marking the border between Haute-Savoie and Savoie, is home to one of the region's lesser-known cheeses (called Tamié, surprisingly enough).

The southern slopes of the Col de Tamié open out into the Combe de Savoie – the heart of Savoie's wine-growing industry. Savoie does not have the prestige of many of France's other wine-producing areas, but many of its wines are very pleasant and well worth tasting. The day ends at St Pierre d'Albigny, a small town dominated by the impressive silhouette of Miolans Castle. This castle-prison, which most famously held the Marquis de Sade in 1772, is open to the public and is worth a visit.

Up until now, the tour has skirted around the edge of the Bauges, but St Pierre d'Albigny provides an excellent starting point from which to explore the heart of the massif. As this is a circular trip, you can leave your luggage behind and enjoy a day of 'lightweight', although still quite strenuous, cycling. The day starts with a stiff climb from the centre of St Pierre up to the Col du Frêne. On the other side of the pass the landscape changes completely: the green fields of the wide valley floor lead the eye to the majestic summit of Mont Trélod at the northern end of the valley. In the middle of this valley lies Ecole-en-Bauges, home to the Bauges Regional Park Flora and Fauna Centre as well as a famous bakery that has exported its bread to hotels as far a-field as London and Paris. The gastronomic theme continues in Aillon-le-Jeune, where the local dairy produces some excellent cheeses, including Tome des Bauges and its own speciality, Bleu des Aillons. You can also visit the dairy to see how the cheese is made.

After Aillon-le-Jeune, the circuit goes over two more passes: the Col des Prés, and the Col du Marocaz. It is worth making a short detour (less than 1km) just before the Col de Marocaz to visit La Thuile and its beautiful lake. The day ends with a steep descent into the Combe de Savoie, followed by 8km of gentle cycling back to St Pierre d'Albigny.

The penultimate day of the tour takes you across the River Isére to Chateauneuf, and then follows the eastern flank of the Combe de Savoie to Montmélian. The old town of Montmélian is small but attractive and the Vine and Wine Museum gives you an opportunity to learn more about Savoie's wines. Five kilometres to the west of Montmélian lies Lake St André, the smallest lake on the tour and a popular picnic spot for the inhabitants of Chambéry. (To visit Chambéry, the former capital of the Dukes of Savoie, follow the

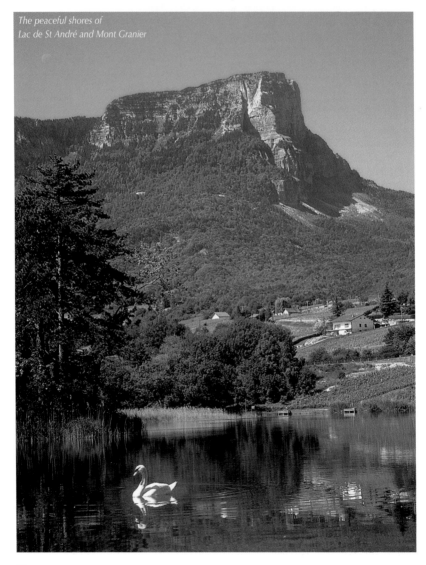

The peaceful shores of
Lac de St André and Mont Granier

'Boucle du Lac de St André' cycling signs into the city centre, and then follow the D912 to rejoin the main route at the Col du Granier. This adds about 15km to the circuit). The lake lies in the shadow of the forbidding north face of Mont Granier, a 700m-high wall of grey limestone which was formed in 1248 by a massive landslide that devastated an area of 20sq km, burying several villages. There are two roads to the Col du Granier from Lake St André, both of which are very steep; the route described here follows the easier and quieter of the two. From the pass, a very pleasant descent leads through Entremont-le-Vieux, with its interesting cave-bear museum, to St Pierre d'Entremont and the spectacular Gorges du Guiers Vif. This penultimate stage ends at Les Echelles/Entre-Deux- Guiers, two adjoining villages that straddle the Guiers Vif. The only hotel is in Les Echelles, the campsite is in Entre-Deux-Guiers.

The final leg takes you through another deep defile and back into the heart of the mountains. Of all the places of interest in the area, the most famous is undoubtedly the Grand Chartreuse Monastery. The monastery itself, which is set well back from the road, is closed to the public, but the adjoining museum provides a fascinating insight into the Spartan lives of the monks. If you have the time (and muscles) to make another short detour, why not visit St Pierre-de-Chartreuse, the 'capital' of the region and home to the Regional Park Visitor Centre, and/or the church at St Hugues, which has a striking collection of modern religious art. There is now only one more major pass to go over, the Col de Porte, before heading back down into the brouhaha of Grenoble.

GETTING THERE

By car
Grenoble is 870km from Calais

By plane
Via Lyon St Exupéry
Bus: There is a shuttle bus every hour
Train: To take the train you have to cycle to La Verpillière (see Appendix A for route details). On average, there is one train every

hour and the journey takes around 1hour 10mins.

Via Geneva
Take the train from the airport to Geneva central station (Cornavin). From Cornavin there is a train every 2–3 hours, either direct or via Culoz and Chambéry. The direct journey takes around 2 hours 15mins.

Via Grenoble
See directions in Appendix A

Via Chambéry
The tour can be started directly from Chambéry airport. Come out of the airport terminal and follow the road to the junction with the N202 (roundabout). Go straight on along the D17 ('Voglans'). Where the D17 turns right, go straight on along a cycle lane ([Boucle de Voglans], no entry for cars) to join the third stage of the tour at Viviers-du-Lac – junction D17/D17B (2.2km from the airport). To get back to the airport from Le Bourget-du-Lac, follow the directions for the start of stage three as far as the roundabout at the junction of the N211 and D17. Turn right here ('Chambéry') onto N202. Turn right at the next roundabout ('Chambéry–Voglans airport') to get to the airport.

WHEN TO GO

All of the passes crossed by this tour are kept open all year round, but it is usually only warm enough for enjoyable cycling from April to October. The roads are never too busy, even during the peak holiday months of July and August but, if you come at this time, it is advisable to book accommodation in advance.

MAPS

Michelin: Local – Sheet 333, Isère, Savoie
Michelin: Regional – Sheet 244, Rhône-Alpes
IGN: Top 100 – Sheet 53: Grenoble, Mont Blanc (the area around Voreppe is not shown on this map. For this you need Sheet 51: Lyon, Grenoble, but the navigation here is easy and this map is not essential).

Day 1 – Grenoble to Aiguebelette-le-Lac

Distance	Location	Directions
0.0	Grenoble station	Leave station via (Centre Ville) exit. Go straight across street in front of station to Rue Casimir Brenier, which you follow to Place Hubert Dubedout.
0.4	Place Hubert Dubedout	Go across square (easiest on foot). Cross River Isère and then turn L to go to gap in fence that leads down to cycleway.
0.6	Cycleway	Turn R onto cycleway and follow it for 2km
2.6	Bridge over cycleway	Turn 180° R and go up under motorway
2.9	St Martin-le-Vinoux: roundabout	Go straight on to join cycleway alongside N75 Follow this cycleway/lane for 11.5km
13.4	Voreppe: N75/D520A	Turn R – D520A (Voreppe – Centre) then (Toutes Directions) to get to roundabout in centre of Voreppe
14.9	Voreppe: roundabout D520A/D520E	Go straight on – D520A (Col de la Placette): 5.5km at 6%
20.4	Col de la Placette	Go straight on
24.5	D520A/D520	Turn L – D520 (Voiron)
28.2	St Etienne-de-Crossey: D520/D49D	Turn R – D49D (St Aupre)
28.7	D49D/D49	Turn R – D49 (becomes D28) (Miribel-les-Echelles). Go through Miribel to Col de la Croix des Mille Martyrs: 5.2km at 6%
42.8	Col des Mille Martyrs	Go straight on
46.1	D28/D49C	Turn 180° R – D49C (Merlas) then (St Bueil)
54.0	Jtn just before St Bueil	Turn R (Voisant) – sign well hidden in hedge on RHS of road. Go through Voissant and down to D82A.
58.3	D82K/D82A	Turn R – D82A (becomes D203) (St Béron). Follow D203 through St Béron to La Bridoire
63.6	La Bridoire	Turn R – D921E (Lac d'Aiguebelette): 2.2km at 5%
65.8	D921E/D921B	Turn R – D912B (Le Gué des Planches)
66.4	D921B/D921	Turn L – D921 (Lac d'Aiguebelette)
66.7	D921/D921B	Turn R – D921D (Lépin-le-Lac) and follow road to Aiguebelette-le-Lac
71.9	Aiguebelette-le-Lac	Village church on RHS of road (Chef Lieu)

Tour of the Chartreuse–Bauges Day 1

The Chartreuse from Col de la Croix des Mille Martyrs

Location	Distance (km)	Water	Shops	Café	Campsite	B&B	Hotel	Bank	Bike Shop
Grenoble	0.0	x	x	x	x	x (1)	x	x	x
St Egrève	4.5	—	x	x	—	—	x	x	—
Voreppe	14.9	x	x	x	—	x	x	x	—
St Etienne-de-Crossey	28.2	x	x	x	x	x	x	—	(2)
Miribel-les-Echelles	38.7	x	x	x	x	x	x	—	—
Merlas	50.0	x	—	x	—	—	—	—	—
St Béron	60.8	—	—	x	x	—	—	—	—
La Bridoire	63.6	—	x	x	—	x	—	—	—
Lépin-le-Lac	66.7	x	x	x	x	x	x	—	—
Aiguebelette-le-Lac	71.9	x	—	—	x	—	x	—	(3)

FACILITIES AND SERVICES

(1) At La Tronche on the north-east edge of Grenoble (about 4km from the station)

(2) At Voiron, 5km west of St Etienne-de-Crossey

(3) Nearest bike shop: Pont de Beauvoisin, 14km from Aiguebelette-le-Lac

Day 2 – Aiguebelette-le-Lac to Le Bourget-du-Lac

As well as being an idyllic place for swimming, Lake Aiguebelette is also renowned as a rowing centre. Like cyclists, rowers prefer wind-free conditions and Aiguebelette boasts 300 windless days per year. As the third largest natural lake in France (after Bourget and Annecy), it regularly hosts international rowing competitions and was the venue for the World Rowing Championships in 1997.

Distance	Location	Directions
0.0	Aiguebelette-le-Lac: Chef Lieu	From in front of church head north along D921D
6.5	D921D/D41: round-about	Go straight on (Novalaise)
7.1	D41/D921: roundabout	Turn R – D921 (Novalaise)
10.8	Novalaise: D921/D916	Go straight on – D921 (Yenne)
17.3	D921/D921C	Bear R – D921C (St Paul-sur-Yenne). Follow this road to Chevelu
25.8	Chevelu: D921C/ N504	Go straight on – D210 (Jongieux)
26.8	Jtn	Turn L, and then bear R 100 metres further on
27.5	Jtn	Bear L
29.5	D210/D44	Turn L (Jongieux)
30.2	Billième: D44/D210	Turn R – D210 (Jongieux) and go through Jongieux to D921
36.0	D210/D921	Turn R – D921 (Chanaz)
44.4	Chanaz: D921/D18	Go straight on – D18 (Conjux)
47.5	Portout: D18/D914	Turn R – D914 (Conjux)
50.5	D914/D18	Follow D914 (St Pierre de Curtille): 9.1km at 4%
52.2	St Pierre de Curtille: D914/D210	Turn L – D914 (Col du Chat)
64.0	D914/D914A	Turn L – D914 (Le Bourget-du-Lac)
67.7	D914/N504	Go straight on (Bourdeau)
67.8	Jtn	Turn R [Chambéry]
68.2	Jtn	Bear L. Do not follow (Le Bourget-du-Lac)
68.5	D13/D14	Turn R – D14
71.5	Le Bourget-du-Lac: Le Port	TO is on the left

Lake Bourget and the Belledonne Mountains from the Col du Chat

FACILITIES AND SERVICES

Location	Distance (km)	Water	Shops	Café	Campsite	B&B	Hotel	Bank	Bike Shop
Aiguebelette-le-Lac	0.0	x	—	—	x	—	x	—	(1)
Novalaise	10.8	x	x	x	—	—	x	x	—
Chevelu	25.8	x	x	x	x	—	x	—	—
Billième	30.2	x	—	—	—	—	—	—	—
Jongieux	32.3	x	—	—	—	x	—	—	—
Chanaz	44.4	x	x	x	x	—	—	—	—
Portout	47.5	—	—	—	—	—	x	—	—
Conjux	50.0	x	—	—	x	—	—	—	—
St Pierre-de-Curtille	52.2	x	—	x	x	x	—	—	—
Le Bourget-du-Lac	71.5	x	x	x	x	x	x	x	(2)

(1) Nearest bike shop: Pont de Beauvoisin, 14km from Aiguebelette-le-Lac

(2) Nearest bike shop: Aix-les-Bains, 10km from Le Bourget-du-Lac or La Motte Servolex, 9km from Le Bourget-du-Lac

Savoie has a flourishing wine industry, largely due to a sales policy that is known as 'in-situ exports': nearly all of the region's wine is sold locally, but a large percentage is drunk elsewhere, taken home as a souvenir by visiting tourists. Of the area's wines, Chignin-Bergeon has the best reputation and is correspondingly expensive. Marestel from Jongieux is another pleasant white wine; if you prefer red, you might like to try a Mondeuse.

Distance	Location	Directions
0.0	Le Bourget-du-Lac TO	Come out of TO and turn L
0.1	Carpark entrance	Turn L into car park then turn R in front of Ecole Française de Voile to join start of cycleway [Aix-les-Bains]
0.7	Bridge	Turn L and go over river [Aix-les-Bains]
3.2	Port entrance	Leave cycleway to join N211. Follow this road to roundabout
3.4	Roundabout: N211/D17B	Go straight on – D17B (Viviers-du-Lac).
4.4	D17B/D17 Jtn with road from Chambéry airport.	Go straight on through Viviers-du-Lac to reach D991.
5.0	D17B/D991	Turn R – D991 (Méry)
5.7	D991/D51	Turn L (Méry): 11.9km at 3%
7.5	Méry: D51/D211	Turn L – D211. Go through Drumettaz and Mouxy
12.1	D211/D913	Bear R – D913 (Le Revard). Go through Trévignin
16.9	D913/D211	Turn L – D211 (St Offenge)
19.9	Montcel: D211/D211A	Turn R– D211A (St Offenge)
23.8	St Offenge Dessous	Go straight on – D211B–D103 (Cusy)
27.5	D103/D911	Turn R – D911 and go through Cusy
37.4	D911/D912	Turn L – D912 (Col de Leschaux): 6.8km at 6%
44.2	Col de Leschaux: D912/D110	Turn L – D110 (Le Semnoz): 13.8km at 5.5%
58.0	Le Semnoz	Go straight on – D41
74.2	Jtn	Turn R (Centre Ville)
74.6	Roundabout	Turn L – Rue des Marquisats (Centre Ville)
75.0	Annecy TO	TO is on L, opposite Hotel de Ville

Tour of the Chartreuse–Bauges Day 3

Lake Annecy from the Semnoz

FACILITIES AND SERVICES

Location	Distance (km)	Water	Shops	Café	Campsite	B&B	Hotel	Bank	Bike Shop
Le Bourget-du-Lac	0.0	x	x	x	x	x	x	x	(1)
Viviers-du-Lac	4.7	x	x	x	—	x	x	x	—
Mouxy	11.7	x	—	—	—	—	—	—	—
Trévignin	16.2	—	—	x	x	—	x	—	—
Montcel	19.9	—	—	x	x	—	x	—	—
Cusy	28.1	—	x	x	x	x	—	—	—
Col de Leschaux	44.2	x	—	x	—	x	—	—	—
Le Semnoz	58.0	—	—	x	—	x	x	—	—
Annecy	75.0	x	x	x	x	x	x	x	x

(1) Nearest bike shop: Aix-les-Bains, 10km from Le Bourget-du-Lac or La Motte Servolex, 9km from Le Bourget-du-Lac

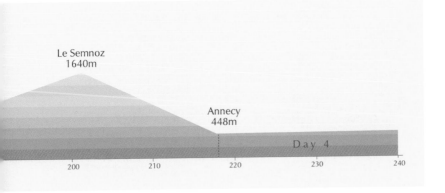

Day 4 – Annecy to St Pierre d'Albigny

Distance	Location	Directions
0.0	Annecy	Come out of TO and turn R onto Rue de Marquisats
0.4	Roundabout	Go straight on – N508, cycle lane
2.6	Sevrier, start of cycleway	Cross N508 to get to start of cycleway
21.1	End of cycleway*	Cross N508 and follow D42 (Vesonne)
21.7	Vesonne	Turn R onto a very narrow minor road
24.5	Faverges: roundabout	Go straight on
25.2	Traffic lights	Turn L
25.7	Jtn	Turn R (Col de Tamié): 10.3km at 4%
36.0	Col de Tamié	Go straight on – D201C
45.5	Frontenex: D201C/D201	Turn R – D201. Follow D201to St Pierre d'Albigny
60.7	St Pierre d'Albigny: D201/D911	Go straight on – D201
61.0	Place Charles Albert	TO is on R

* In April 2004 work started on extending the cycleway to Faverges. They expect the work to have been completed by May 2005 when the diversion through Vesonne will no longer be necessary.

FACILITIES AND SERVICES

Location	Distance (km)	Water	Shops	Café	Campsite	B&B	Hotel	Bank	Bike Shop
Annecy	0.0	x	x	x	x	x	x	x	x
Sevrier	2.6	—	x	x	x	—	x	x	—
Doussard	19.0	—	x	—	x	x	x	x	—
Faverges	25.2	x	x	x	—	x	x	x	x
Col de Tamié	36.0	x	—	x	—	—	—	—	—
Frontenex	45.5	—	x	x	—	—	—	x	—
St Vital	46.8	x	—	—	—	x	—	—	—
Freterive	56.1	x	—	—	—	—	—	—	—
St Pierre d'Albigny	61.0	x	x	x	x	—	x	x	(1)

(1) Nearest bike shop: Albertville, 21km from St Pierre d'Albigny

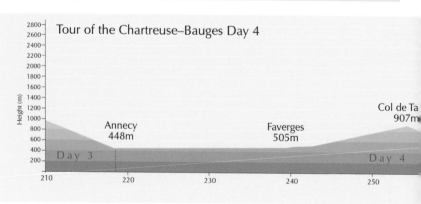

Tour of the Chartreuse–Bauges Day 4

Annecy 448m

Faverges 505m

Col de Ta 907m

Day 3

Day 4

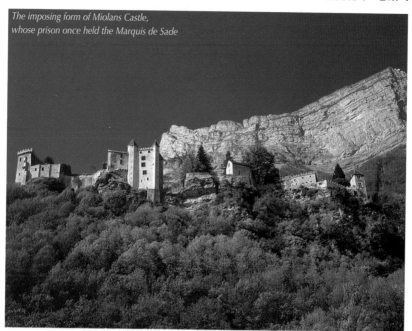

The imposing form of Miolans Castle, whose prison once held the Marquis de Sade

With the exception of an occasional snake, the Bauges and Chartreuse Regional Parks, with their neat little villages and well-kept pastures, are the last places you would expect to encounter potentially dangerous wildlife. Chamois, foxes and hares are common, and there are a few, very discreet lynxes, but nothing to worry these pastoral communities. So, an immense shock-wave spread through the area when wolves were found to have returned. The reintroduction of wolves into the Abruzzi (Italy) and Mercantour (France) National Parks has sparked a bitter argument between environmentalists and shepherds, so the authorities tend not to broadcast the whereabouts of these animals. However, when a wolf is run over by a car, as occurred in the Combe de Savoie, and when wolves attack cattle a few kilometres from Grenoble, it is hard to keep their presence a secret.

To visitors, the boundaries of the 96 *départements* that make up mainland France and Corsica seem to have been rather arbitrarily drawn. For example, part of the Vaucluse *département* forms an enclave within the Drôme and many geographically distinct mountain areas are split between two *départements*. The reasons for this are very varied and often quite complex. The Chartreuse Mountains straddle the boundary between Isère and Savoie, as this used to be the border between France and the Piedmont, of which Savoie was a part. In 1860, when the *département* of Mont Blanc was divided into Haute-Savoie and Savoie, the new *départementale* border followed the boundary between the dioceses of Annecy and Chambéry, splitting the Bauges in two.

Distance	Location	Directions
0.0	St Pierre d'Albigny TO	Turn L and follow Rue Louis Blanc Pinget to D201/D911 jtn
0.3	D201/D911	Turn L – D911 (Col du Frêne): 7.9km at 6%
8.2	Col du Frêne	Go straight on through Routhenes and Ecole-en-Bauges to Pont d'Escorchevel
20.4	Pont d'Escorchevel: D911/D206	Turn L – D206
31.6	D206/D59	Turn R – D206 (Col des Prés) and go through Aillon-le-Jeune to Col des Prés: 4.0km at 6%
35.6	Col des Prés	Go straight on to Les Chavonettes
42.0	Les Chavonettes: D206/D21	Turn L – D21
44.0	D21/D21E	Turn L – D21E and go through Arvey: 3.4km at 5.5%
48.5	D21E/D11	Turn L – D11: 4.5km at 4%
53.0	Col de Marocaz	Go straight on
60.6	Cruet: D11/D201	Turn L and follow D201 (St Pierre d'Albigny)
67.8	St Pierre d'Albigny: roundabout	Turn L at roundabout (Centre Ville)
68.2	Roundabout	Go straight on to church and Place Charles Albert (Centre Ville)
68.3	Town centre	Turn L at T-jtn at top of Place CharlesAlbert
68.4	TO	TO is on R

Looking north towards Mont Trélod from below the Col du Frêne

FACILITIES AND SERVICES

Location	Distance (km)	Water	Shops	Café	Campsite	B&B	Hotel	Bank	Bike Shop
St Pierre d'Albigny	0.0	x	x	x	x	—	x	x	(1)
Ste Reine	10.0	x	—	x	—	—	—	—	—
Ecole-en-Bauges	17.0	x	x	x	—	x	—	—	—
Aillon-le-Vieux	17.8	x	—	—	—	x	—	—	—
Aillon-le-Jeune	31.8	x	x	x	x	x	x	—	—
Puygros	47.0	x	—	—	—	—	—	—	—
Cruet	60.6	x	—	—	—	—	—	—	—
St Pierre d'Albigny	68.4	x	x	x	x	—	x	x	(1)

(1) Nearest bike shop: Albertville, 21km from St Pierre d'Albigny

Despite its modest height (1933m), Mont Granier boasts its own glacier, but it is not a glacier many people see – it is inside the mountain!

Distance	Location	Directions
0.0	St Pierre d'Albigny TO	Turn L and go to Place Charles Albert
0.1	Place Charles Albert	Turn R and go down to L of church
0.2	Roundabout	Turn L – Chemin du Pré de la Cure
0.5	Roundabout	Turn R (1st exit) – D911
1.0	Roundabout	Turn L – D911 (A43). Follow (A43) to traffic lights at D911/N6 jtn
3.5	D911/N6: traffic lights	Go straight on along D202 (Chateauneuf): 1.8km at 5.5%
5.3	Chateauneuf – Eglise D202/D31	Turn R – D31 (Coise)
7.6	D31/D31E	Turn L – D31 (Coise Chef-lieu)
8.5	D31/D204	Turn R – D204 (Montmélian)
17.4	Roundabout	Go straight on – D204 (Montmélian)
17.7	Roundabout	Turn R – D923
17.9	Roundabout	Go straight on – D204 (Montmélian Centre)
18.6	Montmélian: roundabout	Go straight on (Centre Ville)
18.7	Roundabout	Turn L – D201 (Francin)
19.0	Roundabout	Go straight on – D201E (Francin)
19.6	Roundabout	Turn L – D201 (Les Marches)
23.1	Les Marches: D201/N90 traffic lights	Turn L – N90 (Lac de St André)
23.5	N90/D12	Turn R – D12 (Lac de St André). Follow D12 past Lac de St André and through St André.
28.5	D12/D12E	Turn L – D12E (Col du Granier): 7.6km at 8%
36.1	D12E/D912	Turn L – D912 (Col du Granier): 3.0km at 6%
39.1	Col du Granier	Go straight on
49.3	St Pierre d'Entremont: D912/D520C	Turn R – D520C (Les Echelles)
61.0	Entre-Deux-Guiers	Turn R and go through Entre-Deux-Guiers to Les Echelles
61.3	Les Echelles	TO is on L

Tour of the Chartreuse–Bauges Day 6

Vineyards at the foot of
Mont Granier (Day 6)

FACILITIES AND SERVICES

Location	Distance (km)	Water	Shops	Café	Campsite	B&B	Hotel	Bank	Bike Shop
St Pierre d'Albigny	0.0	x	x	x	x	—	x	x	(1)
Chateauneuf	5.3	x	—	—	—	—	—	—	—
La Chavanne	16.3	x	x	x	—	—	—	—	—
Montmélian	18.6	—	x	x	x	—	x	x	—
Les Marches	23.1	—	x	x	—	x	—	—	—
Lake St André	24.6	x	—	x	x	—	—	—	—
Col du Granier	39.1	—	—	x	—	x	—	—	—
Entremont-le-Vieux	44.0	x	x	x	x	x	x	—	—
St Pierre- d'Entremont	49.3	x	x	x	x	x	x	x	—
St Christophe-sur-Guiers	59.3	x	—	x	—	x	—	—	—
Les Echelles	61.3	x	x	x	x	—	x	x	x

(1) Nearest bike shop: Albertville, 21km from St Pierre d'Albigny

Col du Granier
1134m

St Pierre
d'Entremont
640m

Les Echelles
387m

St Laurent-
du-Pont
415m

La Diat
795m

Day 6

Day 7

390   400   410   420   430

There are many very fit retired people in Savoie, so I was somewhat surprised that an ascent of the Col du Granier by an octagenarian should be deemed interesting enough to merit a story on the local TV news – until I found out that he did it on a unicycle!

Distance	Location	Directions
0.0	Les Echelles	Come out of TO and turn R. Go across River Guiers Vif and into Entre-Deux-Guiers.
0.3	Entre-Deux-Guiers	Turn R – Rue de la Poste
0.6	Traffic lights	Go straight on at lights and then take 1st L – D28B (Villette)
5.2	Villette	Bear L – D28. Follow this road to St Laurent-du-Pont
7.0	St Laurent-du-Pont D28/D520	Turn L – D520 (St Pierre de Chartreuse)
7.2	D520/D520B	Turn R – D520B (St Pierre de Chartreuse): 10.1km at 3.8%
17.3	La Diat D520B/D512	Turn R – D512. Follow this road to Col de Porte: 8.5km at 6%
25.8	Col de Porte	Go straight on
28.3	D512/D57	Turn R – D57 (Sarcenas). Follow D57 to jtn with N75
43.1	St Martin-le-Vinoux D57/N75	Turn R – N75
43.3	Place Aristide Briand	Cross River Isère and then Place Hubert Dubedout to get to Rue Casimir Brenier. Go along Rue Casimir Brenier to station.
44.0	Grenoble station	

FACILITIES AND SERVICES									
Location	Distance (km)	Water	Shops	Café	Campsite	B&B	Hotel	Bank	Bike Shop
Les Echelles	0.0	x	x	x	x	—	x	x	x
St Laurent-du-Pont	7.0	x	x	x	x	x	x	x	x
La Diat (St Pierre de Chartreuse)	17.3	x	x	x	—	x	x	—	—
Col de Porte	25.8	—	—	x	—	—	—	—	—
Grenoble	44.0	x	x	x	x	x	x	x	x

Tour of the Chartreuse–Bauges Day 7

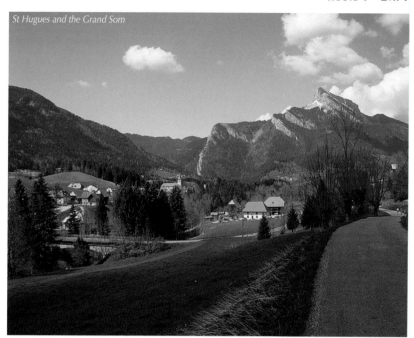

St Hugues and the Grand Som

Extra day: Le Bourget-du-Lac is at the foot of the Mont du Chat, one of the most challenging climbs in the French Alps. The ascent is just over 14km long, with an average gradient of almost 10% for the last 12km. After admiring the view from the summit café, head down the western side of the mountain, turning left after about 7km to go through Vacheresse and over the Col de l'Epine. From the Col de l'Epine, go through St Sulpice and La Motte Servolex to follow the Balcons du Bourget cycling route back to the lake. The circuit can be made a little easier by going back round to Le Bourget-du-Lac via St Paul-sur-Yenne, Chevelu and the Col du Chat.

Grenoble
210m

	460	470	480	490	500

(km)

ACCOMMODATION

Grenoble

Campsites

The nearest campsite is at Seyssins, on the southwest edge of Grenoble:

Les Trois Pucelles (all year), Tel. 04 76 96 45 73

Bed & Breakfast

Mr Cohen, La Tronche, Tel. 04 76 44 78 98

Hotels

There are more than 50 hotels in Grenoble. Contact TO for details.

Lépin-le-Lac/Aiguebelette-le-Lac

Campsites

Des Sirenes, Tel. 04 79 36 06 64

Ferrand (early May to end Oct), Tel. 04 79 36 01 50

Le Curtelet (early May to end Sept), Tel. 04 79 44 11 22

Les Peupliers (early April to end Oct), Tel. 04 79 36 00 48

Bed & Breakfast

Mr and Mrs Viallet-Boutry, Tel. 047 9 36 30 05

Mr and Mrs Dufresne, Tel. 04 79 36 09 62

Hotels

De la Combe de Chez Michelon (**), Tel. 04 79 36 05 02

Du Lac (**), Tel. 04 79 36 03 27

Les Sirenes (**), Tel. 04 79 36 05 09

Le Bourget-du-Lac

Campsites

L'Ile aux Cygnes (end April to end Sept), Tel. 04 79 25 01 76

Le Lamartine (Bourdeau) (mid-June to mid-Sept): 04 79 25 03 41 (town hall)

Bed & Breakfast

Mr and Mrs Van der Hoeven, Tel. 04 79 25 27 72

Mr and Mrs Prud'homme, Tel. 04 79 25 24 19

Mrs Gonay, Tel. 04 79 25 01 72

Hotels

Ombremont (***), Tel. 04 79 25 00 23

Beaurivage (**), Tel. 04 79 25 00 38

Cerisaie (**), Tel. 04 79 25 01 29

Hotel du Port (**), Tel. 04 79 25 00 21

Hotel du Lac, Tel. 04 79 25 00 10

Annecy

Campsites

Le Savoy (mid-April to end Sept), Tel. 04 50 23 62 92

Le Colovry (early June to mid-Sept), Tel. 04 50 23 13 29

Le Belvedere (end March to early Oct), Tel. 04 50 45 48 30

There are many other campsites along the lakeshore between Annecy and Doussard.

Bed & Breakfast

Youth hostel, Tel. 04 50 45 33 19

Hotels

There are more than 40 hotels in Annecy. Contact TO for details.

St Pierre d'Albigny

Campsites

Lac de Carouge (early June to mid-Sept), Tel. 04 79 28 58 16

L'Arclusaz (July/August), Tel. 04 79 28 53 39

Bed & Breakfast

There are no bed & breakfasts in St Pierre d'Albigny

Hotels

Hotel Central (**), Tel. 04 79 28 50 05

Hotel du Commerce, Tel. 04 79 28 50 16

Les Echelles/Entre-Deux-Guiers

Campsites

L'Arc-en-ciel (early March to end Oct), Tel. 04 76 66 06 97

Bed & Breakfast

There are no bed & breakfasts in Les Echelles

Hotels

Hotel du Centre (**), Tel. 04 79 36 60 14

TOURIST INFORMATION

Regional Information

	Telephone	Website
Isere	04 76 54 34 36	www.isere-tourisme.com
Savoie	04 79 85 12 45	www.savoiehautesavoie.com
Haute-Savoie	04 50 51 32 31	www.savoiehautesavoie.com

Tourist Information Offices

Location	Telephone	Website
Grenoble	04 76 42 41 41	www.grenoble-isere-tourisme.com
Voiron	04 76 05 00 38	www.paysvoironnais.info
Lépin-le-Lac	04 79 36 00 02	no website
Yenne	04 79 36 71 54	no website
Le Bourget-du-Lac	04 79 25 01 99	www.bourgetdulac.com
Aix-les-Bains	04 79 88 68 00	www.aixlesbains.com
Annecy	04 50 45 00 33	www.lac-annecy.com
Faverges	04 50 44 60 24	no website
St Pierre d'Albigny	04 79 71 44 07	no website
Aillon-le-Jeune	04 79 54 63 65	www.lesaillons.com
Montmélian	04 79 84 07 31	www.montmelian.com
St Pierre d'Entremont	04 79 65 81 90	no website
Les Echelles	04 79 36 56 24	www.avant-pays-savoyard.com
St Laurent-du-Pont	04 76 06 22 55	perso.wanadoo.fr/st-laurent-du-pont
St Pierre de Chartreuse	04 76 88 62 08	www.st-pierre-chartreuse.com

ROUTE FIVE
TOUR OF THE BELLEDONNE

Day	Route	Distance	Height Gain
1	Grenoble to Allevard	75.8km	1710m
2	Allevard to Albertville	68.6km	1130m
3	Albertville to La Chambre	64.0km	1660m
4	La Chambre to Bourg d'Oisans	60.8km	1670m
5	Bourg d'Oisans to Grenoble	90.8km	1080m
	Totals	**360.0km**	**7250m**

For the purposes of this tour, the name Belledonne has been used in its widest sense to describe the westernmost ramparts of the true Alps between Albertville, Grenoble and La Mure. A closer look at the geography of the area shows that the Arc and Romanche Rivers divide the chain into three separate massifs – from north to south: the Lauzière, the Belledonne and the Taillefer. Three names that may be more familiar to keen cyclists and followers of the Tour de France are the Madeleine, Glandon and Ornon passes, all of which are found along the eastern flank of the Belledonne. Rising to almost 2000m, the Col de la Madeleine and the Col du Glandon are undoubtedly the 'stars' of the Tour of the Belledonne, however they are far from being the only difficulties in this short but strenuous five-day circuit.

Talk to any local cyclist/walker/skier and you will be regaled with stories of how wonderful the Belledonne is. At first sight it is difficult to see what could engender such enthusiasm, as there are few individually striking summits, spectacular cliffs or dramatic gorges; nothing that instantly inspires awe and admiration. This is probably part of the attraction; in a society that increasingly proposes instant gratification and where pleasures are correspondingly fleeting, the Belledonne offers the greatest rewards to those who take the time to get to know it well. Because it has avoided intensive tourist development and never been subject to the restrictions deemed necessary to protect neighbouring national

parks and nature reserves, the Belledonne has retained an unusual degree of authenticity. As could be expected in an area that does not attract a lot of tourists, hotels and campsites can be few and far between and there is only a limited number of potential overnight stopping places.

The Tour of the Belledonne starts and finishes in Grenoble, the self-styled capital of the Alps. Whether or not you agree with such a bold statement, it must be admitted that Grenoble has a unique location, nestled at the foot of three different massifs: the Chartreuse, the Vercors and the Belledonne. Many major cities – of which Grenoble is undoubtedly one, being home to 700,000 people – are unpleasant to cycle around because of the amount of traffic on the roads. However, Grenoble is doubly fortunate in having a well-developed network of cycleways and in being surrounded by steep mountains that funnel most of the traffic along the valley floors. With the exception of one or two roads to the more popular resorts, as soon as you head up into the hills you will rarely be bothered by cars. For more information about Grenoble see the introduction to Route Four.

Day one starts quite gently, following the banks of the River Isère, mostly on cycleways well away from the traffic of the city centre. After about 10km, the rhythm abruptly changes as you leave the valley to climb up into the foothills of the Belledonne, but the hard work is soon rewarded with fantastic views of the Chartreuse Mountains on the

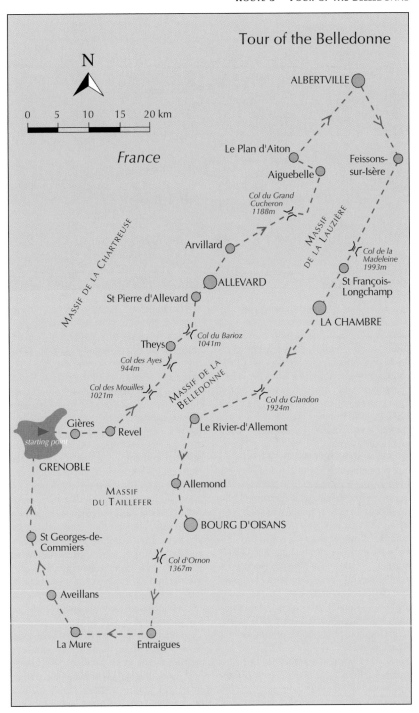

Tour of the Belledonne

N

0   5   10   15   20 km

France

ALBERTVILLE

Le Plan d'Aiton

Aiguebelle

Feissons-
sur-Isère

Col du Grand
Cucheron
1188m

MASSIF DE LA LAUZIÈRE

Arvillard

ALLEVARD

St Pierre d'Allevard

Col de la
Madeleine
1993m

St François-
Longchamp

LA CHAMBRE

Col du Barioz
1041m

Theys

Col des Ayes
944m

MASSIF DE LA
BELLEDONNE

Col des Mouilles
1021m

MASSIF DE LA CHARTREUSE

Col du Glandon
1924m

Gières

Revel

Le Rivier-d'Allemont

starting point

GRENOBLE

MASSIF
DU TAILLEFER

Allemond

BOURG D'OISANS

St Georges-de-
Commiers

Col d'Ornon
1367m

Aveillans

La Mure

Entraigues

The Belledonne seen from near Le Naysord

opposite side of the Grésivaudan Valley. The road goes through a succession of traditional farming villages, following what the French call a 'balcony route' (a traverse across the flanks of a mountain with many good viewpoints along the way). However, the road is by no means flat; you will go over a total of four passes (although one, the Col du Lauteret, is so insignificant that it isn't even marked on most maps) before getting to Allevard.

Although there is little sign of it today, for many centuries Allevard's prosperity was based on the exploitation of iron ore from the nearby Bréda Valley, with the surrounding forests providing fuel for the smelters. Every visitor to Paris will have seen at least one example of Allevard iron as it was used to make the girders with which the Eiffel Tower was built. At the end of the 18th century, the focus of the town's economy began to change with the discovery of the medicinal properties of the local sulphur-rich waters. Allevard-les-Bains is still a spa resort, but it had its heyday at the beginning of the 20th century when it attracted the rich and famous from far and wide. The Musée de Jadis (Museum of Yesteryear) should satisfy the curiosity of those who would like to know more about the history of this surprising and pleasant little town.

From Allevard, the route continues northwards to the village of Arvillard and then through the idyllically pastoral Vallée des Huiles to the Col du Grand Cucheron. Apart from the last 2.5km below the pass, the cycling is quite easy, allowing your legs to warm up gently after the previous day's exertions. The slopes around the pass are very densely forested, but there is one small clearing at the top that gives an excellent view of the Lauzière Mountains to the north. From the pass, the road drops down into St George des Hurtières, a former iron, silver and copper mining village, although cycling through the forests and pastures that surround the village today, it is difficult to imagine it as a mining community. The harsh lives of the miners are vividly portrayed in the village's excellent museum. From St George the road winds down to Aiguebelle, where you cross the Maurienne Valley before climbing back up to Aiton. After a short descent to Le Plan d'Aiton, 13km of easy cycling through the Combe de Savoie takes you to Albertville.

Albertville is a relatively new town which was built in 1856 at the foot of the mediaeval citadel of Conflans. For almost 150 years, this was just another anonymous small town, but, in 1992, Albertville was thrust under the international spotlight when it hosted the 16th Winter Olympics. The Games were a huge success for Albertville, but the biggest rewards, in terms of publicity and international tourism, went to the ski resorts of the Tarentaise Valley (such as Courchevel, La Plagne and Val d'Isère). The story of Albertville's Olympic adventure is told at the Maison des Jeux Olympiques. Despite the large sums of money spent preparing the town for the Olympics, Albertville has little to attract passing tourists, but it is the only town in the area to offer a reasonable range of accommodation. However, Conflans, on the eastern edge of the town, is well worth a visit.

The third stage of the tour takes you south-east along the Tarentaise Valley to the foot of the Col de la Madeleine. Most of the traffic through the valley uses the RN90 dual-carriageway, which was built for the Winter Olympics, so the other roads tend to be very quiet. Once again the day starts gently with less than 250 metres of height gain in the first 20km: a good warm up before you attack the steep initial slopes of the Col de la Madeleine. The climb to the Madeleine is long (25km), but the gradient is quite variable and every few kilometres there are flatter sections where your legs can relax a little. From a tourism marketing point of view it seems to be very important for a pass to be at least 2000 metres high, so a prominent signpost at the top announces 'Col de la Madeleine 2000m', despite the actual height being only 1993 metres. The fact that the pass does not quite make the 2000-metre mark does nothing to spoil the view, especially when it can be enjoyed from the terrace of one of the col's roadside cafés. From the pass it is downhill all the way to La Chambre: a superb but quite technical 18km descent.

La Chambre is only 2km from the foot of the Col du Glandon, the second big climb on the circuit, so your legs have much less time to get warmed up. This is a much stiffer challenge than the Col de la Madeleine, as, apart from 1km through the village of St Colomban-des-Villards, the gradient is unrelenting and the steepest part is right at the top. Up to St Colomban, the road rises through dense forest, so the views are limited.

Above the village, the trees thin out allowing you to appreciate the fabulous countryside around you. Unusually for such a high pass, there are no cafés or refreshment stands at the top, so, outside the holiday season, when the camper vans have gone home, the Glandon has a very wild and isolated atmosphere. If you are in desperate need of refreshment, don't worry, there is a café on the south side of the pass, a few hundred metres from the top. However, you can't afford to relax too much as the hard work is not all over yet: the descent is broken by two short uphill sections. The first, alongside Grand Maison reservoir, is not too difficult, but the second, going up to Le Rivier d'Allemont, has an average gradient of around 10%. To look on the positive side, these two uphill sections mean that the descent will take longer, giving you more time to appreciate one of the most beautiful valleys in the northern Alps. The view of the Grand Pic de la Belledonne from just before Le Rivier d'Allemont is particularly impressive.

Day four ends at Bourg d'Oisans, one of the gateways to the Ecrins National Park. Bourg d'Oisans is a pleasant place that has developed as a tourism centre whilst retaining the charm of a traditional French provincial town. Every year the town is the venue for a major international mineral fair that attracts collectors from all over the world, so it is not surprising that the Mineral and Wildlife Museum should have such a good collection of crystals. Bourg's proximity to so many famous cols (such as Glandon, Croix de Fer and Galibier) has also made it a honey-pot for cyclists. Many of the hotels do special packages that include the sort of substantial breakfast that is so essential before a long day on the bike. The magnet that draws thousands of cyclists to Bourg d'Oisans is Alpe d'Huez, perhaps the most famous mountain stage of the Tour de France. Route Six includes a circuit that starts with the climb to 'L'Alpe'.

The final day of the tour takes you back to Grenoble via the Col d'Ornon and the Valbonnais, a much more pleasant alternative to the direct route along the very busy N91. Although this stage is very long, once

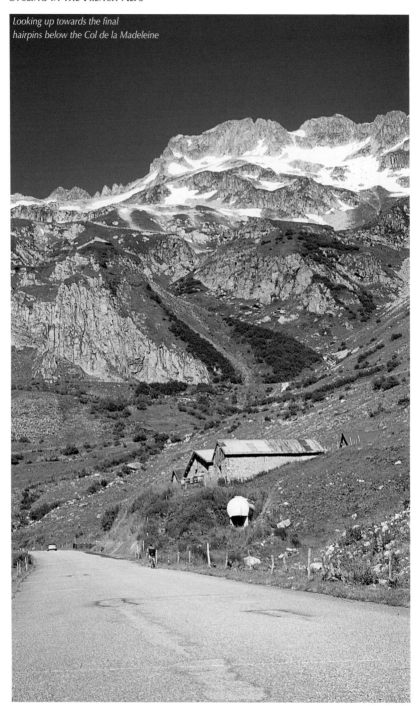

Looking up towards the final
hairpins below the Col de la Madeleine

over the Col d'Ornon most of the cycling is easy; there are no more long or steep climbs. For me, the Col d'Ornon also marks the boundary between the northern and the southern Alps. There is no sudden change in the landscape, but there is a subtle change in the atmosphere, which now has a sunnier, more relaxed Provençale feel. The atmosphere changes once again as you get to La Mure, once an important regional crossroads, but now struggling to come to terms with the decline of the coalfields just to the north of the town. La Mure was a strategic centre during the religious wars of the 16th and 17th centuries, first as a Protestant stronghold and later as a Catholic base for the conversion and persecution of the Calvinist heretics. You can learn more about the town's history, from prehistoric times to the mining era, at the Musée Matheysin. However, if you would like to get a real feel for what life was like for local miners, the place to visit is the Mine-image museum at La Motte-d'Aveillans, which includes an impressive reconstruction of a coalface.

Once past La Motte-Aveillans, the road goes down over the River Vaulx and then up onto the Corniche du Drac, high above the River Drac. The views from here, across to the Vercors Mountains and the tower-like Mont Aiguille, are superb. A 10km descent takes you through the mediaeval village of St Georges-de-Commiers to the valley floor and the industrial complexes around Jarrie. Despite appearances, the enjoyable cycling is not over yet; after a short sprint along the RN85, you leave the factories behind to climb out of the valley and up to the village of Champagnier, from where there is a fabulous panorama across Grenoble to the Chartreuse. Champagnier is only a few short kilometres from the suburbs of Grenoble and the cycleway that will lead you back to the city centre and the end of this superbly varied tour.

GETTING THERE

By car
Grenoble is 870km from Calais

By plane
Via Lyon St Exupéry
 Bus: Shuttle bus every hour.
 Train: To take the train you have to cycle to La Verpillière (see Appendix 1 for route details). On average, there is a train to Grenbole every hour and the journey takes around an hour and ten minutes.

Via Geneva
Take the train from the airport to Geneva central station (Cornavin). From Cornavin there is a train to Grenoble every two to three hours, either direct or via Culoz and Chambéry. The direct journey takes around 2hrs 15mins.

Via Grenoble
See directions in Appendix 1

Via Chambéry
Directions to Chambéry station are given in Appendix 1. There is a very frequent train service from Chambéry to Grenoble with trains every 20mins to one hour, depending on the time of day. The journey takes around 45mins.

WHEN TO GO

This tour can be done at any time from early May to the end of September. In October, it is usually too cold to cycle over such high passes as the Col de la Madeleine and the Col du Glandon and they are closed from midNovember to early May. At the beginning of May, even if the roads are officially still closed, it is usually possible to get through on a bike.

MAPS

Michelin: Local – Sheet 333, Isère, Savoie
  Michelin: Regional – Sheet 244, RhôneAlpes
  IGN: Top 100 – Sheet 53: Grenoble, Mont Blanc

Day 1 – Grenoble to Allevard

Grenoble's tram system provides a fast and efficient way of getting round the city, but its rails can present quite a hazard for the unwary cyclist. Riding across Place Grennette, Grenoble's main shopping square, one day, I tried to cross the tram-lines at too acute an angle. My front wheel slipped into the gap between the rail and the pavement and stopped dead resulting in a very spectacular dismount. The bike went flying, but somehow I managed to stay on my feet, catapulted into a thirty-metre sprint. Fortunately, it was a Sunday and the appreciative audience was not too large.

Distance	Location	Directions
0.0	Grenoble station	Leave the station via the (Centre Ville) exit and go straight across the street in front of the station. Go down Rue Casimir Brenier to Place Hubert Dubedout.
0.4	Place Hubert Dubedout	Go across the square (easiest on foot) and the follow Quai Crequi along the (true) L bank of River Isère. Go straight on to Place Emile de Marcieu.
1.3	Place Emile de Marcieu	Turn L at the traffic lights and go across Place Emile de Marcieu to join the cycle lane along Quai Jonkind.
2.2	Rue Poilus	Turn L onto the cycleway and follow it alongside the Isère (short sections not paved)
10.7	Junction	Turn R and go across the level crossing
10.8	D523	Turn L – D523
11.8	D523/D291	Turn R – D291 (La Pererée): 6km at 6%
20.5	D291/D280b	Turn L – D208b (Revel)
22.8	Revel D208b/D11	Go straight on – D11
24.2	D11/D280	Turn L – D280 (Allevard) Follow this road to St Pierre d'Allevard: a total of 47.9km
46.3	Col des Mouilles	4.1km at 6.5% – up to the pass
53.8	Col des Ayes	1.1km at 6% – up to the pass
64.2	Col du Barioz	6.2km at 7% – up to the pass
72.1	D280/D525	Turn R – D525 (Allevard)
75.0	Roundabout	Go straight on (Centre Ville)
75.8	Allevard	Place de la Resistance

112

Roadside sculptures near Le Mollard

FACILITIES AND SERVICES

Location	Distance (km)	Water	Shops	Café	Campsite	B&B	Hotel	Bank	Bike Shop
Grenoble	0.0	x	x	x	x	(1)	x	x	x
Revel	22.8	x	x	x	—	x	—	—	—
Le Neysord	30.0	—	—	—	x	x	—	—	—
St Mury-de-Monteymond	39.1	x	—	x	x	—	—	—	—
Col des Mouilles	46.3	—	—	x	—	—	—	—	—
Col des Ayes	53.8	x	—	—	x	—	—	—	—
Theys	58.0	x	—	x	x	x	x	—	—
Col du Barioz	64.2	—	—	x	—	—	—	—	—
Allevard	75.8	x	x	x	x	x	x	x	(2)

(1) Nearest B&B: La Tronche on the northeast edge of Grenoble (approx 4km from station)

(2) Nearest bike shop: Goncelin, 10km southwest of Allevard

Day 2 – Allevard to Albertville

There are two ways in which this second day can be made a little more challenging. **1** – turn right in the middle of Aiton to go through Bonvillard (D102, D69). The road climbs quite steeply, gaining 370m in less than 5km, but the views of the Bauges Mountains to the west are truly spectacular. **2** – Cross the Combe de Savoie just after Ste. Hélène-sur-Isère and follow the D201C to the Col de Tamié, 570m above the valley floor. Turn right just before the pass to follow the D104, D104A and D63 down into the centre of Albertville.

Distance	Location	Directions
0.0	Allevard: Place de la Resistance	Turn R in front of church onto Rue du Grand Pont. Go over the river then turn L onto Rue Bir Hakeim.
1.1	Roundabout	Bear R – D209 (Arvillard)
7.0	Arvillard	Go through the centre of the village
7.2	D209/D207E	Turn R – D207E (Presle)
8.8	D207E/D207	Turn R – D207 (Presle) then (Col du Grand Cucheron): 13.7km at 3.5% then 2.6km at 9% just before the pass
25.1	Col du Grand Cucheron	Go straight on
34.8	D207/D73	Turn L – D73 (Aiguebelle)
42.6	Aiguebelle: D73/N6	Turn R – N6
42.8	N6/D72	Turn L – D72 (Randens) then R to go over the River Arc
43.3	Junction	Turn L – D72 (Aiton). Go straight through Aiton and down to Le Plan d'Aiton
49.9	Le Plan d'Aiton: D72/D925	Turn R – D925 (Albertville)
63.4	Grignon: roundabout D925/D64	Turn L – D64 (Gilly-sur-Isère)
65.6	Gilly-sur-Isère: D64/D990	Turn R – D990 (Albertville).
68.6	Albertville*	Railway station

* In the summer of 2004 work started on a new by-pass around Albertville. This work, which is due to take 3 years, should not have any permanent effect on the route into Albertville, but there may be temporary diversions.

Le Bourget-en-Huile

FACILITIES AND SERVICES

Location	Distance (km)	Water	Shops	Café	Campsite	B&B	Hotel	Bank	Bike Shop
Allevard	0.0	x	x	x	x	x	x	x	(1)
Arvillard	7.0	x	x	x	—	—	x	—	—
Bourget-en-Huile	18.0	x	—	—	—	—	—	—	—
St George-des-Hurtières	36.0	x	—	x	—	x	—	—	—
Aiguebelle	42.6	x	x	x	—	—	x	x	—
Le Plan d'Aiton	49.9	—	x	—	—	—	—	—	—
Gilly-sur-Isère	65.6	—	x	x	—	—	—	—	—
Albertville	68.6	x	x	x	x	x	x	x	x

(1) Nearest bike shop: Goncelin, 10km southwest of Allevard

eorges-
Hurtières
80m
Aiguebelle
320m
Le Plan
d'Aiton
300m
Albertville
337m
Day 3

120   130   140   150   160

m)

115

Day 3 – Albertville to La Chambre

Even with all his engineering skills, man's achievements are no match for the forces of nature. Even such sturdy structures as roads sometimes lose the struggle against gravity. A massive landslide at the end of the 1990s definitively swept away one of the roads to the Col de la Madeleine. If you look to your left from La Thuile, you can still see where the road ends abruptly in a very steep scree slope.

Distance	Location	Directions
0.0	Albertville station*	Come out of the station and go straight on along Ave Jean Jaurès. Continue straight on at three sets of traffic lights and at a roundabout – Ave du 8 Mai 1945, and then Route de Tours/D990. Go through La Bathie to Langon Gare.
12.5	Langon Gare: roundabout	Turn R to go over the motorway and the River Isère
13.8	D66B/D66	Turn L – D66. Follow the D66 past Feissonnet – D66–D97
19.1	D97/D94	Turn R – D94 (Col de la Madeleine)
44.4	Col de la Madeleine	Go straight on: 25.3km at 6%
64.0	La Chambre	

* In the summer of 2004 work started on a new by-pass around Albertville. This work, which is due to take 3 years, should not have any permanent effect on the route into Albertville, but there may be temporary diversions.

FACILITIES AND SERVICES								
Location	Distance (km)	Water	Shops	Café	Campsite	B&B	Hotel	Bank	Bike Shop
Albertville	0.0	x	x	x	x	x	x	x	x
La Bathie	9.0	—	x	x	x	—	x	x	x
Celliers	35.0	x	—	x	—	—	x	—	—
Col de la Madeleine	44.4	—	—	x	—	—	—	—	—
St François-Longchamp	49.0	—	x	x	—	x	x	x	—
La Chambre	64.0	x	x	x	x	—	x	x	(1)

(1) Nearest bike shop: St Jean-de-Maurienne, 10km southeast of La Chambre

116

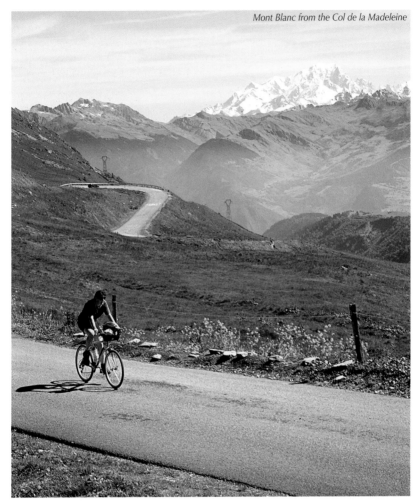

Mont Blanc from the Col de la Madeleine

Day 4 – La Chambre to Bourg d'Oisans

Distance	Location	Directions
0.0	La Chambre	Turn L – D76
0.4	Roundabout	Turn R
0.7	Roundabout	Go straight on
1.2	Roundabout	Go straight on
1.4	Roundabout	Turn R (Col du Glandon)
1.8	Roundabout	Turn L (Col du Glandon): 10.8km at 6%
12.6	St Colomban-des-Villards	Go straight on: 10.4km at 8%
23.0	Col du Glandon	Go straight on
23.3	D927/D926	Turn R – D926-D526 (Allemont)
39.2	Le Rivier-d'Allemont	Go straight on
48.9	D526/D44	Turn R along D526 and go over the dam (Allemont)
50.2	Allemond	Go straight on
53.6	Rochetaillée: D526/N91	Turn L – N91 (Bourg d'Oisans)
60.8	Bourg d'Oisans TO	TO is on the left

FACILITIES AND SERVICES

Location	Distance (km)	Water	Shops	Café	Campsite	B&B	Hotel	Bank	Bike Shop
La Chambre	0.0	x	x	x	x	—	x	x	(1)
St Etienne-de-Cuines	2.5	x	x	x	—	—	x	x	—
St Colomban-des-Villards	12.6	x	x	x	x	x	x	—	—
Col du Glandon	23.0	—	—	x	—	—	—	—	—
Le Rivier-d'Allemont	39.2	x	x	x	—	x	x	—	—
Allemond	50.2	x	x	x	x	x	x	—	—
Rochetaillée	53.6	—	—	—	x	—	—	—	—
Bourg d'Oisans	60.8	x	x	x	x	x	x	x	x

(1) Nearest bike shop: St Jean-de-Maurienne, 10km southeast of La Chambre

Tour of the Belledonne Day 4

Col du Glandon 1924m

St Colomban-des-Villards 1102m

La Chambre 470m

Day 3

Day 4

The V-shaped Villards Valley below the Col du Glandon

Buying and selling minerals has become big business, so much so that people are prepared to risk their lives in decaying mineshafts to collect them. At the beginning of 2005 and after a seven-month inquiry by 45 *gendarmes*, nine people were arrested and charged with illegally extracting minerals from the abandoned mines around Bourg d'Oisans. On searching their homes and garages, the police found a large quantity of dynamite and more than 50 tonnes of minerals. The suspects had even installed rail-mounted wagons in some of the shafts to extract their bounty. As the state is responsible for safety in former mine-workings, it was decided to blow up the mine entrances to seal them permanently. However, voices were immediately raised decrying an act of vandalism that would destroy a vital element in the region's industrial heritage. A petition was signed by 1500 people, including the mayor of Bourg d'Oisans . . . and several of the people who had been arrested!

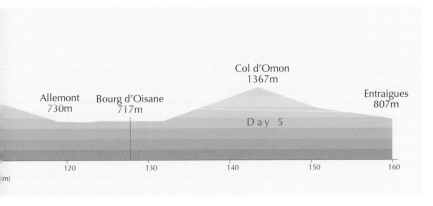

Day 5 – Bourg d'Oisans to Grenoble

Extra day: the most obvious way to extend the tour is to do the circuit through Alpe d'Huez, as described in Route 6. For a less difficult ride, I would recommend the 60km round trip to La Bérarde up the Véneon Valley, arguably one of the most beautiful valleys in the Alps. Apart from short sections after Bourg d'Arud and around St Christophe, the gradient is quite gentle, allowing you to relax and soak up the magnificent surroundings. On the way back, it is worth making a short detour to visit the picturesque village of Venosc.

Distance	Location	Directions
0.0	Bourg d'Oisans TO	Come out of the TO and turn R – N91
2.3	N91/D526	Turn L – D526 (Col d'Ornon): 11.6km at 5.5%
13.9	Col d'Ornon	Go straight on
28.8	Entraigues: D526/D117	Turn R – D526 (La Mure)
36.3	D526/D26	Go straight on along D26 (La Mure)
47.5	La Mure: D26/N85	Turn R – N85 (Grenoble)
48.2	Roundabout	Go straight on
48.4	N85/D529	Turn L – D529 and go through La Motte d'Aveillans and St George de Commiers (Vizille)
71.8	Roundabout: D529/D63A	Turn R – D529 (Grenoble)
76.3	Roundabout: D529/N85	Turn L – N85 (Grenoble)
77.5	N85/D64	Turn R – D64 (Champagnier) then (Grenoble)
82.8	Echirolles: roundabout	Go straight on – D269 (Grenoble)
83.1	Roundabout	Turn R onto cycleway parallel to tramway
85.7	Jtn: cycleway turns R at jtn with Rue de Bretagne	Go across road to go up path that leads to main road and big roundabout. Turn L at roundabout – Ave Edmond Esmonin (Lyon).
86.4	Traffic lights	Go straight on then bear R to go to R of fly-over
86.8	Jtn	Turn R – Ave Paul Verlaine. Follow cycle lane parallel to railway.
88.7	Traffic lights	Turn L to follow cycleway between road and railway
89.0	Jtn	Turn L – Rue Colonel Lanoyerie
89.7	Fork	Bear L (Gare SNCF)
90.2	Grenoble station	Station is on the L

Mt Aiguille, one of the most impressive
mountains in the pre-Alps,
as seen from La Motte d'Aveillans

FACILITIES AND SERVICES									
Location	Distance (km)	Water	Shops	Café	Campsite	B&B	Hotel	Bank	Bike Shop
Bourg d'Oisans	0.0	x	x	x	x	x	x	x	x
La Paute	8.6	x	—	—	—	—	—	—	—
Col d'Ornon	13.9	—	—	x	—	x	—	—	—
Les Daurens	21.2	x	—	x	—	x	—	—	—
Le Perrier	23.9	x	x	x	x	—	—	—	—
Entraigues	28.8	x	x	x	x	x	—	—	—
Valbonnais	32.7	x	—	—	x	x	—	—	—
La Mure	47.5	x	x	x	—	—	x	x	—
Aveillans	54.0	x	x	x	—	—	x	—	—
Notre Dame-de-Commiers	72.7	x	—	—	—	—	—	—	—
St George-de-Commiers	76.4	x	—	—	—	—	—	—	—
Grenoble	90.8	x	x	x	x	(1)	x	x	x

(1) Nearest B&B: La Tronche on the northeast edge of Grenoble (approx 4km from station)

La Mure 855m · Aveillans 964m · St Georges-de-Commiers 384m · Grenoble 210m

(km) 320 330 340 350 360

ACCOMMODATION

Grenoble

Campsites

Les Trois Pucelles, at Seyssins on the southwest edge of Grenoble (all year), Tel. 04 76 96 45 73

Bed and Breakfast

Mr Cohen, La Tronche, Tel. 04 76 44 78 98

Hotels

There are more than 50 hotels in Grenoble. Contact TO for details.

Allevard

Campsites

Idéal Camping (early May to end Sept), Tel. 04 76 97 50 23

Bed & Breakfast

Gîte Auberge, Tel. 04 76 08 83 06

Hotels

There are 13 hotels in Allevard. Contact TO for details.

Albertville

Campsites

La Maladière (mid-Feb to mid-Nov), Tel. 04 79 37 80 44

Les Adoubes (end April to end Sept), Tel. 04 79 32 06 62

Bed & Breakfast

Mr Boisneau, Tel. 04 79 31 23 23

Hotels

There are 10 hotels in Albertville. Contact TO for details.

La Chambre

Campsites (St Martin-sur-La Chambre)

Le Bois Joli (early April to mid-October) Tel. 04 50 45 48 30

Le Petit Nice (all year) Tel. 04 79 56 37 12

Bed & Breakfast

There are no bed & breakfasts or *gites d'étapes* in La Chambre

Hotels

L'Eterlou ** Tel. 04 49 56 20 39

(Le Grand Chatelard, at Saint Marie-de-Cuines, 3km south of La Chambre, Tel. 04 79 59 49 75)

Bourg d'Oisans

Campsites

There are nine campsites in Bourg d'Oisans. Contact TO for details.

Bed & Breakfast

Gîte du Bouthéon 'La Libellule', Tel. 04 76 79 15 57

Mr Arnaud, Tel. 04 76 80 00 10

Mrs Evrard (at La Paute, at the foot of the Col d'Ornon), Tel. 04.76.80.00.10

Mr Guilini (at La Paute, at the foot of the Col d'Ornon), Tel. 04.76.79.11.27

Other B&B style accommodation exists around Bourg d'Oisans. Contact TO for details.

Hotels

There are 9 hotels in Bourg d'Oisans. Contact TO for details.

TOURIST INFORMATION

Regional Information

	Telephone	Website
Isère	04 76 54 34 36	**www.isere-tourisme.com**
Savoie	04 79 85 12 45	**www.savoiehautesavoie.com**

Tourist Information Offices

Location	Telephone	Website
Grenoble	04 76 42 41 41	**www.grenoble-isere-tourisme.com**
Revel	04 76 89 82 09	**www.revel-belledonne.com**
Theys	04 76 71 05 92	**no website**
Allevard	04 76 45 10 11	**www.allevard-les-bains.com**
Aiguebelle	04 79 36 29 24	**www.ot-aiguebelle.com**
Albertville	04 79 32 04 22	**www.albertville.com**
St Francois-Longchamp	04 79 59 10 56	**www.saintfrancoislongchamp.com**
La Chambre	04 79 56 33 58	**www.tourisme-la-chambre.com**
St Colomban-des-Villards	04 79 56 24 53	**www.saint-colomban.com**
Allemont	04 76 80 71 60	**www.allemont.com**
Bourg d'Oisans	04 76 80 03 25	**www.bourgdoisans.com**
Valbonnais	04 76 30 25 26	**no website**
La Mure	04 76 81 05 71	**no website**
La Motte d'Aveillans	04 76 30 72 75	**no website**

The Véneon Valley (Extra day)

ROUTE SIX

TOUR OF THE ECRINS AND GRANDES ROUSSES

Day	Route	Distance	Height Gain
1	St Jean-de-Maurienne to Valloire	26.4km	1129m
2	Valloire to Briançon	55.5km	1241m
3	Briançon to Embrun	61.3km	726m
4	Embrun to St Bonnet-en-Champsaur	64.3km	1340m
5	St Bonnet-en-Champsaur to Bourg d'Oisans	82.0km	1686m
6	Bourg d'Oisans to Bourg d'Oisans	58.2km	1975m
7	Bourg d'Oisans to St Jean-de-Maurienne	79.1km	1962m
	Totals	**426.8km**	**10,059m**

Although not a classic circuit in itself, the Tour of the Ecrins and Grandes Rousses includes some of the most famous mountain passes in the annals of cycling. There cannot be many keen cyclists who do not dream of following in the tracks of Mercx, Hinault and Armstrong on the roads to the Col du Galibier, Col de la Croix de Fer and Alpe d'Huez. Every year, thousands of cyclists attempt to do all three of these climbs in a single day as part of the famous Marmotte event, a 174km circuit with 5000 metres of height gain. Such long-distance challenges can be fun, but at the more gentle pace of the cycle-tourist you have much more time (and energy) to enjoy the surrounding countryside.

Grandes Rousses is the name given to the mountains between the Col du Galibier and the Col de la Croix Fer. It is an area that attracts relatively few visitors despite containing some of the most strikingly elegant summits in the Alps in the shape of the Aiguilles d'Arves. The neighbouring Ecrins Massif, the second highest range of mountains in France and a national park, is much more famous than the Grandes Rousses. The towns of Bourg d'Oisans, Briançon, Embrun and Gap mark the four corners of the massif, which culminates in the 4102 metre-high Barre des Ecrins. During the summer months this area is an extremely popular tourist destination and traffic levels on the main roads

often reach saturation point. Fortunately, with the exception of the descent from the Col du Lautaret to Briançon, cyclists are well served by a network of secondary roads that rarely see much traffic.

The tour starts in St Jean-de-Maurienne, Savoie's third largest city and the birthplace of the House of Savoie. The dynasty was founded by Humbert of the White Hands, who became the first Count of Savoie at the beginning of the 11th century. At its height, the family ruled lands that extended from Bourg-en-Bresse to Turin and from Geneva to Sardinia. Savoie itself became part of France in 1860, but the dynasty lived on with Victor-Emmanuel II becoming King of Italy in 1861. St Jean-de-Maurienne's first cathedral was built in the 6th century to provide a fitting resting-place for the diocese's sacred relics of John the Baptist. The original building was destroyed at the end of the first millennium and replaced in the 11th century by a building that has been greatly modified over the centuries, but which still stands today.

If you arrive in St Jean before the middle of the afternoon, you should have time to reach Valloire that same day. The classic route is through St Michel-de-Maurienne and over the Col du Télégraphe (see Route Eight), however, the only way to get to St Michel is along the main *route nationale* and the road over the Col du Télégraphe can itself be busy at times.

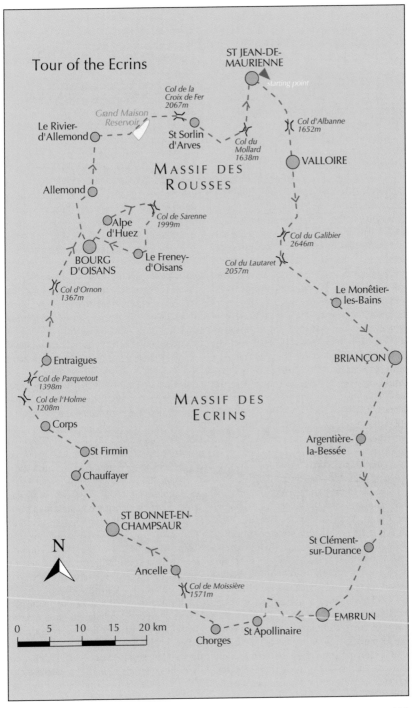

Fortunately, there is an alternative route, via Montricher and the Col de l'Albanne. The gradient is quite severe (an average of 7.5% for 12km) and there is a 2km section on an unpaved forest track (at least 80% can be ridden, even with a road bike), but you are rewarded with virtually deserted roads and a superb view from the pass.

Unlike many ski resorts, Valloire is as busy in summer as it is in winter, partly thanks to its location at the foot of the Col du Galibier. The Galibier has always been one of the great alpine passes and as such attracts tourists from far and wide. Although traffic is rarely a problem, the best time to cycle over the Galibier is the one morning in July (usually the first Thursday of the month) when the pass is closed to cars. However, Valloire also stages other events that may lead to the road being unpleasantly busy or completely closed, even to cyclists. Dates for these events can be found on the village's website.

Whether or not you have the road to yourself, cycling over the Galibier is always a challenge: there are few easy sections and the last kilometre is the steepest. The scenery is magnificent all the way, but very few mountain panoramas can rival the breath-taking view from the top of the pass. The chaotic glaciers and sombre cliffs of the north face of the Meije, just a stone's throw away, have a truly savage beauty that leaves no-one indifferent. The other high summits of the Ecrins seem to cower in the shadow of this monstrous wall of rock and ice. An even more grandiose spectacle is on offer to those who climb the few metres to the tiny summit just west of the pass, as the vista opens out to include the elegant spires of the Aiguilles d'Arves.

After an exhilarating descent to the Col du Lautaret, the route follows the main RN91 down the Guisane Valley to Briançon, the highest town in Europe. Given the number of forts surrounding the town, there can be no doubt as to the location's strategic importance. Many of these forts are open to visitors and guided tours are available. Briançon is a lively place and the town centre can be very busy, especially on a wet summer's day – it has to rain occasionally, even in a town that boasts 300 sunshine days a year! Come rain or shine, there are many interesting things to see including the old town, the forts and the Ski Museum at the Ecrins National Park Centre.

Stage three of the tour, along the Durance Valley from Briançon to Embrun, can be regarded as a semi-rest day as there are no long climbs to tackle. If you would like a more challenging day, the obvious alternative is to

Argentière-la-Bessée: the biggest ice-axe in the world

go over the Col d'Izoard (see Route Eight) and rejoin the main itinerary just before St Clément-sur-Durance.

The first port of call after leaving Briançon is the former mining village of Argentière-la-Bessée. Without completely abandoning its industrial roots, Argentière has successfully turned itself into a centre for outdoor sports, building a white-water canoeing course and holding rock-climbing and ice-climbing competitions. Many of the village's streets have been named after famous mountaineers and the world's largest ice-axe stands proudly in front of the *marie*. A few kilometres south of Argentière lies the hardest climb of the day, a mere 1.5km long but with an average gradient of 12%. Although not completely flat, the rest of the stage is quite easy – time to relax and admire the marvellous scenery.

Embrun is a tiny cathedral city at the north-eastern end of the Serre-Ponçon Reservoir, the largest man-made lake in Europe. Work on the dam began in 1955, a century after the project was first mooted as a way to control the extremely variable flow-rate of the Durance River. The reservoir covers 2800 hectares and feeds 16 hydroelectricity plants, as well as providing irrigation water for 150,000 hectares of agricultural land via the Durance Canal. It is also a huge leisure resource that has transformed the economies of the surrounding villages. Embrun's gothic cathedral was built in the 12th and 13th centuries, but the city has been an archdiocese since the 9th century. The cathedral is one of the most imposing religious buildings in the Alps and well worth a visit. All that remains of the archbishop's palace is the Tour Brune, which now houses an interesting exhibition that explains the evolution of the surrounding landscape.

From Embrun the route follows quiet roads across the flanks of Mt Guillaume, turning left just before Réallon to take in the fabulous view of the lake from St Apollinaire. At this point there is no choice but to descend back into the valley to the pleasant little village of Chorges, and a final opportunity to stock up on calories before attacking the climb to the Col de Moissière. Once again it is possible to avoid the main road by following minor

roads around the northern edge of the village (not marked on either the IGN or Michelin maps). At this relatively low altitude, heat and dehydration can be your worst enemies, especially on the open, south-facing slopes you have to cross to get to the Col de Moissière. Fortunately, the last and steepest part of the ascent is through a cool(er) and shady forest.

The rest of the day's cycling is easy, a 12km descent followed by 11km on the flat. On the edge of the tiny resort of Ancelle, a pancake-smooth patchwork of fields covers the surface of a dried-up lake: an island of visual calm in the midst of this unrelentingly rugged landscape. St Léger-les-Mélèzes, a few kilometres north of Ancelle, is the last village with a full range of services before St Bonnet-en-Champsaur. It also has an excellent little natural history museum. St Bonnet is an attractive but very sleepy little place that seems to spring to life once a year when 300 villagers dress-up in period costumes to demonstrate the arts and crafts of their ancestors. This colourful Fête du Terroir takes place on the first Sunday in August.

Day five starts gently, through the rolling countryside north of St Bonnet, giving your legs time to warm up before tackling the three cols that bar the route to Bourg d'Oisans. The first climb, to the Col des Festraux, is not very long but the first 2km above St Firmin are very steep. After a short descent, the route turns right onto the main RN85, which takes you through Corps. This is the Route Napoléon, the road taken by Bonaparte when he returned from exile on the island of Elba to seize power. With Bonaparte's name splashed across the front of nearly every hotel, restaurant and bar, the visitor is left in no doubt as to the importance of this event in the area's history.

Just after Corps, the route once again leaves the main road to tackle the second major ascent of the day. There are in fact two passes to cross between Corps and Entraigues, but the descent between them is negligible. The road to the first pass, the Col de l'Holme, provides fabulous views of the 2790 metre-high Obiou and the other peaks of the Dévoluy. After the Col de l'Holme, the road very quickly rises again taking you up to

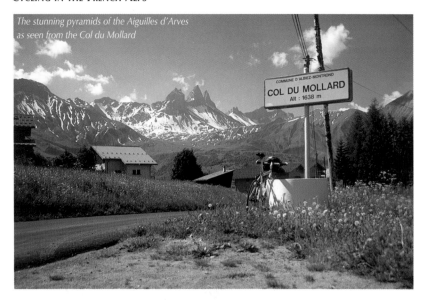

The stunning pyramids of the Aiguilles d'Arves as seen from the Col du Mollard

COMMUNE D'ALBIEZ-MONTROND
COL DU MOLLARD
Alt : 1638 m

(and above!) the Col de Parquetout. The descent from this second pass is very steep and narrow with a lot of blind corners, so be wary of vehicles coming the other way. The final climb of the day, over the Col d'Ornon, is long but quite easy, although the gradient increases slightly a few kilometres below the summit. If you are feeling too weary to continue, a night spent at the *gite d'étape* at Les Daurens is highly recommended. It was here that I first experienced a true *table d'hote*, where guests at a hotel or restaurant eat at the same table as their hosts. If you are lucky enough to have hosts like Mr and Mrs Marin, this is an excellent way to get a feel for French life. For those who make it all the way to the pass, the reward comes in the form of the wonderful descent to the Romanche Valley and Bourg d'Oisans.

Bourg d'Oisans is renowned amongst cyclists as the starting point for the climb to Alpe d'Huez. (see the introduction to Route Five for more about Bourg d'Oisans). Every day during the summer, dozens if not hundreds of cyclists pit themselves against the 21 hairpins, 13km and 1120 metres of ascent. Alpe d'Huez is a must if only because of its legendary reputation, but you often have to share the road with a lot of tourist traffic, especially in July and August. The climb to

Alpe d'Huez is also the first part of a magnificent but strenuous circuit over the Col de Sarenne, one of the wildest passes in the Alps. The views of the Roche de Muzelle from the eastern side of the pass are truly spectacular, but the first part of the descent can be quite dangerous as there is a lot of gravel on the road. Just after Mizoën the route briefly joins the main RN91 before turning right at Le Freney-d'Oisans to follow the D211A above the Gorges de l'Infernet. The section across the Rochers d'Armentier is particularly dramatic: hanging 600 metres above the valley floor, the road seems to cling to the mountainside by its fingernails.

Day seven, over the Col de la Croix de Fer, is another long day that has been made even longer by the roadworks that will close the direct route back to St Jean-de-Maurienne every summer until at least 2007. Many people, including Lance Armstrong, consider the Croix de Fer to be one of the most beautiful passes in the Alps. At first the road runs through dense forest and it is only when you get to Le Rivier d'Allemond that the magnificent scenery is fully unveiled in all its glory. A roadside café 2.5km below the pass marks the junction with the road to the Col du Glandon, a mere 17 metres above you. If you are truly on your last legs, it is always possible to turn left here and go over the Col du Glandon to the railway station at La Chambre; otherwise, there is another café at the Col de la Croix Fer, giving you the opportunity to refuel before freewheeling down to the foot of the last climb of the tour. The road up to the Col du Mollard has the unwelcome characteristic of getting steeper and steeper as you approach the top, with the last 2.5km being at an average gradient of more than 10%. This time the compensation for your efforts is two-fold: a magnificent view of the Aiguilles d'Arves and a final exhilarating 18km descent back to St Jean-de-Maurienne.

GETTING THERE

By car
St Jean-de-Maurienne is 980km from Calais.

By plane
Via Lyon
Bus/Train: Bus to Chambéry then train from Chambéry to St Jean-de-Maurienne. There are five or six busses per day and the journey takes about one hour. There is a train every two to three hours from Chambéry to St Jean-de-Maurienne and the journey takes 50mins to one hour.

Cycle/Train: You can also take the train by cycling to Bourgoin Jallieu (see Appendix 1 for route details), however, there are only two or three trains per day train – check the SNCF website to see if they are compatible with your flight times. The train journey takes between two and three hours, depending on connections.

Via Geneva
Train: Take the train from the airport to Geneva central station (Cornavin). There are only two or three trains per day from Cornavin to St Jean and you will always have to change at Chambéry and possibly Bellegarde and/or Culoz as well. The journey takes between three and four hours, depending on connections.

Via Chambéry
Directions to Chambéry station are given in Appendix 1. There are about five or six trains per day from Chambéry to St Jean-de-Maurienne. The journey takes around one hour.

WHEN TO GO
This tour can only be done from the middle of June to October as the Col du Galibier is closed for the other seven months of the year. The Col de la Croix de Fer usually opens in early May, about one month before the Galibier. Apart from the section from Valloire to Briançon, the tour follows secondary roads that do not normally see a lot of traffic, even during the main holiday periods.

MAPS
Michelin: Local – Sheet 333: Isère, Savoie; and Sheet 334: Alpes-de-Haute-Provence, Hautes-Alpes

Michelin: Regional – Sheet 244: Rhône-Alpes and Sheet 245: Provence, Côte d'Azur

IGN: Top 100 – Sheet 53: Grenoble, Mont Blanc and Sheet 54: Grenoble, Gap

Day 1 – St Jean-de-Maurienne to Valloire

Under the French Revolution all place-names with superstitious origins had to be changed, hence Saint Jean-de-Maurienne briefly became known as Arc.

Distance	Location	Directions
0.0	St Jean-de-Maurienne Station	Come out of station, turn R then immediately L to go past the EDF office
0.2	Roundabout	Turn L – Rue Germain Sommeiller (Toutes Directions)
0.3	Jtn	Turn R – Quai de l'Arvan (Vallée de l'Arvan)
0.9	Jtn	Turn L – D906 (Torino)
2.2	Roundabout	Go straight on (Toutes Directions)
2.3	Roundabout	Turn L second exit (Montricher–Albanne)
3.9	Roundabout D81/D80	Go straight on – D81 (Montricher–Albanne)
4.5	Roundabout	Go straight on (Montricher–Albanne)
6.6	Le Bochet	Bear R towards centre of village
6.7	Jtn	Turn R – D81 (Montricher): 12.5km at 7.5%
13.9	Montricher: D81/D81B	Turn L – D81 (Albanne)
19.2	Col de l'Albanne	Go straight on
20.3	Albanne: jtn	Turn R (Albannette)
22.6	Jtn with forest track	Jtn is at apex of LH hairpin – go straight on along track [Valloire]
24.5	Jtn with paved road	Go straight on
26.1	Valloire	Take the road on the L, just after river, to town centre
26.4	Jtn	Turn R and TO is on R

FACILITIES AND SERVICES

Location	Distance (km)	Water	Shops	Café	Campsite	B&B	Hotel	Bank	Bike Shop
St Jean-de-Maurienne	0.0	x	x	x	x	—	x	x	x
Le Bochet	6.6	x	—	—	—	—	—	—	—
Montricher	13.1	x	—	x	—	—	x	—	—
Albanne	20.1	x	—	x	—	—	—	—	—
Valloire	26.4	x	x	x	x	x	x	x	x

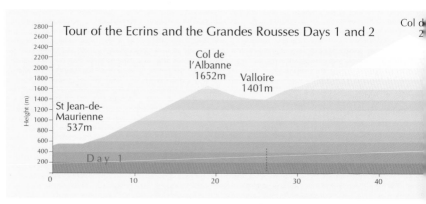

Tour of the Ecrins and the Grandes Rousses Days 1 and 2

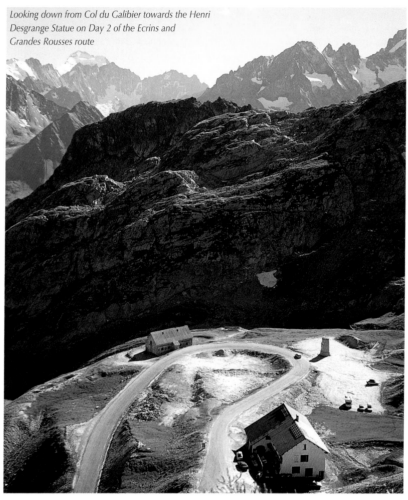

Looking down from Col du Galibier towards the Henri Desgrange Statue on Day 2 of the Ecrins and Grandes Rousses route

131

Day 2 – Valloire to Briançon

Briançon's main street is known as 'La Grande Gargouille' after the open channel that runs down the middle. The channel's most important function was not as a drain, but as a way of supplying water to fight fires. La Grande Gargouille, which has an average gradient of 8% for 1km, has been the scene of many exciting finishes of stages of both the Tour de France and the Dauphiné Libéré.

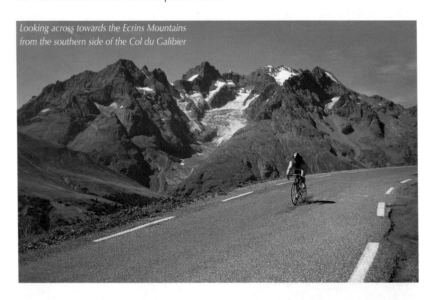

Looking across towards the Ecrins Mountains from the southern side of the Col du Galibier

Distance	Location	Directions
0.0	Valloire TO	Come out of TO and turn R – D902: 17.5km at 7%
17.5	Col du Galibier	Go straight on
26.2	Col du Lauteret	Turn R – N91. Follow this, and then D994 into Briançon
53.0	Briançon – roundabout	Turn R (Gap)
54.5	Traffic lights	Turn L onto D2 (Gare SNCF)
54.8	Roundabout	Turn R
55.0	Roundabout	Go straight on
55.5	Briançon station	Station is on the R

FACILITIES AND SERVICES								
Location	Distance (km)	Water	Shops	Café	Campsite	B&B	Hotel	Bank	Bike Shop
Valloire	0.0	x	x	x	x	x	x	x	x
Col du Lauteret	26.2	—	x	x	—	—	—	—	—
Monêtier-les-Bains	39.7	x	x	x	—	x	x	x	x
Chantemerle	48.0	x	x	x	x	x	x	x	—
Briançon	55.5	x	x	x	x	(1)	x	x	x
(1) At Villard St Pancrace, 2km south of Briançon									

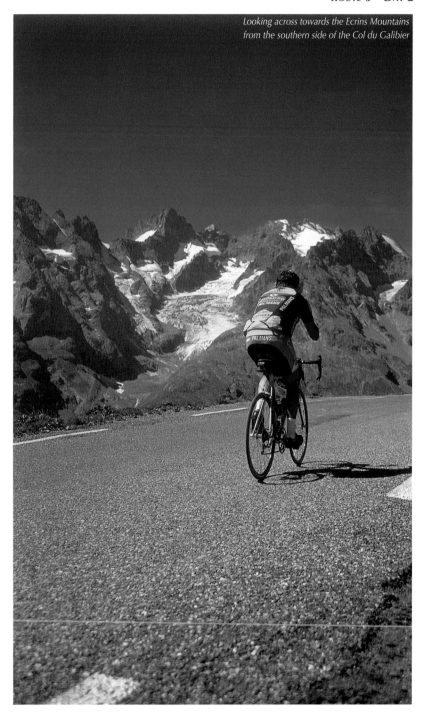

Looking across towards the Ecrins Mountains from the southern side of the Col du Galibier

Distance	Location	Directions
0.0	Briançon station	Come out of the station and go straight on (Villar St Pancrace)
0.1	Roundabout	Turn R – D36 (Villar St Pancrace)
0.3	Roundabout	Go straight on (Villar St Pancrace)
0.8	Roundabout	Turn L (Villar St Pancrace)
1.0	Villard St Pancrace	Turn R at the roundabout (Centre Village)
1.4	Roundabout	Go straight on
1.9	Jtn	Go straight on along Routes des Espagnols
7.8	Roundabout	Turn L (Prelles)
7.9	Jtn	Turn L – N2094 (Prelles)
8.2	N2094/N94	Turn R – N94 (Briançon)
8.9	N94/D4	Turn L – D4 (Vallouise): 2.2km at 5%
17.1	D4/D994E	Turn L – D994E (Argentière)
21.7	Argentière-la-Bessée	Go straight through the village: D994E–D104
22.5	Roundabout	Turn L – D104
23.5	Roundabout	Go straight on – D138A (Champcella)
26.7	D138A/D38	Go straight on – D38: 1.5km at 12%
29.4	Pallon	Turn L – D38 (Champcella)
30.9	Jtn	Bear L – D38 (St Crépin)
35.4	Jtn (after bridge)	Turn L
35.7	Jtn	Turn R along D38 (St Clément)
39.6	Jtn	Go straight on – D38 (St Clément)
43.8	D38/N94	Turn L – N94
44.2	N94/D994D	Turn R – D994D (St André-sur-Embrun)
54.9	D994D/D139	Turn R – D994D (Embrun)
58.8	Jtn	Turn R over wooden bridge, and then follow road round to L and then to R to go up hill.
60.8	Embrun	Turn L – N94 (Centre Ville)
61.1	Jtn	Turn L to go into pedestrian zone – Rue Clovis Hugues
61.2	Jtn	Turn R to get to TO
61.3	Embrun TO	TO is in front of you

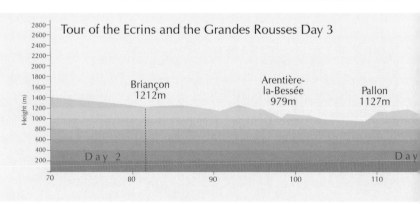

Tour of the Ecrins and the Grandes Rousses Day 3

Looking north from Chanteloube

FACILITIES AND SERVICES

Location	Distance (km)	Water	Shops	Café	Campsite	B&B	Hotel	Bank	Bike Shop
Briançon	0.0	x	x	x	x	(1)	x	x	x
Prelles	8.9	x	x	—	—	—	—	—	—
Les Vigneaux	16.5	x	x	—	x	x	—	—	—
Argentière-la-Bessée	21.7	x	x	x	x	x	x	x	x
Pallon	29.5	x	—	x	x	—	x	—	—
St Clément-sur-Durance	43.8	x	x	—	x	x	—	—	—
Embrun	61.3	x	x	x	x	x	x	x	x

(1) At Villard St Pancrace, 2km south of Briançon

St Clément-sur-Durance 870m

Embrun 869m

St Apollinaire 1275m

D a y 4

130   140   150   160   170

(km)

In recent years, a great many ski resorts have pursued the 'big is beautiful' road to development, linking up with their neighbours to create immense ski areas with dozens of lifts. Other resorts, such as Ancelle, have decided to remain small and to use their 'traditional village' status to attract a new sort of clientele. Studies have shown that at least 20 percent of visitors to ski resorts come to the mountains to relax and soak up the scenery rather than to ski. The 'authentic mountain experience' these visitors are looking for is easier to provide when there are fewer ski lifts to mar the views.

Distance	Location	Directions
0.0	Embrun TO	Come out of the TO, turn R and then R again – Rue des Ecuries. This road leads to the N94. Turn L – N94
0.8	N94/D9	Turn R – D9 (Puy-Sanières) then (Réallon): 6.6km at 5.5%, and then 4km at 2.5%
13.5	Les Méans D9/D41	Turn L – D9 (Chorges)
27.0	Jtn	Turn R (Briançon)
27.6	Chorges: jtn	Turn R (Le Bourget)
27.8	Jtn	Turn L (Gap)
27.9	Jtn	Turn R to go past car park (Le Martouret) then take first left: 5.5km at 2.5%
30.0	Jtn	Go straight on – D614 (no sign)
33.7	D614/D214	Go straight on – D214 (Les Aubins): 7.5km at 8%
41.2	Col de Mossière	Go straight on
45.3	Ancelle: D214/D12	Go straight on over bridge and then turn R – D13 (Pont du Fossé)
50.2	St Léger les Mélèzes: roundabout: D12/D113	Turn L – D113 (St Bonnet)
53.2	D113/D944	Turn L (St Bonnet) and then take the first R (Chabottes)
53.8	Jtn	Turn L – D945 (St Bonnet)
54.6	D945/D43A	Turn L – D945 (St Bonnet)
63.9	St Bonnet: jtn	Turn L (Centre Ville)
64.1	Jtn	Turn L and go down to Place Cheveril
64.2	Place Cheveril	Turn R beside fountain to get to Place Grenette
64.3	Place Grenette	TO is on L under covered market place

Tour of the Ecrins and the Grandes Rousses Day 4

Ancelle, on the 'shores' of a dried-up lake.

FACILITIES AND SERVICES

Location	Distance (km)	Water	Shops	Café	Campsite	B&B	Hotel	Bank	Bike Shop
Embrun	0.0	x	x	x	x	x	x	x	x
Les Truchets	6.1	x	—	—	—	—	—	—	—
Les Rousses	15.3	x	—	—	—	—	—	—	—
St Apollinaire	19.1	x	x	x	x	—	—	—	—
Chorges	27.6	x	x	x	x	x	x	x	—
Les Aubins	35.6	x	—	—	—	—	—	—	—
Ancelle	45.3	x	x	x	x	x	x	x	—
St Léger-les-Mélèzes	50.2	x	x	x	x	x	x	—	x
La Plaine	53.8	—	x	—	—	—	—	—	—
St Bonnet-en-Champsaur	64.3	x	x	x	x	x	x	x	x

Day 5 – St Bonnet-en-Champsaur to Bourg d'Oisans

Bourg d'Oisans is one of the few places in the Alps where it is possible to rent road bikes that are of good enough quality for multi-day cycle touring in the mountains. Contact 'Cycles et Sports' (04 76 79 16 79) for prices and bookings. If you come to the Alps without a bike and you would like to start your tour in Bourg d'Oisans, there is a regular coach service from Grenoble (go to **www.vfd.fr for details**).

Distance	Location	Directions
0.0	St Bonnet TO	Come out of TO and go past fountain. Turn L in front of Crédit Agricole onto Rue St Eusèbe.
0.1	Jtn	Turn R (Autres Directions)
6.2	D23/D123	Turn L – D23 (Chauffayer)
12.6	D23/D316	Turn R – D316 (Les Blachus)
16.4	D316/D16A	Turn L – D16A (St Firmin)
16.8	D16A/D16	Turn R – D16 (La Chapelle)
16.9	D16/D216	Turn L – D216 (St Firmin): 4km at 6.5%
18.9	St Firmin: jtn	Go straight on (Les Reculas)
19.6	Jtn	Turn L – D58 (Aspres-les-Corps)
21.4	Col des Festraux	Go straight on
26.5	D58/N85	Turn R – N85 Go through Corps
30.6	N85/D212	Turn R – D212 (Ste Luce): 7.6km at 4%
38.2	Col de l'Holme	Go straight on
41.0	D212/D212F	Turn R – D212F (Valbonnais): 2.8km at 8%
43.4	Col de Parquetout	Go straight on
43.8	High point	Go straight on
50.0	Les Angelas: D212F/C9	Turn R – D212F
51.1	D212F/D526	Turn R – D526
53.2	Entraigues: D526/D117	Turn L – D526 (Bourg d'Oisans): 13.6km at 4%
68.1	Col d'Ornon	Go straight on
79.7	D526/N91	Turn R – N91 (Bourg d'Oisans)
82.0	Bourg d'Oisans	TO is on the L

Tour of the Ecrins and the Grandes Rousses Day 5

The Dévoluy Mountains as seen from the Col de l'Holme

FACILITIES AND SERVICES

Location	Distance (km)	Water	Shops	Café	Campsite	B&B	Hotel	Bank	Bike Shop
St Bonnet-en-Champsaur	0.0	x	x	x	x	x	x	x	x
Chauffayer	12.6	—	x	—	—	—	x	—	—
St Firmin	18.9	x	x	x	x	x	x	x	—
Corps	29.6	—	x	x	x	—	x	x	—
Ste Luce	37.2	x	—	—	—	—	—	—	—
Entraigues	53.2	x	x	x	x	x	—	—	—
Le Perrier	58.1	x	x	x	x	—	—	—	—
Les Daurens	60.8	x	—	x	—	x	—	—	—
Col d'Ornon	68.1	—	—	x	—	x	—	—	—
La Paute	73.4	x	—	—	—	—	—	—	—
Bourg d'Oisans	82.0	x	x	x	x	x	x	x	x

Day 6 – Bourg d'Oisans to Bourg d'Oisans

The climb to Alpe d'Huez was first included in the Tour de France in 1952 and it has been part of the race 23 times since 1976. It is renowned as the Dutch Mountain, as cyclists from that flat country tend to do extraordinarily well here; however, the country with the most victories is Italy. In 2004, and for the first time, Alpe d'Huez was ridden as a time-trial, giving Lance Armstrong the opportunity to seal his sixth victory in the Tour de France. He covered the 15.5km course in 39mins 41secs: an average speed of 23.4km/hr. However fast you do the climb, during the summer months a professional photographer will be waiting beside the road to immortalize your ascent of 'L'Alpe'.

Distance	Location	Directions
0.0	Bourg d'Oisans TO	Come out of TO and turn L – N91
0.7	N91/D211	Turn L – D211 (Alpe d'Huez): 13.5km at 8.5%
13.9	Alpe d'Huez TO	Go straight on past TO and follow road around to L (Centre Station)
14.2	High point	Go straight on
15.0	Jtn	Turn R in front of La Belle Aurore (no sign)
15.1	Roundabout	Go straight on
15.4	Roundabout	Turn R past Residence Azur
15.7	Roundabout	Turn L (Col de Sarenne)
16.1	Jtn	Turn L and follow road up, past Club Med and altiport: 3.1km at 8% just before col
24.1	Col de Sarenne	Go straight on
31.3	Clavans-le-Haut	Turn R – D25A (Bourg d'Oisans)
33.6	D25A/D25	Turn R – D25 (Bourg d'Oisans)
37.1	D25/N91	Turn R – N91 (Grenoble)
39.9	Le Freney-d'Oisans: N91/D211A	Turn R – D211A (Auris-en-Oisans): 3.5km at 9%, short descent, and then 3.4km at 5.5%
46.8	Jtn	Turn L (Bourg d'Oisans)
48.0	Jtn	Go straight on – D211A (Bourg d'Oisans)
54.1	La Garde: D211A/D211	Turn L – D211 (no sign)
57.5	D211/N91	Turn R – N91 (Grenoble)
58.2	Bourg d'Oisans TO	TO is on the R

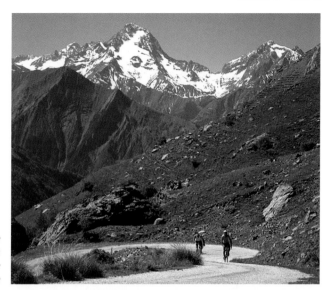

*View of the Roche de
la Muzelle from
below the
Col de Sarenne*

FACILITIES AND SERVICES

Location	Distance (km)	Water	Shops	Café	Campsite	B&B	Hotel	Bank	Bike Shop
Bourg d'Oisans	0.0	x	x	x	x	x	x	x	x
La Garde	4.1	x	—	—	—	—	—	—	—
Huez	10.0	x	—	—	—	x	—	—	—
Alpe d'Huez	13.9	x	x	x	—	x	x	x	x
Clavans-le-Bas	32.7	x	—	x	—	—	x	—	—
Mizoën	35.8	x	x	x	x	x	—	—	—
Le Freney-d'Oisans	39.9	—	x	x	x	—	x	—	—
La Garde	54.1	x	—	—	—	—	—	—	—
Bourg d'Oisans	58.2	x	x	x	x	x	x	x	x

Day 7 – Bourg d'Oisans to St Jean-de-Maurienne

Extra day: If you would like to prolong your stay in Bourg d'Oisans, the ride up the Véneon Valley is an excellent day out (see route 5). However, if you prefer a change of scene, why not use St Bonnet as a base from which to explore the limestone plateaux and mountains of the Dévoluy. The circuit: St Bonnet–Col du Noyer–St Disdier–St Etienne-en-Dévoluy–Ambel–Le Glaizil–St Bonnet takes in some of the most beautiful scenery and avoids the busy *route nationale* as much as possible (approx 65km, 1100m height gain).

Distance	Location	Directions
0.0	Bourg d'Oisans TO	Come out of the TO and turn R – N91
7.2	Rochetaillée: N91/D526	Turn R – D526 (Allemont). Go through Allemont and over the dam
11.9	D526/D44	Turn L – D526 (Le Rivier d'Allemont) D526 later becomes D926 7km at 7%
21.6	Le Rivier d'Allemont	Go straight on
22.7	High point	Go straight on
24.2	Low point	Go straight on 9.1km at 6.5%, short descent, and then 5.6km at 6%
37.5	D926/D927	Go straight on
40.2	Col de la Croix de Fer	Go straight on through St Sorlin d'Arves and St Jean d'Arves
54.5	D926/D80	Turn R – D80 (Albiez-le-Vieux): 5.9km at 7%*
60.4	Col du Mollard	Go straight on
62.0	Albiez-le-Vieux: D80/D110	Turn L – D110 (St Jean-de-Maurienne)
77.4	Roundabout	Go straight on (no sign)
77.6	Roundabout	Go straight on (Toutes Directions)
77.7	Roundabout	Turn R (Gares)
78.2	Jtn	Turn R (Gare SNCF)
78.3	Jtn	Turn L (Gare SNCF)
78.8	Crossroads	Go straight on (Gares SNCF/Routière)
79.1	St Jean-de-Maurienne	Station is on the right

* From 2007 onwards, it should once again be possible to follow the D926 all the way back to St Jean-de-Maurienne. This avoids the climb to the Col du Mollard, but be careful, there are (currently) two unlit tunnels on the D926, one of which is around 800 metres long.

Tour of the Ecrins and the Grandes Rousses Day 7

High Point 1339m

Bourg d'Oisans 717m

Allemont 722m

Le Rivier-d'Allemont 1265m

Day 6

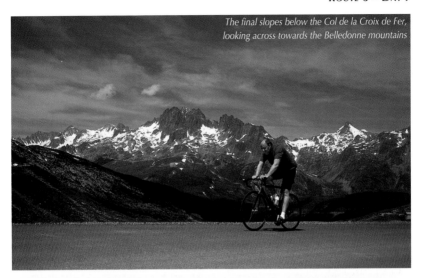

*The final slopes below the Col de la Croix de Fer,
looking across towards the Belledonne mountains*

FACILITIES AND SERVICES

Location	Distance (km)	Water	Shops	Café	Campsite	B&B	Hotel	Bank	Bike Shop
Bourg d'Oisans	0.0	x	x	x	x	x	x	x	x
Rochetaillée	7.2	—	—	—	x	—	—	—	—
Allemont	13.0	x	x	x	x	x	x	—	—
Le Rivier d'Allemond	21.6	x	x	x	—	x	x	—	—
Col de la Croix de Fer	40.2	—	—	x	—	—	—	—	—
St Sorlin d'Arves	46.8	x	x	x	x	x	x	x	—
St Jean d'Arves	50.5	x	—	—	—	x	x	—	—
Col du Mollard	60.4	x	x	x	—	x	—	—	—
Albiez-le-Vieuz	62.0	x	x	—	—	—	x	—	—
St Jean-de-Maurienne	79.1	x	x	x	x	—	x	x	x

Col de la
Croix de Fer
2067m

Col du
Mollard
1638m

Belleville
1227m

St Jean-de-
Maurienne
537m

Day 7

(km)   390   400   410   420   430

143

ACCOMMODATION

St Jean-de-Maurienne

Campsites

Camping des Grands Cols (mid-May to end Sept), Tel. 04 79 64 28 02

Bed & Breakfast

There are no bed & breakfasts in St Jean-de-Maurienne

Hotels

St Georges (***), Tel. 04 79 64 01 06

Bernard (**), Tel. 04 79 64 01 53

Du Nord (**), Tel. 04 79 64 02 08

Dorhotel (**), Tel. 04 79 64 23 83

De l'Europe (**), Tel. 04 79 64 06 33

Des Voyageurs, Tel. 04 79 64 02 35

De la Chemin de Fer, Tel. 04 79 64 01 84

Des Sports, Tel. 04 79 64 02 40

De la Gare, Tel. 04 79 83 21 83

Valloire

Campsites

Sainte Thecle (early June to end Sept), Tel. 04 79 83 30 11

Bed & Breakfast

Gite d'étape des Plans, Tel. 04 79 59 00 60

Hotels

There are 13 hotels in Valloire. Contact TO for details.

Briançon

Campsites

Les Cinq Vallées (early June to end Sept), Tel. 04 92 21 06 27

Bed & Breakfast

La Riolette (at Villard St Pancrace), Tel. 04 92 20 58 68

Le Bois de Barracan (*Gite d'étape* at Villard St Pancrace), Tel. 04 92 21 27 79

Hotels

There are 18 hotels in Briançon. Contact TO for details.

Embrun

Campsites

La Clapière (early May to end Sept), Tel. 04 92 43 01 83

La Vieille Ferme (dates not known), Tel. 04 92 43 04 08

La Tour (mid-June to end Aug), Tel. 04 92 43 17 66

Le Moulin (early June to mid-Sept), Tel. 04 92 43 00 41

Les Esparons (mid-June to end Aug), Tel. 04 92 43 02 73

Bed & Breakfast

Le Vieux Chalet, Tel. 04 92 43 00 17

Le Pigeonnier, Tel. 04 92 43 89 63

Jennif'air, Tel. 04 92 43 37 80

Mrs Mathery, Tel. 04 92 43 39 76

Hotels

Les Bartavelles (***), Tel. 04 92 43 20 69

Le Rex (**), Tel. 04 92 43 00 06

La Mairie (**), Tel. 04 92 43 20 65

Notre Dame (**), Tel. 04 92 43 08 36

Le Tourisme (*), Tel. 04 92 43 20 17

Le Lion d'Or (*), Tel. 04 92 43 02 68

Du Commerce, Tel. 04 92 43 54 54

St Bonnet-en-Champsaur

Campsites

Le Roure ('summer'), Tel. 04 92 50 01 86

Les Rives du Drac (mid-April to end Sept), Tel. 04 92 50 19 73

Bed & Breakfast

La Combe Fleurie, Tel. 04 92 50 53 97

Les Rives du Drac, Tel. 04 92 50 19 73

Hotels

La Crémaillère (**), Tel. 04 92 50 00 60

Les Chênets (**), Tel. 04 92 50 03 15

Auberge du Connetable, Tel. 04 92 49 00 62

Bourg d'Oisans

Campsites

There are nine campsites in Bourg d'Oisans. Contact TO for details.

Bed & Breakfast

Gîte du Bouthéon 'La Libellule', Tel. 04 76 79 15 57

Mr Arnaud, Tel. 04 76 80 00 10

At La Paute, 2km west of Bourg d'Oisans:

Mrs Evrard, Tel. 04.76.80.00.10

Mr Guilini, Tel. 04 76 79 11 27

Hotels

There are 9 hotels in Bourg d'Oisans. Contact TO for details.

TOURIST INFORMATION

Regional Information

	Telephone	Website
Savoie	04 79 85 12 45	www.savoiehautesavoie.com
Hautes-Alpes	04 92 53 62 00	www.hautes-alpes.net
Isère	04 76 54 34 36	www.isere-tourisme.com

Tourist Information Offices

Location	Telephone	Website
St Jean-de-Maurienne	04 79 83 51 51	www.saintjeandemaurienne.com
Valloire	04 79 59 03 96	www.valloire.net
Serre Chevalier	04 92 24 98 98	www.serre-chevalier.com
Briançon	04 92 21 08 50	www.ot-briancon.fr
L'Argentière-la-Bessée	04 92 23 03 11	no website
Embrun	04 92 43 72 72	www.ot-embrun.fr
Chorges	04 92 50 64 25	www.otchorges.com
Ancelle	04 92 50 83 05	www.ancelle.fr
St Léger-les-Mélèzes	04 92 50 43 77	http://st-leger05.fr
St Bonnet-en-Champsaur	04 92 50 02 57	www.saint-bonnet-en-champsaur.net
St Firmin	04 92 55 23 21	no website
Corps	04 76 30 03 85	no website
Valbonnais	04 76 30 25 26	no website
Bourg d'Oisans	04 76 80 03 25	www.bourgdoisans.com
Allemont	04 76 80 71 60	www.allemont.com
St Sorlin d'Arves	04 79 59 71 77	www.saintsorlindarves.com
Albiez-le-Vieux	04 79 59 30 48	www.albiez-montrond.com

Cyclists are made to feel welcome in Bourg d'Oisans (Day 6)

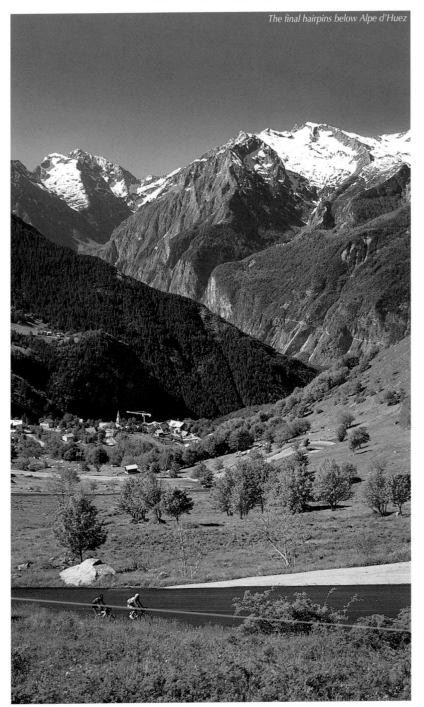

The final hairpins below Alpe d'Huez

TOUR OF THE SOUTHERN ALPS

Day	Route	Distance	Height Gain
1	Barcelonnette to Vinadio	64.9km	864m
2	Vinadio to Isola	43.9km	1455m
3	Isola to Puget-Theniers	68.7km	1240m
4	Puget-Theniers to Guillaumes	72.9km	1525m
5	Guillaumes to Barcelonnette	63.5km	1549m
	Totals	**313.9km**	**6633m**

If there were a competition for the world's best cycling holiday destination, the Ubaye Valley would be a hot contender for the gold medal. Naturally the valley's bid would vaunt the proximity of numerous high passes (including the Cime de la Bonette, the highest paved road in Europe), its relatively quiet roads and the area's mild and sunny climate. It might also include the facilities provided to make cyclists feel welcome – for example, kilometre posts showing altitudes and gradients, *brévets* (certificates) for cyclists who have done all seven of the valley's passes and hotels that cater especially for cyclists. However, its trump card would be something much less tangible and difficult to quantify: even when your legs are turning to rubber at the end of a long, hard day, cycling in the valley is surprisingly relaxing. Life in the Ubaye seems to proceed at a slower pace than elsewhere, and this (more natural?) rhythm quickly casts its spell over the visitor. Even Barcelonnette, a bustling little town in summer, somehow avoids the hectic atmosphere that infuses so many other popular holiday destinations.

Of course, the Ubaye Valley is only a small part of the southern Alps, defined here as the area between the Col de Vars and the Mediterranean. Much of this area falls within the boundaries of the Mercantour Natural Park, a haven for wildlife and the site for the highly controversial reintroduction of wolves to the Alps. The tour described here focuses on the highest passes in the area between the Ubaye and Var valleys, with a short incursion into the hills south of the Var. Despite being difficult to get to by public transport, Barcelonnette was chosen as the start point for the tour as it allows you to go over the easiest of the high passes, the Col de Larche, on the first day, reserving the Col de la Cayolle, in my opinion the most beautiful pass in the Alps, as a wonderful finale.

Being the Ubaye Valley's main tourist centre, Barcelonnette is a lively place and during the summer there is always something going on. The pedestrianized town centre is very pleasant and there are numerous shady cafés and restaurants where you can enjoy a coffee and croissant while watching the world go by.

The town was founded in 1231 by the Count of Provence, Raimond Béringer V, who named it after his hometown of Barcelona. It has become the most Mexican of alpine towns, as between 1814 and 1955 a great many people from the Barcelonnette area emigrated to Mexico to make their fortunes. Most decided to remain in their adopted home – 5000 families from the Ubaye Valley are now registered with the French consulate in Mexico – but some came back and built themselves luxurious Mexican-style villas. You can find out more about the town's history and the Mexican exodus at the local museum.

Day one of the tour starts very gently, following the banks of the River Ubaye past Jausiers (see the introduction to Route Eight) and La Condamine-Châtelard. It is not until you get to the confluence of the Ubaye and

The gentle slopes up through the village of Larche

Ubayette that the climb to the Col de Larche really begins. This strategic location, at the foot of two major passes (Vars and Larche) and close to the Italian border, is surveyed by the Fort de Tournoux, a marvel of military architecture that has been likened to the Palace of Versailles for the intricacy and ingenuity of its design. Of all the high passes in the French Alps, the Col de Larche is probably the easiest to cycle over, as it is neither particularly steep nor too long. However, it is one of the region's few cross-border routes and local cyclists consider it to be the busiest road in the area. (That being said, whenever I have been on this road, the traffic has always been very light). From the col the road sweeps down into Italy and through Argentera, Bersezio and Pietraporzio to Vinadio.

Vinadio is a very small village protected by a very large fort, which, although less spectacular than Tournoux, is still well worth a visit as it often houses interesting art, photography and local history exhibitions. The narrow streets that wind through the village centre are picturesque: the perfect place for a pre-dinner stroll. There is no better cycling fuel than pasta, and nowhere better to eat pasta than its traditional home (there is some evidence to suggest that pasta, like so many other things, was actually invented in the Arab world), so why not round off this first day with a good Italian meal in one of the village's restaurants.

On the other hand, it would be unwise to have a big breakfast immediately before starting out on stage two, as the uncompromisingly steep climb to the Col de la Lombarde starts barely a kilometre from Vinadio. This is a much more challenging pass to cycle over than the Col de Larche, with the first 8km through the spectacular gorges of the Santa Anna Valley being particularly steep. After an all too brief respite, the gradient steepens again as the second half of the climb takes you through the larch forests and more open slopes of the upper part of the valley. The pass is a very wild and wind-blown place, but offers spectacular views past the Santa Anna Monastery to the north and across the Tinée Valley to the west. As the road down to Isola 2000 is used as a ski run in winter, the surface is of very mediocre quality, in marked contrast to the second part of the descent, which is billiard table smooth and a joy to race down.

Isola, with its superbly restored facades (many of them with *trompe-l'oeil* designs) is a gem of a mountain village. Although small, it is a wonderful place to explore, as you seem to stumble upon delightful surprises around nearly every corner. French-speakers may like to join one of the free guided tours to learn more about this fabulous little corner of the Alps. Ask at the tourist office for details.

From Isola to St Sauveur-sur-Tinée the road gently descends through a steep-sided valley that sees little sun and is therefore often chilly in the mornings. However, all thoughts of being cold will soon be forgotten as you start the ascent to the Col de la Couillole, one of the area's lesser-known passes. The road is unrelentingly steep, rising almost 1200 metres in 16km, and there is very little shade from the Mediterranean sun. After the first few hairpins, the village of Roubion, perched improbably high above the valley, comes into view. The village centre lies just above the main road, but it is worth making the short detour as this is one of the few places to rival Isola for the title of most charming village in the area. Roubion has been inhabited for almost 3000 years, but the oldest remaining buildings date

Filling water bottles at one of Isola's decorative fountains

Looking back towards Roubion from just below the Col de la Couillole

from the Middle Ages. As well as its mediaeval lanes and fabulous views, the village also has a very pleasant little café in which to enjoy a welcome break before tackling the last few kilometres to the col.

Once at the pass, the hard work for the day is behind you, but the scenic delights continue as you descend into the Cians Gorge, a deep and often extremely narrow ravine with walls of vivid red sandstone. The road goes through several tunnels, but cyclists can skirt around most of them and enjoy views that are hidden to car drivers. Towards its southern end, the gorge opens out slightly as the geology changes and the red sandstone gives way to grey limestone. Unfortunately, to get to Puget-Théniers from the end of the gorge there is no alternative but to follow the main RN202 along the Var Valley, however the road is flat and this 8km section is quickly covered.

The penultimate leg of the tour gives a brief taste of the delightful cycling to be had in the hills south of the River Var. This is a very sparsely populated corner of the world where many of the roads tend to be almost deserted, guaranteeing a peaceful day. Unsurprisingly, shops, cafés and drinking fountains are few and far between, so you will need to be self sufficient for the few hours it takes to go over the St Raphaël, Trébuchet and Félines Passes.

The countryside is always pretty, but extremely arid due to the warm, dry Mediterranean climate – these conditions would seem to suit ostriches given the number of farms that have been set up in the area. However, the most spectacular prospect is incontestably that of Entrevaux from below the Col des Félines. It is unlikely that Vauban, Louis XIV's celebrated military architect, was thinking of aesthetics when he designed the fort that watches over the mediaeval village, but the view of the resulting ensemble is breathtaking. Access to the walled village, with its gothic cathedral and cobbled square, is via a drawbridge over the river. Whether or not you are interested in military architecture, it is worth climbing the steep, zig-zag ramp that leads to the fort for the bird's-eye view of the village.

From Entrevaux, the route follows the River Var, through the Daluis Gorge, to Guillaumes. Slicing through the same red sandstones as Cians, the Daluis Gorge is, if anything, even more spectacular than its near neighbour. The road starts level with the river and gradually climbs out of the valley floor, clinging to the walls of the canyon or tunnelling through the cliffs (most of the tunnels can be avoided by cyclists) high above the river. There are many fabulous viewpoints, but one of the best is from the Pont de la Mariée

(Bride's Bridge), named in remembrance of the tragic events of 30th July 1927. Late on the evening in question, a couple of newly-weds on honeymoon in Guillaumes decided to visit the gorge. A short time later the husband returned, alone, in a state of panic. He claimed that in the gathering darkness his wife had tripped and fallen off the bridge into the gorge 80 metres below. After an enquiry, it was concluded that the young woman's death had in fact been an accident. Today, people still plummet off the bridge – firmly attached to a bungee cord.

Guillaumes is a pleasant little place that has had the excellent idea of installing a free, open-air exhibition on the village's history in the communal wash-house (*lavoir*). As well as looking after its visitors, Guillaumes seems to take care of its livestock too: the motto '*Village des Bêtes Heureuses*' (village of happy animals) is proudly carved above the fountain opposite the tourist office.

Guillaumes lies 33km south of the Col de la Cayolle, the final pass of the tour. The first half of the climb is quite gentle, allowing your legs to warm up slowly before the serious work begins just after Entraunes. Despite being part of the Route des Grandes Alpes (see Route Eight), the road over Col de la Cayolle is one of the quietest in the area, as many motorists prefer the more prestigious Cime de la Bonette to the east. It is not unusual to find herds of cows or donkeys on the road – be careful, they can be quite aggressive – or even sleeping marmots! The last 15km of the climb can feel quite long if your legs are tired after the exertions of the previous four days, but it is always a pleasure to cycle through such wonderful scenery and there are plenty of places to take a break and have a drink or a snack. The descent from the pass is particularly beautiful, winding across barren moorland, past lightly wood pastures and through rocky gorges. All too soon you find yourself back in the bustle of Barcelonnette at the end of this marvellous voyage.

GETTING THERE

By car
Barcelonnette is 1100km from Calais.

By plane
Barcelonnette is not easily accessible by public transport. The best alternative is to start in Italy flying to Turin and taking the train to Borgo san Dalmazo, which is 39km from Vinadio. Contact Turin airport (**www.aeroportoditorino.it**) and/or Italian railways (**www.trenitalia.com**) for information about connections from Turin to Borgo san Dalmazo.

Via Nice
It is also possible to start by flying into Nice, although this would add at least two days to the tour. Turn left in front of the airport terminal and head towards the N7 in order to cross the River Var (extremely busy roads). Once across the river, head north along the Var Valley, and then follow the D1 to Roquesteron (hotel, campsite). From Roquesteron, follow the D17 to join the main itinerary just after Pont des Miolans. To get back to Nice, the best option is to follow the last two days of the Grand Traverse (Route Eight) from Isola through Levens and then Levens to Nice.

WHEN TO GO

The route can be done from the middle of May until the end of September. Even this far south, it is generally too cold to enjoy cycling over high passes in October, and the roads over the Col de la Lombarde, Col de la Couillole and Col de la Cayolle are closed until early May. At the beginning of May, even if the roads are officially still closed, it is usually possible to get through on a bike. Barcelonnette can be very busy during the summer holidays, so in July and August it is best to book accommodation in advance, even if you are camping.

MAPS

Michelin: Local – Sheet 334, Alpes-de-Haute-Provence, Hautes-Alpes

Michelin: Regional – Sheet 245, Provence, Côte d'Azur

IGN: Top 100 – Sheet 61: Nice, Barcelonnette

From 2000 to 2003 the Col de Larche was closed to pedestrians and cyclists (but not to cars) because of road works. This was again the case in 2005, although the pass should be open again from 2006. You can find out if the pass is open by downloading the excellent Guide du *Vélo en Ubaye* from the Barcelonnette website, **www.barcelonnette.net**. If the Col de Larche is closed, Isola can still be reached via the Cime de la Bonette. The day's cycling that is lost by following this short cut can be compensated for by following the alternative route described on page 162.

Distance	Location	Directions
0.0	Barcelonnette: Place Manuel	Go past the Café St Tropez to follow the road out of Barcelonnette
0.3	Jtn	Go straight on – D900 (Jausiers)
16.0	D900/D902	Follow road round to the R – D900 (Col de Larche): 16.4 km at 4%
32.4	Col de Larche: Franco-Italian border	Go straight on – SS21
64.9	Vinadio: Hotel Monte Nebius	The hotel is on the R

FACILITIES AND SERVICES									
Location	Distance (km)	Water	Shops	Café	Campsite	B&B	Hotel	Bank	Bike Shop
Barcelonnette	0.0	x	x	x	x	x	x	x	x
Jausiers	8.6	x	x	x	x	x	x	x	x
La Condamine-Châtelard	16.0	x	x	x	x	x	x	—	—
Larche	26.1	x	x	x	x	x	x	—	—
Col de Larche	32.4	—	x	—	—	—	—	—	—
Bersezzio	42.4	x	x	x	x	x	x	—	—
Pietraporzio	50.8	x	—	x	x	x	x	—	—
Vinadio	64.9	x	x	x	—	—	x	x	(1)

(1) Nearest bike shop is in Cuneo, 35km east of Vinadio

154

Pietraporzio

Day 2 – Vinadio to Isola

With the exception of the Col d'Allos, the high passes of the southern Alps have not often featured in the Tour de France. Therefore, 1993 was an exceptional year, as the 11th stage went over the Col d'Izoard, the Col de Vars, and then took in both the Cime de la Bonette and the climb to Isola 2000. The stage was won by Tony Rominger, who had already won the previous stage over the Cols du Glandon and Galibier, just ahead of Miguel Indurain. A certain Lance Armstrong, in his first Tour de France, came in 97th, almost 29 minutes behind Rominger. This was to be the last stage that Armstrong completed in that year's Tour, but his future team manager, Johan Bruyneel, finished seventh overall. 1993 was Indurain's third successive Tour de France victory and his second successive Giro-Tour de France double.

Distance	Location	Directions
0.0	Vinadio: Hotel Monte Nebius	Come out of the hotel and turn L – SS21
0.3	Jtn	Turn L (Colle Lombarda) 22.8km at 6.5%
14.8	Jtn	Turn L (Colle Lombarda)
23.1	Col de la Lombarde	Go straight on
27.0	Isola 2000	Follow D97 through Isola 2000 (Isola–Village)
43.8	Isola: jtn	Turn R (Isola Centre Ville)
43.9	Isola: *mairie*	*Mairie* is on the R

FACILITIES AND SERVICES

Location	Distance (km)	Water	Shops	Café	Campsite	B&B	Hotel	Bank	Bike Shop
Vinadio	0.0	x	x	x	—	—	x	x	(1)
Isola 2000	27.0	x	—	x	—	—	—	—	—
Isola	43.9	x	x	x	x	x	x	x	(2)

(1) Nearest bike shop is in Cuneo, 35km east of Vinadio

(2) Nearest bike shop is in Nice, 70km south of Isola on the N202

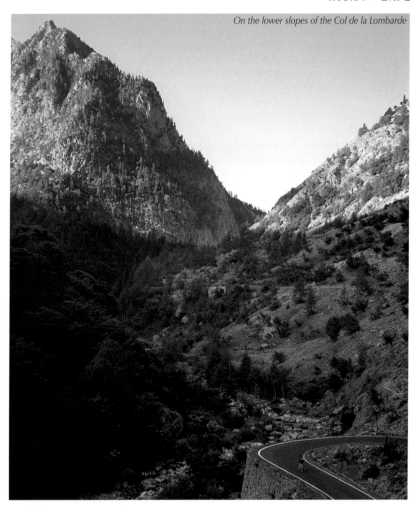
On the lower slopes of the Col de la Lombarde

le

Isola 2000
2056m

Isola
873m

St Sauveur-
sur-Tinée
510m

Col de la
Couillole
1678m

D a y   3

100   110   120   130   140

Day 3 – Isola to Puget-Théniers

When cycling in poorly inhabited areas such as the southern Alps, it is essential to be self-reliant for minor repairs. This I learned the hard way when exploring the minor roads between Isola and Nice. A puncture is not usually a problem as I always carry a spare inner tube. Of course, one tube is not sufficient if you puncture both tyres at the same time. It was 35° in the shade, the road was deserted and it was 11km to the nearest village. No choice, but to start walking ...

Distance	Location	Directions
0.0	Isola *mairie*	Come out of the *mairie* and turn R (Toutes Directions)
0.2	Roundabout	Turn L – D2205 (St Sauveur-sur-Tinée)
14.3	St Sauveur-sur-Tinée: D2205/D30	Turn R – D30 (Col de la Couillole): 16km at 7.5%
30.7	Col de la Couillole	Go straight on
38.1	Beuil: D30/D28	Go straight on – D28 (Puget-Théniers)
60.5	D28/N202	Turn R – N202 (Puget-Théniers)
68.7	Puget-Théniers: jtn	N202/Ave Remond

FACILITIES AND SERVICES									
Location	Distance (km)	Water	Shops	Café	Campsite	B&B	Hotel	Bank	Bike Shop
Isola	0.0	x	x	x	x	x	x	x	(1)
St Sauveur-sur-Tinée	14.3	x	x	x	x	—	x	—	—
Roubion	25.7	x	x	x	—	x	—	—	—
Col de la Couillole	30.7	—	—	—	—	x	—	—	—
Beuil	38.7	x	x	x	—	—	x	—	—
Pra-d'Astier	52.3	x	—	—	—	—	—	—	—
Puget-Théniers	68.7	x	x	x	x	—	x	x	(2)

(1) Nearest bike shop is in Nice, 70km south of Isola

(2) Nearest bike shop is in Nice, 65km southeast of Puget-Théniers

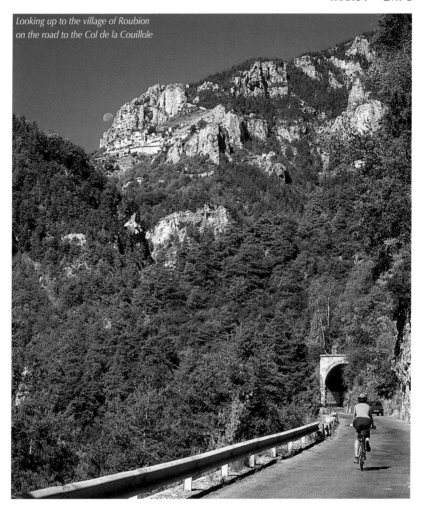

*Looking up to the village of Roubion
on the road to the Col de la Couillole*

Pra d'Astier
561m

Puget-Théniers
410m

Col de
St Raphaël
876m

Day 4

160   170   180   190   200

ɔ)

Day 4 – Puget-Théniers to Guillaumes

Distance	Location	Directions
0.0	Puget-Théniers: jtn N202/Ave Remond	Turn L – N202
0.1	N202/D2211A	Turn R – D2211A (Col de St Raphäel): 8.4km at 5.5%
8.5	Col de St Raphäel	Go straight on – D2211A (La Penne)
15.2	D2211A/D10	Turn R – D10 (Castellet St Cassien): 7.5km at 4% then 3.2km descent followed by 6.2km at 4.5%
32.1	Col du Trébuchet	Go straight on
37.7	D10/D911	Turn R – D911 (Entrevaux): 2.7km at 3.5%
40.4	Col des Félines	Go straight on
47.4	Entrevaux: D911/N202	Turn L – N202 (Annot)
52.9	N202/D902	Turn R – D902/D2202 (Guillaumes)
72.9	Guillaumes TO	TO is on the R

A short but sweet descent past the village of La Penne

Tour of the Southern Alps Day 4

Col de St Raphaël 876m

La Rochette 930m

Puget-Théniers 410m

Day 3

Day 4

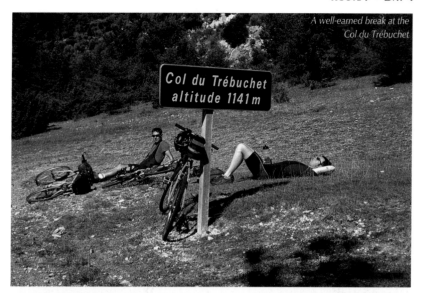

A well-earned break at the
Col du Trébuchet

Col du Trébuchet
altitude 1141m

FACILITIES AND SERVICES

Location	Distance (km)	Water	Shops	Café	Campsite	B&B	Hotel	Bank	Bike Shop
Puget-Théniers	0.0	x	x	x	x	—	x	x	(1)
La Penne	10.8	x	—	—	—	—	x	—	—
La Rochette	22.7	x	—	x	—	—	—	—	—
Castellet-St Cassien	36.7	x	—	—	—	—	—	—	—
Entrevaux	47.4	x	x	x	x	—	x	x	—
Daluis	61.3	x	—	—	—	—	—	—	—
Guillaumes	72.9	x	x	x	x	x	x	x	(2)

(1) Nearest bike shop is in Nice, 65km southeast of Puget-Théniers

(2) Nearest bike shop is in Barcelonnette, 64km north of Guillaumes

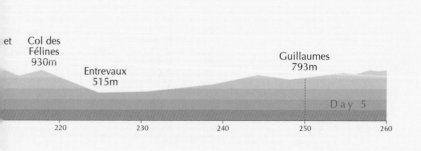

et Col des
Félines
930m

Entrevaux
515m

Guillaumes
793m

Day 5

220   230   240   250   260

Day 5 – Guillaumes to Barcelonnette

Extra day: it is difficult to do a day trip of a reasonable length from any of the overnight stops on this tour. However, a day can be added to the tour by extending the excursion into the superb countryside to the south of the Var Valley. Day 4 would then become Puget–Théniers–Roquesteron–Bouyon–Coursegoules–Gréolières (One hotel, two B&Bs, no campsite – **www.greolieres.fr**). Day 5 would be Gréolières –St Auban–Briançonnet–Col de Félines–Entrevaux–Guillaumes.

Distance	Location	Directions
0.0	Guillaumes TO	Come out of TO and turn R – D2202 (Col de la Cayolle): 12km at 2%, 5.9km at 3.5%, and then 15.1km at 7%
33.0	Col de la Cayolle	Go straight on – D902
60.6	D902/D908	Turn R – D902 (Barcelonnette)
62.8	Pont du Plan	Go straight on over bridge
63.2	Jtn	Turn L (past fountain) to go into pedestrian area
63.3	Jtn	Turn R onto main pedestrian street
63.5	Barcelonnette: Place Manuel	

FACILITIES AND SERVICES								
Location	Distance (km)	Water	Shops	Café	Campsite	B&B	Hotel	Bank	Bike Shop
Guillaumes	0.0	x	x	x	x	x	x	x	(1)
St Martin-d'Entraunes	12.0	x	x	x	—	x	x	—	—
Entraunes	17.9	x	—	x	x	—	x	—	—
Estenc	25.4	x	—	x	—	x	x	—	—
Col de la Cayolle	33.0	x	—	x	—	x	—	—	—
La Bayasse	42.3	x	—	x	—	x	—	—	—
Uvernet-Fours	59.0	x	x	x	—	x	x	—	—
Barcelonnette	63.5	x	x	x	x	x	x	x	x

(1) Nearest bike shop is in Barcelonnette, 64km north of Guillaumes

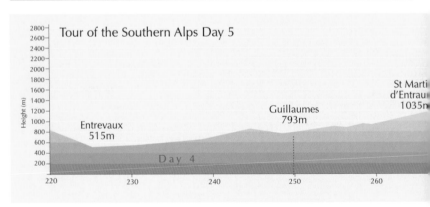

Tour of the Southern Alps Day 5

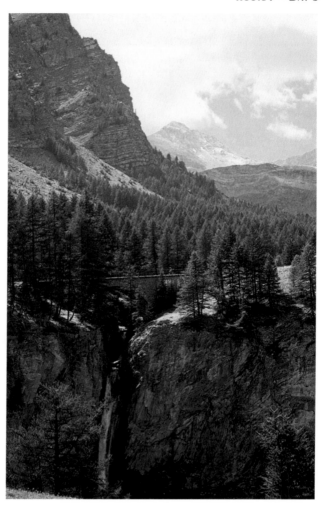

*Looking up towards
the Col de la Cayolle*

Col de la Cayolle
2326m

stenc
785m

La Bayasse
1783m

Barcelonnette
1136m

Day 5

280   290   300   310   320

ACCOMMODATION

Barcelonnette

Campsites

Le Plan (dates not known), Tel. 04 92 81 08 11

Le Tampico (Christmas to end Oct), Tel. 04 92 81 02 55

Le Peyra (early May to end Oct), Tel. 04 92 81 24 06

Bed & Breakfast

L'Establoun, Tel. 04 92 81 13 57

Le Bosquet, Tel. 04 92 81 41 28

Odel Var, Tel. 04 92 81 03 33

La Pare, Tel. 06 80 66 59 27

Hotels

Azteca (***), Tel. 04 92 81 46 36

La Grande Epervière (***), Tel. 04 92 81 00 70

Le Cheval Blanc (**), Tel. 04 92 81 00 19

Le Grand (**), Tel. 04 92 81 03 14

L'Europe (**), Tel. 04 92 81 03 37

L'Aupillon, Tel. 04 92 81 01 09

Choucas, Tel. 04 92 81 15 20

Le Touring, Tel. 04 92 81 07 57

Vinadio

Campsites

The nearest campsite is the Centro Sentieri in Pietraporzio, 14km north-west of Vinadio (dates not known), Tel. 0171 96512

Bed & Breakfast

There are no bed and breakfasts in Vinadio

Hotels

Albergo Italia (***), Tel. 0171 959148

Albergo Ligure (**), Tel. 0171 959149

NB Both the above hotels are closed on Mondays

Albergo Ristorante Ciastella, Tel. 0171 959253

Albergo Strepeis, Tel. 0171 95831

Isola

Campsites

Lac des Neiges (all year), Tel. 04 93 02 18 16

Bed & Breakfast

Au Vieux Chalet, Tel. 04 93 23 99 99

Gite d'étape at Lac des Neiges campsite, Tel. 04 93 02 18 16

Hotels

Hotel de France (*), Tel. 04 93 02 17 04

Hotel d'Isola, Tel. 04 93 02 17 03

Puget-Théniers

Campsites

Municipal (all year), Tel. 04 93 05 10 53

Bed & Breakfast

There are no bed & breakfasts in Puget-Théniers

Hotels

Alizé (**), Tel. 04 93 05 06 20

Laugier (**), Tel. 04 93 05 01 00

Guillaumes

Campsites

Pont de la Mariée (early April to end Sept), Tel. 04 93 05 53 50

Bed & Breakfast

Gîte d'étape de Villeplane, Tel. 04 93 05 56 01

Hotels

Les Chaudrons, Tel. 04 93 05 50 01

La Renaissance, Tel. 04 93 05 59 89

TOURIST INFORMATION

Regional Information

	Telephone	Website
Alpes de Haute-Provence	04 92 31 57 29	**www.alpes-haute-provence.com**
Alpes Maritimes	04 93 37 78 78	**www.guideriviera.com**

Tourist Information Offices

Location	Telephone	Website
Barcelonnette	04 92 81 04 71	**www.barcelonnette.com**
Jausiers	04 92 81 21 45	**www.jausiers.com**
Larche	no telephone	**www.haute-ubaye.com**
Bersazio/Pietraporzio/Vinadiono	telephone	**www.ghironda.com/valstura**
Isola 2000	04 93 23 15 15	**www.isola2000.com**
Isola	04 93 02 18 97	**www.isola2000.com**
St Sauveur-sur-Tinée	04 93 02 00 22	**no website**
Roubion	04 93 02 10 30	**www.roubion.com**
Beuil	04 93 02 32 58	**http://members.aol.com/beuil/**
Puget-Théniers	04 93 05 05 05	**www.provence-val-dazur.com**
Guillaumes	04 93 05 57 76	**www.pays-de-guillaumes.com**
Entraunes-Estenc	04 93 05 51 26	**no website**

ROUTE EIGHT

GRAND TRAVERSE OF THE FRENCH ALPS

Day	Route	Distance	Height Gain
1	Geneva to Thonon-les-Bains	51.1km	200m
2	Thonon-les-Bains to La Clusaz	78.7km	1660m
3	La Clusaz to Beaufort	51.3km	1240m
4	Beaufort to Bourg St Maurice	45.7km	1410m
5	Bourg St Maurice to Bessans	68.7km	2020m
6	Bessans to Valloire	70.8km	1180m
7	Valloire to Briançon	55.5km	1250m
8	Briançon to Guillestre	51.8km	1150m
9	Guillestre to Jausiers	42.5km	1110m
10	Jausiers to Isola	65.3km	1650m
11	Isola to Levens	77.8km	1340m
12	Levens to Nice	37.1km	200m
	Totals	**696.3km**	**14,410m**

However enjoyable circular tours may be, there is something uniquely satisfying about completing a true 'journey', especially when that journey takes you through an area as fabulously beautiful as the French Alps. The Grand Traverse from Lake Geneva to the Mediterranean is one of Europe's great cycle tours, covering almost 700km over some of the continent's highest mountain roads.

The idea of traversing the Alps by road was first mooted by the Touring Club de France in 1911 as a way of developing motorised tourism. Their idea of driving the whole length of the French Alps from Thonon-les-Bains to Menton was extremely ambitious as most alpine passes were not at all practicable for motorcars. In 1913 a major road-building programme was launched, culminating in 1937 with the inauguration of the Col de l'Iseran, at the time the highest road in Europe. The Route des Grandes Alpes was an immediate success and it is still a highly popular itinerary, especially with motorcyclists. Several guides to the route have been produced, details of which can be found at **www.routedesgrandesalpes.com** (in

French only). Of course, these new roads did not only benefit cars and motorbikes; before the Second World War cycling on mountain roads often had more in common with mountain biking than modern road cycling.

The itinerary described here is slightly different to the classic Route des Grandes Alpes as, in order to facilitate access by public transport, it goes from Geneva to Nice rather than from Thonon-les-Bains to Menton. Additional changes were made in order to avoid the very busy road over the Col des Gets (south of Thonon-les-Bains) and to include the Cime de la Bonette, currently the highest paved road in Europe. From St Sauveur-sur-Tinée, the itinerary goes through Utelle and Levens to Nice rather than to Menton via St Martin-Vésubie and Sospel.

As the most pleasant road from Geneva to Thonon-les-Bains is along the shores of Lake Geneva, the first stage of the Grand Traverse follows the same route as the Tour of the Chablais–Aravis (see Route Two).

Day two, although it does not take you over any really high passes, will enable you to assess your fitness as there are nevertheless

166

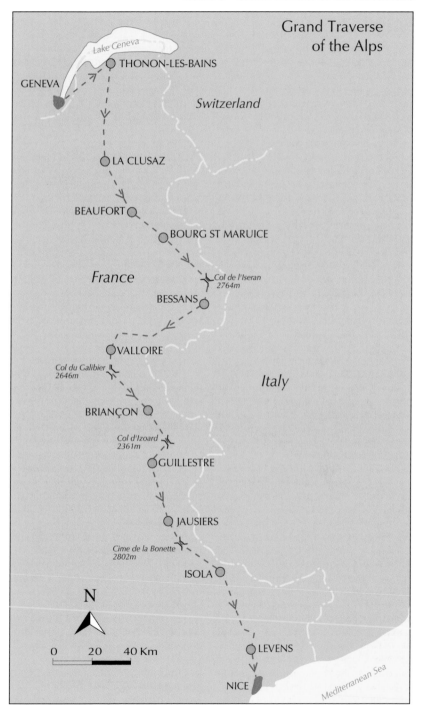

Grand Traverse
of the Alps

Lake Geneva

THONON-LES-BAINS

GENEVA

Switzerland

LA CLUSAZ

BEAUFORT

BOURG ST MARUICE

France

Col de l'Iseran
2764m

BESSANS

VALLOIRE

Col du Galibier
2646m

Italy

BRIANÇON

Col d'Izoard
2361m

GUILLESTRE

JAUSIERS

Cime de la Bonette
2802m

ISOLA

N

0   20   40 Km

LEVENS

NICE

Mediterranean Sea

several hills to climb. The first of these, the Col des Moises, is only 16km from Thonon and the road starts climbing as soon as you leave the town. Fortunately, the gradient is gentle at first, but the slope steepens significantly for the last 6km of the ascent. Once over the pass, the route runs down through the Vallée Verte, a picturesque vale of green fields dotted with traditional chalets. The second, much shorter ascent takes you to what is without a doubt the most obscure pass on the entire traverse: the Col de Ludran. Admittedly, this pass is not a major geographical feature (it is not even marked on most road maps), but it does offer a stunning view of Mont Blanc and the Chamonix Aiguilles. After descending to Viuz-en-Sallaz there is a third, even easier climb to negotiate before freewheeling down into the Arve Valley. Although it is not the most picturesque of towns, Bonneville is a bustling little place that is especially lively on market days (Tuesday and Friday mornings) and, if your legs are feeling a little too weary to face the easy-angled, but long climb to La Clusaz, the town offers a full range of accommodation. The Gorges des Eveaux, south of Bonneville, can seem dark and forbidding, even on a bright summer's day, as the trees overhanging the road block the small amount of sunlight that manages to penetrate this steep-sided, north-facing valley. Once past Le Petit-Bornand, the valley widens slightly, but it is not until you get near St Jean-de-Sixt that the views open out and you can appreciate the craggy summits of the Aravis Mountains. More information about the Aravis Mountains and La Clusaz is given in the introduction to Route Two.

Day three takes you over one of the most popular passes in the Alps, the Col des Aravis. During July and August it is a good idea to make an early start from La Clusaz to reach the pass before it becomes a giant car park. The scenery is magnificent, but it is harder to appreciate it if the roads are busy. A short, but technical descent with numerous hairpin bends takes you to La Giettaz, one of the few ski resorts to have truly retained a traditional village atmosphere. After La Giettaz, the gradient eases as you go through the Gorges de l'Arondine to Flumet, where you start the second climb of the day, to the Col des Saisies.

Once over the col, and after a good night's sleep in Beaufort (see Route Three), it is time to face the most spectacular and the most strenuous part of the traverse. Beaufort is the gateway to the high Alps and during the next 400km the cyclist will have to overcome an unrelenting succession of mighty passes, culminating in the 2808 metres-high Cime de la Bonette.

The first of these, the Col du Pré, is only a few metres higher than the Col des Saisies, but the ascent is much more challenging with the last 7km having an average gradient of 9%. After a short descent, the road follows the edge of the extremely picturesque Roseland Reservoir before climbing up to the Cormet de Roseland, the first truly alpine pass of the traverse. The summit is quite open, but the sunny south-facing pastures on the left of the col never seem to reflect enough warmth to ease the forbidding chill of the austere cliffs and barren slopes of the north-facing combes on the right. The cold here is not just metaphorical, as the Cormet de Roseland is well known for its exceptional snowfall: you will often see people skiing here right up until the end of June.

As well as being the first high pass, the Cormet de Roseland also provides the first really long descent, with 20km of sweeping curves and tight hairpins between the summit and Bourg St Maurice (see Route Three for more information about Bourg St Maurice).

Bourg St Maurice is only 45km from Beaufort, but it takes a lot of courage to start up the Col de l'Iseran the same day. The Iseran is a true giant amongst alpine passes, rising 1957 metres above the town. When the short descents after Séez and the Tignes dam are taken into account, climbing the Col de l'Iseran actually involves more than 2000 metres of ascent. Traffic on the first part of the climb is often quite heavy as this is the only road to Tignes and Val d'Isère, two of the biggest resorts in Savoie. In the 1930s, before the first ski lift was installed, Val d'Isère was a poor mountain village without running water or electricity. As the ski area grew and the village was modernised Val d'Isère began to rival Megève as *the* fashionable winter sports destination for the rich and famous. Its final consecration came in 1992, when the resort was chosen to host some of the most prestigious events of the Albertville Winter Olympics.

Above Val d'Isère the road is never particularly steep, but when your legs are tired at the end of a long climb the kilometre posts slip by all too slowly. The view from the top of the pass is sensational, but it can be a cold and desolate place. On windy days the summit café provides a welcome refuge while you catch your breath and put on an extra layer of clothing before sweeping down into the Maurienne Valley. The climb to the pass is most spectacular in June as the road is often sandwiched between towering walls of snow that can be six-metres high or more. At this altitude, snow can fall at any time of year: in July 1996, a stage of the Tour de France had to be considerably shortened because both the Col de l'Iseran and the Col du Galibier were blocked by snow.

In marked contrast to Val d'Isère, the villages of the Haute Maurienne Valley have remained quiet backwaters and have not been submerged by the high-rise constructions of the 1970s ski boom. Of course, there has been some modern development in the valley, but it has been much lower key than in many other areas. Bonneval-sur-Arc, at the head of the valley, remains an idyllic mountain hamlet of slate-roofed wooden chalets, and Bessans, the 'capital' of this part of the valley, has developed a much lower impact form of tourism based around hiking, mountain biking and, especially, cross-country skiing.

You cannot spend much time in the Haute Maurienne without encountering one of the innumerable statues and paintings of the four-horned Bessans Devil. Legend has it that a craftsman from Bessans, called Joseph, signed a contract to build a bridge over the River Arc. The work dragged on and on as the work was beset by unforeseen problems and Joseph was frightened that he would be sent to prison for not fulfilling the contract on time. The day before the half-finished bridge was due to be opened the Devil's emissary appeared before him and offered to finish the work. In exchange, the Devil would be allowed to take the soul of the first person to cross the bridge. Eventually Joseph agreed, and when he arrived at work the next day he found the bridge had been finished. Standing on the far side was the Devil himself: a hideous creature with long horns. Approaching the bridge was a small boy at the head of the troop of soldiers who were to march across the bridge for its inauguration. Knowing what would happen to the boy if he crossed the river first, Joseph's wife chased a huge billy goat from a neighbouring field

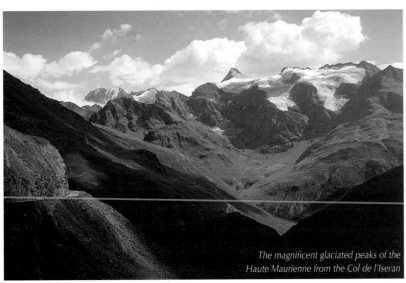

The magnificent glaciated peaks of the Haute Maurienne from the Col de l'Iseran

onto the bridge. The goat saw the Devil and took him for a rival come to steal his flock. He put his head down and charged, piercing the Devil's skull with his horns. The Devil fled and has never been seen in Bessans again, but now he is always depicted as having four horns.

From Bessans, the route follows the River Arc all the way to St Michel-de-Maurienne at the foot of the Col du Télégraphe. After going through the villages of Lanslevillard and Lanslebourg, jointly known as the resort of Val Cenis, the route merges with the main N6 road, but a few kilometres after Termignon it is possible to leave the N6 for the much quieter D83. In the 19th century Savoie was still an independent state, but the people of Savoie knew that the French had designs on their lands. Aussois was seen as a strategic point in the Arc Valley from which to defend the Piedmont. To that end, a complex of five forts, all facing west, was built between 1817 and 1834. When Savoie became part of France in 1860, these forts were abandoned without having seen action. One has now been restored and turned into a magnificent *gîte d'étape* and the ruins of the remaining four are open to visitors, with Fort Victor-Emmanuel being the most extensive and the most interesting.

The road between the industrial towns of Modane and St Michel-de-Maurienne is the least interesting part of the entire traverse. There is no option but to follow the main RN6 road, although the new motorway has significantly reduced traffic levels on the *route nationale*. The main street through Modane is not particularly attractive, but it does have a bakery that sells fabulous homemade ice cream.

Often considered a mere warm-up on the way to the mighty Col du Galibier, the Col du Télégraphe is actually quite a difficult climb in its own right. The gradient averages 7% for more than 12km and there is no real respite until you get to the top. The road is mostly surrounded by thick forest, but occasional clearings give superb views of the precipitous cliffs of the Croix des Têtes. From the summit it is a pleasant 5km descent to Valloire.

Of all the passes in the Alps, the Col du Galibier is undoubtedly the most famous, perhaps because it has been part of the Tour de France a record 53 times, and has gained a worldwide reputation as one of the most difficult ascents in the Alps. Fittingly, a monument to Henri Desgranges, the founder of the Tour de France, has stood on the south side of the Galibier since 1949. The summit is 38km from Briançon, perhaps the most interesting town on the route in which to spend a rest day. See Route Six for more information about the Col du Galibier and Briançon.

The next giant to conquer is the Col d'Izoard, another of the Tour de France's classic alpine stages. The Izoard is certainly less formidable than either the Iseran or the Galibier, but the ascent is nevertheless no push-over. By taking it easy for the first 10km where the gradient is very variable, your legs should be nicely warmed up for the second, more difficult part of the climb. Just below the pass the road emerges from the shade of the forest and the full force of the southern sun makes itself felt. The only shelter is to be found at the Refuge Napoléon, a mountain hut and cycling museum combined. From the summit the road plunges down into the Casse Déserte, a breathtaking landscape of barren scree and contorted rock towers. This is the most famous part of the Col d'Izoard, but the whole route, from the pastures and forests around Cervières to the spectacular gorges of the Combe de Queyras, is fabulously beautiful.

Guillestre is a very lively village in summer, mainly thanks to the thousands of white-water sports, hiking and mountain biking enthusiasts who are attracted by the fabulous countryside. For visitors looking for less strenuous ways of passing a few hours in Guillestre, there is little to do but browse around the pleasant village centre. If you were to spend a spend a rest day here, I would recommend visiting Mont Dauphin, 4km to the west (see author note p.192).

As Guillestre sits at the very foot of the Col de Vars there is no warm-up before attacking the steepest part of the climb. The gradient eases after 9km, but those 9km are testing, especially if your legs are feeling tired after eight days of hard cycling. The views to the north are splendid, with the snow-covered peak of Mont Pelvoux rising high above the

Jausiers, one of many picturesque villages in the Southern Alps

Durance Valley. After a short breather the gradient increases again as you continue towards Vars, a modern ski resort with little to attract the passing cyclist. The last 3km, past a tiny lake and a second Refuge Napoléon, are wonderfully picturesque. The Refuges Napoléon were so named because they were built to honour the terms of Napoleon's last will and testament. The former emperor had bequeathed a sum of money to the *départements* that had suffered the most from the wars during his reign. This money was to be used to create something that would benefit the population and provide a permanent reminder of Napoleon's benevolence. After long deliberations, the Hautes-Alpes *département* decided to build mountain huts at the summits of six mountain passes, including the Col de Vars and the Col d'Izoard.

The Col de Vars is the gateway to the Ubaye Valley and one of seven major passes that surround the valley's main town, Barcelonnette. Barcelonnette tourist office issues a certificate to cyclists who have climbed all seven of these passes, the 'proof' being provided by a card the cyclist gets stamped at a box at the summit of each pass. There is one of these boxes at the Col de Vars, but, of course, first you have to descend to Barcelonnette to get the card!

As this is a short day, there is plenty of time to enjoy a drink or a snack at the summit café before starting the descent. From just below the pass, there are superb views of the Brec de Chambeyron, one of the highest summits in the southern Alps.

The stage ends in Jausiers, a pretty and unpresuming village with a wonderfully friendly and relaxing atmosphere. Despite its obviously limited means, the village museum has put together some interesting exhibits that are well worth the 1.50 Euro entrance fee. If you feel like stretching your legs a little, I would recommend a stroll up to the orientation table behind the bell-tower for the panorama it offers of the whole Ubaye Valley. For those looking for a livelier place to spend the night, Barcelonnette is only 9km down the road (see Route Seven).

Even if it were not the highest paved road in Europe, the 2808 metre-high Cime de la Bonette would be a great climb, through a magnificent corner of the Alps. The high point of the road is neither a true pass nor the summit of the mountain; the road was extended to this point from the true Col de la Bonette simply to steal the Col de l'Iseran's throne as the highest road in France. The extra height was not gained easily and the gradient over the last few hundred metres provides a stiff test

171

for tired legs. The view from the roadside is quite spectacular, but it is worth making the effort to walk the last 50 metres to reach the true Cime for the glorious 360° panorama of the southern Alps. An orientation table will help you get your bearings: on a clear day you can see the Mediterranean, 100km to the south.

On the southern side of the Bonette the billiard-table smooth surface of the recently resurfaced road is a delight to cycle down. One of the joys of cycling in the mountains is the exhilarating feeling of effortlessly flying down a mountainside and here that sensation can be enjoyed to the full with 26km of free-wheeling descent all the way to St Etienne-de-Tinée. St Etienne is a very pleasant village with an imposing baroque church and a maze of picturesque cobbled lanes. On leaving St Etienne, the road goes gently uphill for a short distance before descending once again towards Isola (see Route Seven).

Day 11 is the last hard day of the traverse, but it starts easily with 34km of gentle down-hill or flat cycling along the Tinée Valley. With properly warmed-up leg muscles, and compared to the efforts of the previous days, the climb to La Tour-sur-Tinée should not feel too difficult (be careful not to miss the turn off

– it is just before a tunnel). La Tour is a real gem of a village and it is easy to see why it has been listed as an historic monument. The Grand Place in the centre of this hamlet of 300 souls is surrounded by perfectly restored mediaeval buildings with brightly painted facades. A number of narrow, cobbled lanes lead away from this square towards the edge of the village, from where there are fabulous views of the surrounding countryside.

After a short descent, the road climbs again to go over an unnamed pass and into the wild and sun-baked Carbonnières Valley. The narrow road (which, in places, is poorly main-tained) runs through a desiccated landscape of grey limestone, stunted trees and thorny scrub. Despite its modest altitude, this is an impres-sively remote and inhospitable place so the more 'civilised' landscape that emerges as you approach Utelle is strangely comforting. At this point the road surface also improves dra-matically and the descent to St Jean-la-Rivière is great fun.

There are surprisingly few hotels and campsites in the countryside north of Nice, except for those beside the main road in the Var Valley (mostly dual-carriageway and dan-gerous to cycle along). Although it does not have a campsite, Levens, just south of the

Col de la Bonette

Typical perched village in the Gorges de la Vésubie, near Levens

Vésubie Valley, is one of the few villages to offer a choice of accommodation. The road to Levens follows the left bank of the Vésubie Gorge, above the spectacular cliffs of the Saut des Français, so-called because local fighters, who resisted the 'invasion' by French Revolutionary soldiers from 1793 to 1794, forced their prisoners to jump off the cliff. Levens is a fortified mediaeval village sitting high above the Vésubie. If you were not lucky enough to glimpse the Mediterranean from the Cime de la Bonette, you will almost certainly see it from here.

The final day can be taken at a relaxing pace as Levens is only 37km from Nice, and most of the cycling is downhill. The route goes through several villages, including Aspremont, a pretty little place that spirals around the top of a small hill, just above the outskirts of Nice – one last chance to relax in a quiet country café and contemplate the magnificent journey you have just completed before entering the hubbub of France's fifth largest city.

Like all large cities, Nice is surrounded by anonymous and sprawling suburbs, but the old town is very pleasant and the city has several interesting museums, including one dedicated to the work of Henri Matisse. Nice's most famous landmark is undoubtedly the Promenade des Anglais, a wide boulevard overlooking the Mediterranean and home to some of the Riviera's most exclusive hotels. However, the city's most sumptuous (and unexpected) building is its ornate Russian Orthodox church. Hotels can be expensive, but Nice has a great many reasonably priced restaurants: what better way to celebrate the end of such an epic journey than with a glass of champagne and a good meal in the glow of a Mediterranean sunset?

GETTING THERE

By car
Geneva is 760km from Calais

By plane
Via Geneva
The route starts directly from Geneva airport

LEAVING NICE

The route ends at Nice airport. There are direct flights from here to many European destinations, including Geneva and several cities in the UK. It is also possible to take the train from Nice to Geneva, via Marseille.

173

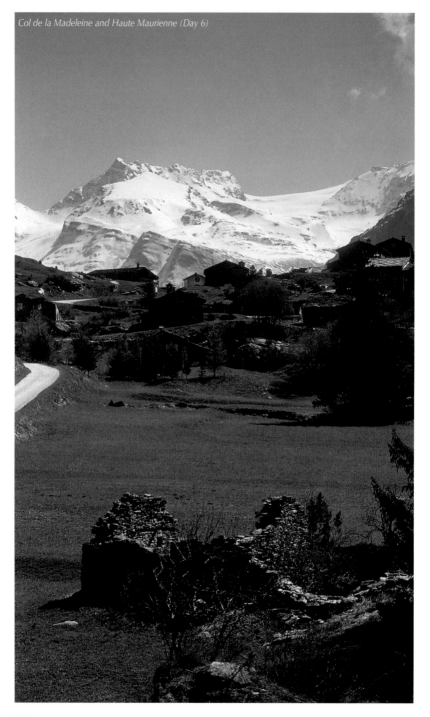

Col de la Madeleine and Haute Maurienne (Day 6)

Nice–St Augustin railway station is less than 1km from the airport (see Day 12 route card). There is a frequent service to the centre of Nice

WHEN TO GO

The best times to do this tour are in June and early July, or from late August to the end of September.

Unsurprisingly, the traffic on such a famous route can be heavy during the holiday season, with the sections between La Clusaz and Flumet, Bourg St Maurice and the Col de l'Iseran, and Modane and Briançon being particularly busy. All of the high passes are

closed from the middle of October to early or mid-June.

MAPS

Michelin: Local – Sheet 328 Ain, Haute-Savoie, Sheet 333 Isère, Savoie; Sheet 334 Alpes-de-Haute-Provence, Hautes-Alpes; Sheet 341 Alpes Maritimes
Michelin: Regional– Sheet 244 Rhône-Alpes, and Sheet 245 Provence, Côte d'Azur
IGN: Top 100 – Sheets 45 Annecy, Lausanne, 53 Grenoble, Mont Blanc, 54 Grenoble, Gap and 61 Barcelonnette, Nice

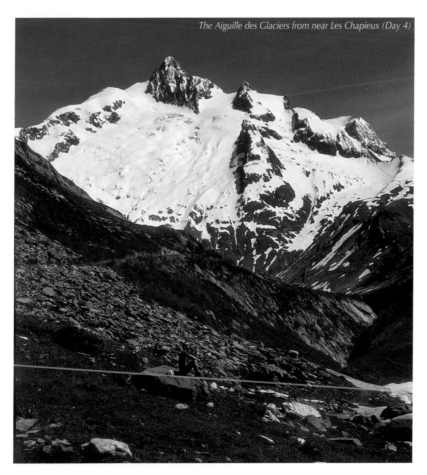
The Aiguille des Glaciers from near Les Chapieux (Day 4)

Day 1 – Geneva to Thonon-les-Bains

One of the best ways to enjoy the scenery around Lake Geneva, and perhaps visit some of the other interesting towns and villages along its shores, is to take a boat trip across the lake. The Compagnie Générale de Navigation runs a large number of cruises, including shuttle services from Geneva to Yvoire and Thonon-les-Bains. In May 2005, second-class single tickets cost 10.30 Euros and 20.30 Euros respectively. Bicycles are accepted on all of the company's boats, except for those marked with a 'V' (V = vedette, a small motor launch) in the timetable. There is a 6CHF (approx. 4 Euros) supplement for bicycles. For further information, download the *Horaires d'été: Genève–Lausanne–Ouchy–St Gingolph* timetable from the company's website, **www.cgn.ch**.

Distance	Location	Directions
0.0	Geneva airport	For directions from airport to Franco–Swiss border see Appendix 1
22.5	Hermance: Franco–Swiss border	Go straight on – D25
24.7	Chens-sur-Léman: D25/D20	Turn L – D25 (Thonon). Follow D25 through Messery, Yvoire and Excenevex to Sciez.
39.5	Sciez: D25/N5	Turn L – N5 (Thonon)
41.0	N5/D325	Turn L – D325/Route du Port (Port de Sciez-Plage)
41.6	Roundabout	Turn R (Le Chatelet)
43.2	Roundabout	Turn R (Thonon)
43.6	Jtn	Turn R – D35/Route du Port de Sciez
43.9	Séchex: jtn	Turn L – Rue Centrale/D35
45.8	Anthy-sur-Léman	Turn L in centre of village [Tour du Bas Chablais]. Follow these blue cycling signs to Thonon-les-Baines.
50.5	Thonon: roundabout	Go straight on (Office de Tourisme)
50.7	Jtn	Turn R onto Rue Vallon (Centre Ville-Rue Pietonnée). Follow road around to L and turn immediately R into square with large fountain. Go across square and then straight on along Rue St Sebastien.
51.0	Jtn	Turn R onto Place du Marché
51.1	Thonon TO	TO is on the L

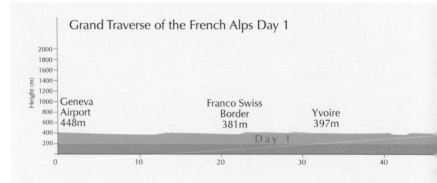

Grand Traverse of the French Alps Day 1

Thonon, view from the town over the marina

FACILITIES AND SERVICES

Location	Distance (km)	Water	Shops	Café	Campsite	B&B	Hotel	Bank	Bike Shop
Geneva	0.0	—	x	x	x	x	x	x	x
Vésenaz	13.7	—	x	x	—	—	x	x	x
Hermance	21.9	—	x	x	—	—	x	—	—
Chens-sur-Léman	25.7	x	x	x	x	—	x	—	—
Yvoire	32.2	x	x	x	x	—	x	—	—
Excenevex	35.5	—	x	x	x	x	x	—	—
Sciez (1)	39.2	—	x	x	x	x	x	x	(2)
Séchex	43.6	x	—	x	x	—	—	—	—
Thonon-les-Bains	50.8	x	x	x	x	x	x	x	x

(1) There are campsites and hotels in several places between Sciez and Thonon

(2) The bike shop is actually in Bonnatrait, 1km from Sciez

Col des Moises 1121m
Col de Ludran 938m
on-
ains
ı
Boëge 740m
Peillonnex 686m
Day 2
60   70   80   90   100
(km)

Distance	Location	Directions
0.0	Thonon TO	Come out of TO and turn R. After 50m, turn L onto Rue des Granges.
0.1	Roundabout	Go straight on – Boulevard G. Andrier (Morzine)
0.3	Jtn after railway line	Turn R – N5 (Annecy)
0.7	Roundabout	Go straight on
1.0	Traffic lights	Turn L – D903 (Habère-Poche)
1.7	Roundabout D903/D12	Go straight on – D12 (Habère-Poche): 8.5km at 3%
10.2	D12/D246	Turn L (Col des Moises): 5.8km at 7%
16.0	Col des Moises	Go straight on
17.3	D246/D12	Turn R (Col de Cou)
17.6	D12/D40	Turn L (Burdignin)
26.9	Boëge	Turn L – D22/Rue de Saxel
27.0	Jtn	Go straight on (Villard)
27.2	D22/D220	Turn R (St André)
29.0	Jtn	Turn L. Follow (Viuz-en-Sallaz): 2.9km at 6.5%
31.9	Col de Ludran	Go straight on
35.1	Sardagne	Turn R to follow (Boisinges) then (Brégny)
37.5	Jtn	Turn L (Bucquigny)
38.8	Jtn	Turn R – D12 (Annemasse)
39.4	D12/D907	Go straight on – D12 (Bonneville): 3.1km at 3.5%
50.4	D12/N205	Turn L – N205 (Bonneville)
52.4	Bonneville: roundabout	Turn R (Cluses); go straight on at next two roundabouts
53.0	Roundabout	Turn L – start of cycleway (Cluses)
53.4	N205/D27	Turn R – D27 (Pontchy–Dessus)
56.3	Jtn: D27/D12	Turn L – D12 (no sign: T-jtn just after river): 22 km at 3%
64.7	Le Petit Bornand	Go straight on
74.9	D12/D4	Turn R – D4 (La Clusaz)
75.7	St Jean-de-Sixt: round-about	Turn L (La Clusaz)
78.4	La Clusaz: roundabout	Turn L then R (Centre Village)
78.7	La Clusaz TO	TO is on the R

View of Mont Blanc and Le Môle from Col de Ludran

FACILITIES AND SERVICES

Location	Distance (km)	Water	Shops	Café	Campsite	B&B	Hotel	Bank	Bike Shop
Thonon-les-Bains	0.0	x	x	x	x	x	x	x	x
Allinges	8.9	—	x	x	—	—	—	—	—
Boëge	26.9	x	x	x	—	—	—	x	—
Sardagne	35.1	x	x	—	—	—	—	—	—
Viuz-en-Sallaz	39.4	—	x	x	—	—	x	x	—
Peillonnex	42.9	—	x	x	—	—	—	—	—
Faucigny	45.3	x	—	x	—	—	—	—	—
Bonneville	52.4	x	x	x	x	—	x	x	—
Le Petit Bornand	64.7	x	x	x	x	x	x	—	—
St Jean-de-Sixt	75.7	x	x	x	x	x	x	x	x
La Clusaz	78.7	x	x	x	x	x	x	x	x

Col des Aravis 1486m

La Clusaz 1040m

Le Petit Bornand 728m

Peillonnex 686m

Bonneville 450m

Day 3

100   110   120   130   140

(km)

Day 3 – La Clusaz to Beaufort

Distance	Location	Directions
0.0	La Clusaz TO	Come out of TO and turn R to go past police station
0.1	Jtn	Turn R onto Route de l'Etale and go past cinema: 2.5km at 7%
1.7	Jtn	Bear L onto Route de Sence (just after tiny chapel on R)
2.6	Jtn	Turn L – D16 (no sign)
2.7	D16/D909	Turn R (Col des Aravis): 4.5km at 6%
7.2	Col des Aravis	Go straight on
19.1	Flumet: jtn	Turn R (Toutes Directions)
19.5	Roundabout	Turn L – N212 (Mégeve)
19.8	Roundabout: N212/D218	Turn R – D218 (Les Saisies): 2.1km at 6.5%
21.9	D218/D218A	Turn R – D218 (Les Saisies): 7.1km at 6% then 5km at 4%
34.8	Col des Saisies	Go straight on
41.8	D218/D218B	Turn L (Hauteluce)
42.8	Hauteluce: D218B/D70	Go straight on – D70
43.6	Jtn	Turn R – D70 (Beaufort)
50.8	D70/D925	Turn R – D925
51.3	Beaufort TO	TO is on the L

Notre Dame de Bellecombe, on the way up to the Col des Saisies

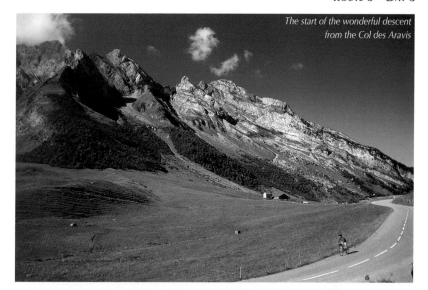

The start of the wonderful descent from the Col des Aravis

FACILITIES AND SERVICES

Location	Distance (km)	Water	Shops	Café	Campsite	B&B	Hotel	Bank	Bike Shop
La Clusaz	0.0	x	x	x	x	x	x	x	x
Col des Aravis	7.2	x	x	—	—	—	—	—	—
La Giettaz	13.0	x	x	x	x	x	x	—	—
Flumet	19.1	x	x	x	x	x	x	x	—
Notre Dame-de-Bellecombe	23.2	x	x	x	—	x	x	—	x
Les Saisies	35.5	x	x	x	—	x	x	x	—
Hauteluce	42.8	x	x	x	—	x	x	x	—
Beaufort	51.3	x	x	x	x	x	x	x	(1)

(1) Nearest bike shop is in Albertville, 20km southwest of Beaufort

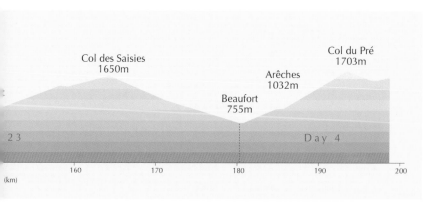

Day 4 – Beaufort to Bourg St Maurice

Cycling between La Clusaz and the Col du Pré you can see two of the works of Gargantua, a gluttonous and truculent giant who features in a great many French myths (including the myth of the 'mermaid of the vines', see Route 1). It is said that in a fit of pique while walking through the Aravis, the giant gave the mountains an enormous kick and sent a huge lump of rock flying through the air. The gap that was left forms the Porte des Aravis (above the Col des Aravis) and the detached block landed in the Beaufortain to form the tooth-like Pierre Menta.

Distance	Location	Directions
0.0	Beaufort TO	Come out of TO and turn L – D218 (Arêches-Le Planay): 4.0km at 6.5%
5.0	Arêches: D218/D85	Go straight on – D218 (Col du Pré): 7.3km at 9%
12.3	Col du Pré	Go straight on
15.7	Low point	Go straight on
17.7	Col de Meraillet: D217/D925	Turn R – D217 (Bourg Saint Maurice): short descent then 5.9km at 6.5%
25.9	Cormet de Roseland	Go straight on (D217 becomes D902)
45.6	Bourg St Maurice: roundabout: D902/N90	Turn R – N90 (Aime)
45.7	Bourg St Maurice TO	TO is on the R

FACILITIES AND SERVICES

Location	Distance (km)	Water	Shops	Café	Campsite	B&B	Hotel	Bank	Bike Shop
Beaufort	0.0	x	x	x	x	x	x	x	(1)
Arêches	5.0	x	x	x	x	x	x	—	—
Col du Pré	12.3	—	—	x	—	—	—	—	—
Col de Meraillet	17.7	—	—	x	—	—	—	—	—
Bourg St Maurice	45.7	x	x	x	x	—	x	x	x

(1) Nearest bike shop is in Albertville, 20km southwest of Beaufort

Grand Traverse of the French Alps Day 4

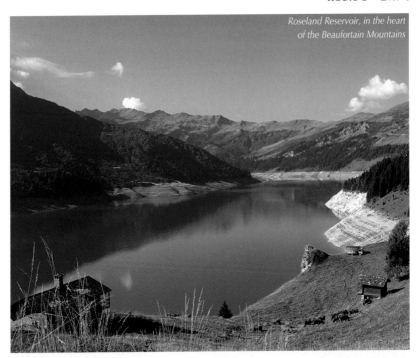

Roseland Reservoir, in the heart of the Beaufortain Mountains

The only time I have experienced the unpleasant effects of hypoglycaemia (weak legs, dizziness and nausea) was on a long ride over the Cormet de Roseland and the Col de l'Iseran. The Cormet burnt up the few cereal bars I had, but I wasn't worried, there are plenty of bakeries in Val d'Isère. My expectations were quickly shattered: it being the end of the season all the shops were closed. On rubber legs, I struggled up to the pass, drawn on by the thought of bilberry tarts at the summit café. It was cold and windy… and the café was shut! Devastated, I slumped down to Bonneval and wobbled through Bessans to Lanslebourg, where I eventually found somewhere to refuel.

Day 5 – Bourg St Maurice to Bessans

When it was finished, in 1952, the Tignes Dam was the biggest in Europe, an engineering marvel that was to provide half of Savoie's electricity. However, the project was not welcomed by everyone and the inhabitants of the village of Tignes, whose homes were to be submerged below the reservoir's 235 million cubic metres of water, fought hard, but in vain, to prevent its construction. The fresco of Hercules supporting the dam on his shoulders was not added until 1989.

Distance	Location	Directions
0.0	Bourg St Maurice TO	Come out of TO and turn L – N90
0.1	Roundabout	Go straight on – (Italie)
2.8	N90/D902	Turn R – D902 (Col de l'Iseran): 15.8km at 6%
23.9	D902/D87A	Go straight on (Val d'Isère)
31.0	Val d'Isère*	Go straight on: 16.4km at 6%
47.4	Col de l'Iseran	Go straight on
68.0	D902/D902A	Turn R – D209 (Bessans)
68.7	Bessans TO	The TO is on the L

* The road system through Val d'Isère may change over the next few years as there are plans to turn the village into a 'car-free' resort

Location	Distance (km)	Water	Shops	Café	Campsite	B&B	Hotel	Bank	Bike Shop
Bourg St Maurice	0.0	x	x	x	x	—	x	x	x
Seez	2.6	x	x	x	x	x	x	—	—
Ste Foy-Tarentaise	11.9	—	x	x	—	—	x	—	—
La Thuile	14.6	—	—	—	—	—	x	—	—
Val d'Isère	31.0	x	x	x	—	x	x	x	x
Col de l'Iseran	47.4	—	—	x	—	—	—	—	—
Bonneval-sur-Arc	60.0	x	x	x	—	x	x	—	—
Bessans	68.7	x	x	x	x	x	x	—	(1)

FACILITIES AND SERVICES

(1) Nearest bike shop is in Lanslebourg, 11.7km west of Bessans

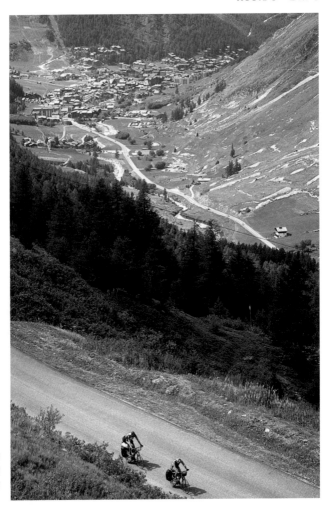

Looking down on Val d'Isère from the Col de l'Iseran road

Day 6 – Bessans to Valloire

Distance	Location	Directions
0.0	Bessans TO	Come out of TO and turn L – D209
1.9	D209/D902	Turn R – D902 (Modane)
4.6	Col de la Madeleine	Go straight on
11.7	Lanslebourg: D902/N6	Go straight on – N6
19.7	N6/D83	Turn R – D83 (Sardières): 4.5km at 5%
28.5	Aussois	Go straight on – D215 (Modane)
36.0	Modane: traffic lights	Turn L (Centre Ville)
36.2	Jtn	Turn R – N6 (Centre Ville)
53.4	St Michel-de-Maurienne: N6/D902	Turn L – D902 (Valloire): 12.3km at 7%
65.7	Col du Télégraphe	Go straight on
70.6	Valloire: roundabout	Turn R
70.8	Valloire TO	TO is on the R

FACILITIES AND SERVICES

Location	Distance (km)	Water	Shops	Café	Campsite	B&B	Hotel	Bank	Bike Shop
Bessans	0.0	x	x	x	x	x	x	x	(1)
Lanslevillard	8.8	x	x	x	—	—	x	—	—
Lanslebourg	11.7	x	x	x	x	x	x	x	—
Termignon	17.8	x	x	x	x	x	x	—	—
Sardières	24.3	x	—	x	—	x	—	—	—
Aussois	28.5	x	x	x	x	x	x	x	—
Modane	36.0	x	x	x	x	—	x	x	x
St Michel-de-Maurienne	53.4	x	x	x	—	x	x	x	—
Col du Télégraphe	65.7	x	—	x	—	—	—	—	—
Valloire	70.8	x	x	x	x	x	x	x	x

(1) Nearest bike shop is in Lanslebourg, 11.7km west of Bessans

Grand Traverse of the French Alps Day 6

Bessans 1705m
Col de la Madeleine 1750m
Lanslebourg 1399m
Auss 147

Day 5   Day 6

Looking across to the 600m high cliffs of the Croix des Têtes from the Col du Télégraphe

187

The Col du Galibier was first included in the Tour de France in 1911 as part of a 336km stage from Chamonix to Grenoble. The winner that day, Emile Georget, recorded an average speed of almost 27km/hr, an impressive performance given the bikes that were being used (only two gears and to change between them involved turning the back wheel round!) and the quality of the roads. The last man to finish got to Grenoble a full 8hrs and 33 minutes after the winner! With high-tech bikes and a much improved road surface, today's elite riders can cover the 18km from Valloire to the top of the Galibier in around 50 minutes. Rather surprisingly, given the importance of the mountain stages in determining the overall winner of the race, on only five occasions has the first rider to cross the Galibier gone on to win the Tour.

Distance	Location	Directions
0.0	Valloire TO	Come out of TO and turn R – D902: 17.5km at 7%
17.5	Col du Galibier	Go straight on
26.2	Col du Lauteret	Turn L – N91. Follow this road, and then D994 into Briançon
53.0	Briançon – roundabout	Turn R (Gap)
54.5	Traffic lights	Turn L onto D2 (Gare SNCF)
54.8	Roundabout	Turn R
55.0	Roundabout	Go straight on
55.5	Briançon station	Station is on the R

FACILITIES AND SERVICES								
Location	Distance (km)	Water	Shops	Café	Campsite	B&B	Hotel	Bank	Bike Shop
Valloire	0.0	x	x	x	x	x	x	x	x
Col du Lautaret	26.2	—	x	x	—	—	—	—	—
Monêtier-les-Bains	39.7	x	x	x	—	x	x	x	x
Chantemerle	48.0	x	x	x	x	x	x	x	—
Briançon	55.5	x	x	x	x	(1)	x	x	x

(1) At Villard St Pancrace, 2km south of Briançon

Grand Traverse of the French Alps Day 7

The arid country on the southern side of the Col du Galibier

Alpine passes were often dangerous and forbidding places so it is not surprising that they have given rise to numerous myths and legends, not all of which can be attributed to the overactive imagination of more superstitious times. A number of car drivers crossing the Col du Lautaret on stormy nights have told of a mysterious woman, dressed all in white and with her face completely hidden by a white shawl, hitch-hiking beside the road. Several drivers, touched by the apparent distress of the hitchhiker, have given her a lift, but none of them have heard her speak a word or seen her face. Forced to concentrate on the road by the terrible weather, they only realise that the woman has disappeared when they arrive, safely, at their destination. It is said that those who refuse to give the White Lady a lift are not always so lucky!

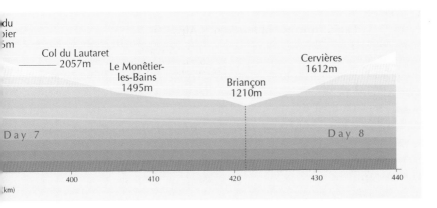

Day 8 – Briançon to Guillestre

The parched and desolate scenery of the Casse Déserte, below the Col d'Izoard, has such an otherworldly aura that it does not seem surprising that some of the geomorphological processes to which it is subject are thought to be analogous to those observed on Mars. The yellowy-grey rock of the contorted towers that emerge from the surrounding scree was formed by the partial dissolution of the original dolomitic limestone by the sulphate-rich waters that flowed through the neighbouring beds of gypsum. Such formations are not rare – the towers near Sardières (Day 6) were formed in a similar way – but rarely do they produce such a spectacular landscape.

Distance	Location	Directions
0.0	Briançon station	Come out of the station and turn L (Toutes Directions)
0.5	Jtn	Turn R (Col d'Izoard)
0.7	Jtn	Turn R (no sign)
0.9	Roundabout	Turn R – D902 (Col d'Izoard): 9.4km at 4.2%
10.3	Cervières	Go straight on: 10.1km at 7.5%
20.4	Col d'Izoard	Go straight on
34.8	D902/D947	Turn R – D902 (Guillestre)
51.1	Roundabout	Turn R (Guillestre–Centre Historique)
51.8	Guillestre TO	TO is on the R

FACILITIES AND SERVICES

Location	Distance (km)	Water	Shops	Café	Campsite	B&B	Hotel	Bank	Bike Shop
Briançon	0.0	x	x	x	x	(1)	x	x	x
Cervières	10.3	x	—	—	x	x	—	—	—
Col d'Izoard	20.4	x	—	x	—	x	x	—	—
Brunissard	27.6	x	—	x	x	x	—	—	—
Arvieux/La Chalp	30.8	x	x	x	x	x	x	x	—
Guillestre	51.8	x	x	x	x	x	x	x	x

(1) At Villard St Pancrace, 2km south of Briançon

Grand Traverse of the French Alps Day 8

Col d'Izoard 2361m

Le Monêtier-les-Bains 1495m

Briançon 1210m

Cervières 1612m

Day 7

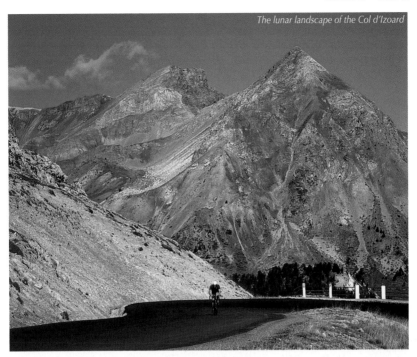
The lunar landscape of the Col d'Izoard

For 370 years, Briançon was the capital of the Republic of the Escartons, a federation of 51 municipalities between Grenoble, Gap and Turin. In 1343, this area was part of an independent state known as the Dauphiné, but its ruler, Humbert II, was living beyond his means and was thus in great financial difficulty. The municipalities took advantage of Humbert's weakness to buy their freedom and set up their own system of government based on the protection of collective and individual rights and fair taxation. In 1349, Humbert seceded his lands to the king of France, but the republic survived until 1713, when its lands were divided between France and the Duchy of Savoie under the terms of the Treaty of Utrecht.

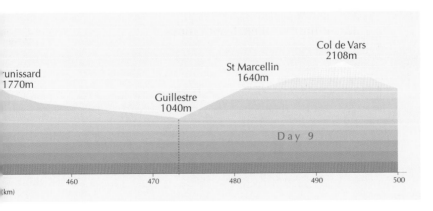

Day 9 – Guillestre to Jausiers

Mont Dauphin (just outside Guillestre) is much more than another fort; it is an entire walled village, perched on a small plateau overlooking the strategic crossroads formed by the confluence of the Durance and Guil Rivers. The fort was designed in 1693 by Vauban (like so many Alpine forts), although his original plans were constantly developed and perfected throughout the 18th and 19th centuries. Cars are not allowed into what is now an historic monument, making a stroll around the well-preserved village/fort an extremely pleasant experience. It is easy to spend at least half a day here wandering around the streets, visiting the exhibition on the fort's history, enjoying the superb views across the valley and, of course, sipping a relaxing drink outside the village café.

Distance	Location	Directions
0.0	Guillestre TO	Come out of the TO and turn R. Follow road round to the L (Vars): 20.1km at 5.5%
0.4	Roundabout	Turn L – D902A (Vars)
0.7	Roundabout	Turn R – D902 (Vars)
20.1	Col de Vars	Go straight on
34.9	D902/D900	Turn R – D900 (Jausiers)
42.4	Jausiers	Bear L off the D900 to go into the centre of Jausiers
42.5	Jausiers TO	TO is on the R

FACILITIES AND SERVICES								
Location	Distance (km)	Water	Shops	Café	Campsite	B&B	Hotel	Bank	Bike Shop
Guillestre	0.0	x	x	x	x	x	x	x	x
Ste Marie-de-Vars	12.4	x	x	x	—	—	x	—	—
Vars: resort	15.3	x	x	x	—	x	x	x	—
Col de Vars	20.1	—	—	x	—	—	—	—	—
St Paul-sur-Ubaye	28.6	x	x	x	x	x	x	—	—
La Condamine-Chatelard	37.4	x	x	x	x	x	x	—	—
Jausiers	42.5	x	x	x	x	x	x	x	x

192

*Attacking the
Col de Vars, with
Mont Pelvoux in
the background*

193

Day 10 – Jausiers to Isola

For a village of barely 1000 souls, Jausiers has a remarkably good bike shop. As well as providing standard spare parts and repair services, Chardon Bleu Sports rents reasonable quality road bikes and sells specially designed Col de la Bonette cycling jerseys.

Distance	Location	Directions
0.0	Jausiers TO	Come out of TO and turn L. Go through pedestrian area to jtn with D900
0.1	Jtn	Bear R – D900
0.2	D900/D64	Bear R (Nice): 23.6km at 6.5%
23.8	Cime de la Bonette	Go straight on
45.5	D64/D2205	Turn L – D2205 (St Etienne de Tinée)
49.7	St Etienne-de-Tinée	Turn R to go into village
49.8	Jtn	Turn L (Nice par le village)
50.1	Jtn	Turn R to go past church
50.3	Jtn	Turn R – D39 (Nice)
52.0	Roundabout: D39/D2205	Go straight on – D2205 (Nice)
65.2	Isola	Turn L (Isola Centre Ville)
65.3	Isola *mairie*	The *mairie* is on the R

FACILITIES AND SERVICES								
Location	Distance (km)	Water	Shops	Café	Campsite	B&B	Hotel	Bank	Bike Shop
Jausiers	0.0	x	x	x	x	x	x	x	x
Halte 2000	11.2	x	—	x	—	—	—	—	—
Cime de la Bonette	23.8	—	—	(1)	—	—	—	—	—
Boussieyas	36.8	x	—	x	—	x	—	—	—
St Etienne-de-Tinée	49.7	x	x	x	x	x	x	x	—
Isola	65.3	x	x	x	x	x	x	x	(2)

(1) Refreshment stall, open during July and August

(2) Nearest bike shop is in Nice, 70km south of Isola

Grand Traverse of the French Alps Day 10

Jausiers 1213m

Day 9   Day 10

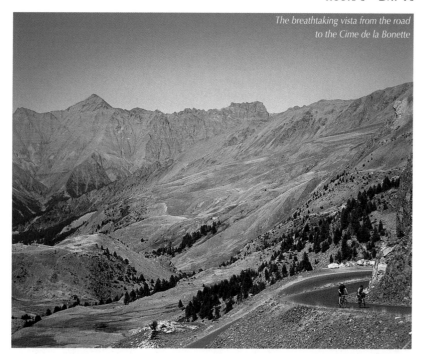

*The breathtaking vista from the road
to the Cime de la Bonette*

The main itinerary describes a direct route to Nice, but there are several ways to extend the tour through the Southern Alps, for example via the Col St Martin and the Col St Roche (20km north of Monaco). For a more adventurous alternative: 22km after the Bonette turn right to St Dalmas-le-Selvage (hotel). Continue to the Col de la Moutière (2454m, 11km at 9%). Turn right after the pass and descend the rough, but cycleable track to Bayasse (*gite d'étape*). Turn left to go over the Col de la Cayolle (2326m, 9km at 6%) to Guillaumes (see Route 7). Go through Péone to Valberg (1673, 14.5km at 6%), and then through Beuil to the Col de la Couillole. Re-join the main itinerary at St Sauveur-sur-Tinée. Allow one or two extra days.

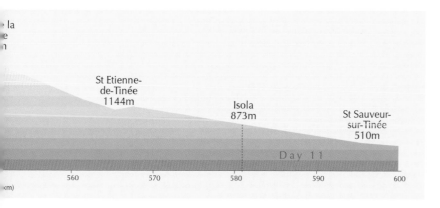

195

Day 11 – Isola to Levens

Distance	Location	Directions
0.0	Isola Mairie	Come out of the Mairie and turn R (Toutes Directions)
0.2	Roundabout	Turn L – D2205(St Sauveur-sur-Tinée)
33.9	D2205/D32	Turn L – D32 (Utelle) (the jtn is easy to miss, it is just before a tunnel): 6.8km at 5.5%
40.7	La Tour-sur-Tinée	Go straight on through village – cobbled streets
41.0	Jtn	Turn R – D32 (Utelle)
44.0	Low point	Go straight on 1.9km at 9.5%
45.9	High point	Go straight on
47.5	Low point	Go straight on 6.1km at 6.5%
53.6	High point	Go straight on
54.7	Utelle	Go straight on
63.4	St Jean-la-Rivière	Turn L to go across bridge (Toutes Directions)
63.5	D32/D2565	Turn R – D2565 (Nice)
63.9	D2565/D19	Turn L – D19 (Levens) 2.4km at 10%, short descent, then 8.9km at 4%
76.8	Levens	Turn R (Levens Centre)
77.3	Jtn	Turn L (Centre Ville)
77.8	Levens TO	TO is on the R

FACILITIES AND SERVICES

Location	Distance (km)	Water	Shops	Café	Campsite	B&B	Hotel	Bank	Bike Shop
Isola	0.0	x	x	x	x	x	x	x	(1)
St Sauveur-sur-Tinée	14.6	x	x	x	x	-	x	x	-
Pont-de-Clans	28.6	x	x	x	-	-	-	-	-
La Tour	40.7	x	-	x	-	x	-	-	-
Utelle	54.7	x	x	x	-	-	x	-	-
St Jean-la-Rivière	63.4	x	-	-	-	-	-	-	-
Levens	77.8	x	x	x	-	-	x	x	(2)

(1) Nearest bike shop is in Nice, 70km south of Isola

(2) Nearest bike shop is in Aspremont, 15km south of Levens

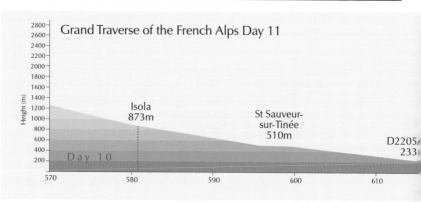

Grand Traverse of the French Alps Day 11

Isola 873m

St Sauveur-sur-Tinée 510m

D2205/ 233

Day 10

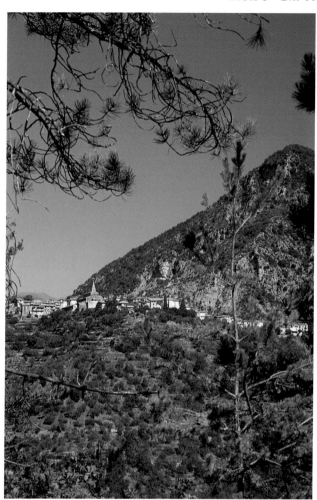

The superbly situated and extremely pretty village of La Tour-sur-Tinée

Tour
03m

Utelle
800m

St Jean-la-
Rivière
288m

Levens
560m

Day 11

Day 12

630 640 650 660 670

(km)

If you would like to continue your journey south from Nice, there is only one option: take the ferry to France's *Ile de beauté* and explore the fabulous mountain roads of Corsica.

Distance	Location	Directions
0.0	Levens TO	Come out of the TO and turn L. Follow the road down to jtn with D19.
0.5	Jtn	Turn R – D19
1.8	D19/D14	Turn R – D14 (St Blaise)
12.2	Jtn	Go straight on – D14 (Aspremont)
13.4	Jtn	Turn L – D14 (Aspremont)
15.4	Aspremont: D14/D414	Turn R – D414 (Colomars)
18.6	Jtn	Turn R – D414 (Colomars)
19.5	Jtn	Turn R – D414 (Colomars)
20.6	Colomars: D414/D714	Turn L – D714 (Nice St Romain-de-Bellet)
21.2	Roundabout	Go straight on (Nice)
25.5	Traffic lights	Go straight on
26.7	Roundabout	Turn R – Ave Joseph Durandy (RN202)
28.0	Jtn	Turn R – Chemin de la Ginestière (RN202)
28.7	Jtn	Turn R – Route de Grenoble
30.0	Jtn (at hairpin bend)	Turn L – Corniche Fleurie
33.1	Roundabout	Turn R (Nice Centre)
33.8	Traffic lights	Turn R (Nice Ouest)
34.4	Traffic lights	Go straight on – Boulevard Napoleon III
34.9	Traffic lights	Turn L – Ave Henri Matisse
35.0	Roundabout	Turn R (A8 Péage)
35.6	Traffic lights	Get off your bike and cross three pedestrian crossings (on the LHS of the road) to get to the furthest lane of traffic. Turn L and go under the railway.
35.7	Traffic lights	Go straight on
36.0	Traffic lights	Bear R (Arenas)
36.9	Roundabout	Turn L to go into airport car parks
37.1	Nice Airport: roundabout	Go straight on (no-entry for cars). Airport arrivals is in front of you. The departures area is 50 metres to your L.

198

Enjoying the descent from the
Cime de la Bonette (Day 10)

FACILITIES AND SERVICES

Location	Distance (km)	Water	Shops	Café	Campsite	B&B	Hotel	Bank	Bike Shop
Levens	0.0	x	x	x	—	—	x	x	(1)
Aspremont	15.4	x	x	x	—	—	x	—	x
Colomars	20.6	—	x	x	—	x	x	—	—
Nice	37.1	—	x	x	(2)	x	x	x	x

(1) Nearest bike shop is in Aspremont, 15km south of Levens

(2) The campsite is approx. 8km north of the airport, beside the N202. To get there, take the D414 in Colomars, and then the D514.

Nice Airport
0m

Day 12

| 700 | 710 | 720 | 730 | 740 |

(km)

ACCOMMODATION

Geneva

Campsites

Pointe-à-la-Bise – in Vesenaz, 6km north-east of the city centre (early April to early Oct), Tel. (022) 752 12 96

Bois de Bay – in Satigny, 4km west of Geneva airport (all year), Tel. (022) 341 05 05

Val de l'Allondon – in Satigny, 4km west of Geneva airport (early April to end Oct), Tel. (022) 753 15 15

Bed & Breakfast

Geneva youth hostel, Tel. (022) 732 62 60

Hotels

There are more than 100 hotels in Geneva. Contact TO for details.

Thonon-les-Bains

Campsites

Le Lac Noir (June to Sept), Tel. 04 50 26 07 28

Le Morcy (Easter to mid-Sept), Tel. 04 50 70 44 87

Saint Disdille (early April to end Sept), Tel. 04 50 71 14 11

Bed & Breakfast

La Clématite, Tel. 04 50 71 85 95

Centre International de Séjour (hostel, sleeps 200), Tel. 04 50 71 77 80

Hotels

There are 16 hotels in Thonon-les-Bains. Contact TO for details.

La Clusaz

Campsites

Le Plan du Fernuy (early June to early Sept), Tel. 04 50 02 44 75

Le Cret (at St Jean-de-Sixt) (mid-June to mid-Sept), Tel. 04 50 35 80 54

Bed & Breakfast

Youth hostel, Tel. 04 50 02 41 73

Mme Suize, Tel. 04 50 02 42 81

La Ferme du Var, Tel. 04 50 02 26 56

La Trace, Tel. 04 50 02 46 76

Hotels

There are more than 20 hotels in La Clusaz. Contact TO for details.

Beaufort

Campsites

Le Domelin (June to end Sept), Tel. 04 79 38 33 88

Bed & Breakfast

There are no bed & breakfasts/gites d'étapes in Beaufort

Hotels

Le Doron (**), Tel. 04 79 38 33 18

Hotel du Grand Mont (**), Tel. 04 79 38 33 36

La Cascade (**) 3km west of Beaufort on D925, Tel. 04 79 38 70 00

Hotel de la Roche (*), Tel. 04 79 38 33 31

Bourg St Maurice

Campsites

Le Versoyen (mid-May to end Oct), Tel. 04 79 07 03 45

Bed & Breakfast

There are no bed & breakfasts in Bourg St Maurice.

Hotels

There are nine hotels in Bourg St Maurice. Contact TO for details.

Bessans

Campsites

L'Illaz (early June to mid-Sept), Tel. 04 79 05 83 31

Bed & Breakfast

Le Petit Bonheur, Tel. 04 79 05 06 71

La Batisse (2km north of the village), Tel. 04 79 05 95 84

Hotels

La Vanoise (**), Tel. 04 79 05 96 79

Le Grand Fond (**), Tel. 04 79 05 83 05

Le Mont Iseran (**), Tel. 04 79 05 95 97

Le Chamois (**), Tel. 04 79 05 94 87

Valloire

Campsites

Sainte Thecle (early June to end Sept), Tel. 04 79 83 30 11

Bed & Breakfast

Mr and Mrs Souille, Tel. 04 79 59 01 02

Les Plans, Tel. 04 79 59 00 60

Les Reaux, Tel. 04 79 59 06 64

Gîte d'étape Pierre-Paul (at Les Verneys, 2km south of Valloire), Tel. 04 79 59 01 02

Hotels

There are 13 hotels in Valloire. Contact TO for details.

Briançon

Campsites

Les Cinq Vallées (early June to end Sept), Tel. 04 92 21 06 27

Bed & Breakfast

La Riolette – at Villard St Pancrace, Tel. 04 92 20 58 68

Le Bois de Barracan – *Gîte d'étape* at Villard St Pancrace, Tel. 04 92 21 27 79

Hotels

There are 18 hotels in Briançon. Contact TO for details.

Guillestre

Campsites

Le Villard (all year), Tel. 04 92 45 06 54

La Longeagne (early Feb to end Oct), Tel. 04 92 45 07 62

La Rochette (mid-May to mid-Sept), Tel. 04 92 45 02 15

Saint James les Pins (all year), Tel. 04 92 45 08 24

La Ribière (mid-June to mid-Sept), Tel. 04 92 45 25 54

Le Serre Altitude 1000 (mid-May to end Sept), Tel. 04 92 45 00 40

Le Vivier (mid-June to mid-Sept), Tel. 04 92 45 01 47

Les Bouleaux (dates not known), Tel. 04 92 45 04 32

Bed & Breakfast

Le Villard, Tel. 04 92 45 20 54

Clos de Phazy, Tel. 04 92 45 25 66

Hotels

Les Barnières (***), Tel. 04 92 45 04 87

Le Catinat Fleuri (**), Tel. 04 92 45 49 29

La Maison du Roy (**), Tel. 04 92 45 08 34

Le Martinet (**), Tel. 04 92 45 00 28

Le Chalet Alpin (**), Tel. 04 92 45

Jausiers

Campsites

Le Planet (mid-June to mid-Sept), Tel. 04 92 81 06 57

Bed & Breakfast

Les Bartavelles, Tel. 04 92 84 69 86

La Cordée, Tel. 04 92 84 61 34 9 (*Gite d'étape*)

La Mexicaine, Tel. 04 92 84 69 63

Hotels

Le Bel Air (**), Tel. 04 92 81 06 35

Le Sans Souci (*), Tel. 04 92 81 06 20

Villa Morélia, Tel. 04 92 84 67 78

Isola

Campsites

Lac des Neiges (all year), Tel. 04 93 02 18 16

Bed & Breakfast

Au Vieux Chalet, Tel. 04 93 23 99 99

Gite d'étape at Lac des Neiges campsite, Tel. 04 93 02 18 16

Hotels

Hotel de France (*), Tel. 04 93 02 17 04

Hotel d'Isola, Tel. 04 93 02 17 03

Levens

Campsites

There are no campsites in Levens, but there is a small campground at Pont Charles-Albert/La Roquette-sur-Var. It is beside the RN202, approximately 13km southwest of Levens. Tel. 04 93 08 91 57.

Bed & Breakfast

There are no bed & breakfasts in Levens

Hotels

La Vigneraie (**), Tel. 04 93 79 70 46

La Chaumière, Tel. 04 93 79 71 58

Le Mas Fleuri, Tel. 04 93 79 70 35

Nice

Campsites

Le Terry (all year), Tel. 04 93 08 11 58

Bed & Breakfast

Mrs Martiny, Tel. 04 93 85 98 37

Mrs Golle, Tel. 04 93 37 94 31 or 06 70 06 53 31

Youth hostel, Espace Magnan, approx. 5km northeast of airport (open mid-June to mid-Sept), Tel. 04 93 86 28 75

Hotels

There are more than 200 hotels in Nice. Contact TO for details.

TOURIST INFORMATION

Regional Information

	Telephone	Website
Haute-Savoie	04 50 51 32 31	www.savoiehautesavoie.com
Savoie	04 79 85 12 45	www.savoiehautesavoie.com
Hautes-Alpes	04 92 53 62 00	www.hautes-alpes.net
Alpes de Haute-Provence	04 92 31 57 29	www.alpes-haute-provence.com
Alpes Maritimes	04 93 37 78 78	www.guideriviera.com

Tourist Information Offices

Location	Telephone	Website
Geneva	022 909 70 00	www.geneve-tourisme.ch
Thonon-les-Bains	04 50 71 55 55	www.thononlesbains.com
Boëge/Viuz-en-Sallaz	04 50 31 90 94	www.alpesduleman.com
Bonneville	04 50 97 38 37	no website
Le Petit Bornand	04 50 03 52 38	www.tourisme.fr/petit-bornand
St Jean-de-Sixt	04 50 02 70 14	www.saintjeandesixt.com
La Clusaz	04 50 32 65 00	www.laclusaz.com
La Giettaz	04 79 32 91 90	www.la-giettaz.com
Flumet	04 79 31 61 08	www.flumet-montblanc.com
Notre-Dame-de-Bellecombe	04 79 31 61 40	www.ot-ndb.com
Les Saisies	04 79 38 90 30	www.lessaisies.com
Arêches–Beaufort	04 79 38 37 57	www.areches-beaufort.com
Bourg St Maurice	04 79 07 04 92	www.lesarcs.com
Ste Foy-Tarentaise	04 79 06 95 09	www.saintefoy.net
Val d'Isère	04 79 06 06 60	www.valdisere.com
Bessans	04 79 05 96 52	www.bessans.com
Lanslebourg	04 79 05 23 66	www.valcenis.com
Aussois	04 79 20 30 80	www.aussois.com
Modane	04 79 04 05 01	www.modane-valfrejus.com
St Michel-de-Maurienne	04 79 56 53 42	www.saint-michel-de-maurienne.com
Valloire	04 79 59 03 96	www.valloire.net
Serre Chevalier	04 92 24 98 98	www.serre-chevalier.com
Briançon	04 92 21 08 50	www.ot-briancon.fr
Arvieux	04 92 46 75 76	www.arvieux.com

Guillestre	04 92 45 04 37	www.pays-du-guillestrois.com
Vars	04 92 46 51 31	no website
St Paul-sur-Ubaye	no telephone	www.haute-ubaye.com
Jausiers	04 92 81 21 45	www.jausiers.com
St Etienne-de-Tinée	04 93 02 41 96	www.auron.com
Isola	04 93 02 18 97	no website
St Sauveur-sur-Tinée	04 93 02 00 22	no website
Levens/Aspremont	04 93 79 71 00	www.canton-de-levens.com
Nice	08 92 70 74 07	www.nicetourism.com

Mending a slate roof in Bonneval (Day 5)

APPENDIX 1

AIRPORT ACCESS ROUTES

1A: FROM GENEVA AIRPORT TO FRANCO–SWISS BORDER AT HERMANCE		
Distance	**Location**	**Directions**
0.0	Geneva airport terminal	Come out of the terminal and turn R – Route de l'Aeroport
1.2	Jtn	Turn R onto cycleway
1.3	Jtn	Turn L (Vernier–Meyrin)
1.4	Jtn	Turn L (Vernier)
1.7	Jtn	Go straight on and through underpass
1.9	Chemin de la Croisette/Route de Vernier	Go straight on past Café de la Croisette
2.0	Jtn	Turn L (no bike path and no signs)
2.3	Jtn	Turn L back onto cycleway. Follow cycleway to and along Route de Vernier to a major flyover
3.9	Flyover	Go straight on under flyover (Genève) and then turn R – Ave de Châtelaine
5.4	Place des Charmilles	Bear R – Rue des Charmilles
5.5	Jtn	Turn R – Rue de Miléant
5.7	Jtn (blocked by bollards)	Turn L – Ave des Tilleuls (pedestrian zone but bikes are allowed)
6.1	Pont des Délices	Turn R, and then L – Rue de St Jean
6.6	Jtn	Turn R – Rue de la Pisciculture
6.7	Jtn	Turn L – Quai du Seujet
7.4	Jtn	Turn R and cross River Rhone [Rive Gauche]
7.7	Jtn	Turn L – Quai Général Guisan
8.0	Place du Port	Turn R and then L – Rue du Rhône. To do this you have to go straight on at the traffic lights and do a U-turn after 20 metres to get back to Rue du Rhône
8.5	Place des Eaux Vives	Go across the square in bus lane and turn L onto Rue des Eaux Vives
9.4	Jtn	Turn R to follow minor road beside Quai Gustave Ador. Follow this minor road and then the cycleway to Versenaz.
14.0	Versenaz	Turn L (Hermance)
22.5	Franco–Swiss border	Go straight on

1B: FROM FRANCO–SWISS BORDER AT COLLONGES TO GENEVA AIRPORT

Distance	Location	Directions
0.0	Franco–Swiss border	Go straight on to roundabout
0.3	Roundabout	Go straight on (Compesières)
1.6	Roundabout	Turn R – Route de Saconnex d'Arve. Follow (Genève) for 2.5km.
4.1	Roundabout and tramline	Go straight on to follow the road to the L of the tramline
4.6	Roundabout	Go straight on into Lancy
6.2	Underpass	Road to airport goes through underpass. Bear R to go over underpass then rejoin airport road.
7.3	Jtn	Follow LH cycleway (Aeroport) to cross River Rhone and follow Ave de l'Ain to traffic lights under flyover (bear R where airport road goes up onto flyover)
9.0	Lights under flyover	Turn L – Route de Vernier (Vernier–Meyrin)
10.5	Route de Vernier/ Chemin de la Croisette	Turn R – Chemin de la Croisette (Gare de Cointrin) [Aeroport]
10.7	Jtn	Go straight on along Chemin de Champs-Prévost
11.0	Jtn	Turn R (Aeroport)
11.1	Jtn	Turn R (Vernier)
11.2	Jtn	Turn L
12.4	Geneva airport	Terminal is on the L

2A: LYON ST EXUPÉRY TO MEXIMIEUX

Distance	Location	Directions
0.0	St Exupéry Airport: TGV train station main entrance	Come out of the station and go across the concourse and bus lanes to turn R onto road out of carparks. Follow road round to L, but get into RH lane. Follow (Lyon-nord) then (Janneyrias) to third roundabout.
4.7	Roundabout	Turn L – D517 (Pusignan)
6.1	Pusignan: D517/D6E	Turn R – D6E (Villette d'Anthon)
6.8	Roundabout	Turn L – D6E (Villette d'Anthon)
7.2	Lights	Go straight on – D6E (Jons)
11.5	Jons: D6E/D6	Turn R – D6 (Montluel)
11.7	Roundabout: D6/D6E	Turn L – D6E-D61 (Montluel)
13.5	D61/C16	Turn R – C16 (Balan)
16.7	Balan: C16/D84B	Turn L – D84B (Montluel)
17.0	D84B/D84C	Turn R – D84B (Dagneux)
19.5	Dagneux: D84B/N84	Turn R – N84 (Meximieux)
19.6	N84/D84B	Turn L onto Rue de Bressolles
20.1	Jtn	Turn L – D84B(Bressolles)
22.5	Bressolles: tn	Go straight on (Faramans)
24.1	Jtn (at foot of electric pylon)	Turn R
27.2	Jtn	Go straight on
28.3	Bourg St Christophe: jtn	Go straight on – D4C (Pérouges)
30.5	D4C/D4	Turn R – D4 (Meximieux)
31.3	D4/N84	Turn L – N84
31.6	Roundabout	Go straight on (Centre Ville)
31.9	Meximieux TO	TO is on the L just after a small roundabout (turn R to go down to station)

2B: MEXIMIEUX TO LYON ST EXUPÉRY

Distance	Location	Directions
0.0	Meximieux TO	Come out of the TO and turn R. Go straight on at the roundabout – N84
0.3	Roundabout	Go straight on
0.6	N84/D4	Turn R – D4 (Pérouges)
1.4	D4/D4C	Turn L – D4C (Bourg St Christophe)
3.6	Bourg St Christophe: jtn	Go straight on (Bressolles)
4.7	Jtn	Go straight on (Bressolles)
7.8	Jtn (at foot of electric pylon)	Turn L
9.4	Bressolles: jtn	Go straight on (Dagneux)
11.8	Jtn	Turn L (N84)
12.2	Jtn	Turn R – N84
12.7	N84/D84B	Turn L – D84B (Balan)
15.2	D84B/D84C	Turn L – D84B (Balan)
15.5	Jtn	Turn R to go past the *mairie*
18.7	Jtn	Turn L – D61-D6E (Jons)
20.5	D6E/D6	Turn R – D6 (St Exupéry)
20.7	D6/D6E	Turn L – D6E (St Exupéry)
25.0	Lights	Go straight on into Pusignan
25.4	Roundabout	Turn R – D6E (St Exupéry)
26.1	Pusignan: D6E/D517	Turn L – D517 (St Exupéry)
27.5	Roundabout: D517/D517A	Turn R – D517A (St Exupéry)
31.9	T-junction	Go straight across the main road to go into Parc P6. Turn L and go across the car park to the TGV station.
32.3	St Exupéry Airport:	TGV station main entrance

3A: LYON ST EXUPÉRY TO LA VERPILLIÈRE/BOURGOIN-JALLIEU

Distance	Location	Directions
0.0	St Exupéry Airport: TGV train station main entrance	Come out of the station and go across the concourse and bus lanes to turn R onto road out of car parks. Follow road round to L, but get into RH lane. Follow (Lyon-nord) then (Janneyrias) to third roundabout.
4.7	Roundabout	Turn R – D517 (Janneyrias)
6.5	Janneyrias: D517/D124	Turn R – D124-D155 (La Verpillière)
9.8	Saugnieu	Turn L then R – D155 (Satolas et Bonce)
11.3	D155/D26	Go straight on – D155-D124 (Satolas et Bonce)
16.9	Roundabout: D124/C8	Turn L – C8 (Le Chaffard)
17.9	Le Chaffard: C8/D75	Turn L – D75
18.6	D75/D163A	Turn R – D163A-D163 (Frontonas)
32.0	D163/D126	

(The route now splits depending on whether you are going to La Verpillière or Bourgoin-Jallieu)

For Bourgoin-Jallieu		
22.0	D163/D126	Go straight on – D163 (Frontonas)
22.4	D163/D126	Turn R – D163 (Bourgoin-Jallieu)
27.5	Roundabout: D163/D208A	Turn R – D208A (L'Isle d'Abeau)
29.5	D208A/D208	Turn L – D208 (Morestel)
31.8	Roundabout: D208/D522	Go straight on – D208 (Champfleuri)
33.1	Roundabout	Turn R (Centre Ville)
34.1	Roundabout	Go straight on through three sets of lights (Centre Ville)
35.1	4th set of lights	Go straight on (Gare SNCF) then turn R to go up ramp that leads to the station
35.3	Bourgoin-Jallieu station	

For La Verpillière		
22.0	D163/D126	Turn R – D126 (La Verpillière)
24.8	Roundabout	Go straight on along cycleway [La Verpillière]
25.4	End of cycleway	Turn L
25.7	D126/N6	Turn L then R (Gare SNCF)
26.1	La Verpillière station	

3A: LA VERPILLIÈRE/BOURGOIN-JALLIEU TO LYON ST EXUPÉRY

Distance	Location	Directions
From Bourgoin-Jallieu		
0.0	Bourgoin-Jallieu	Come out of the station and turn R. Go down ramp and turn R at lights to get to major jtn.
0.1	Traffic lights	Go straight on
1.2	Roundabout	Go straight on (Bourg-en-Bresse)
2.2	Roundabout	Turn L – D208 (Bourg-en-Bresse)
3.5	Roundabout	Go straight on (Pierre Louve)
5.8	Roundabout: D208/	Turn R – D208A (St Marcel-Bel-Accueil) D208
8.0	Roundabout: D208A/D163	Turn L – D163 (Frontonas)
13.1	D163/D126	Turn L – D163 (La Verpillière)
13.5	D163/D126	Go straight on – D163*

*Junction with route from La Verpillière – see below (reset odometer to zero)

Distance	Location	Directions
From La Verpillière to Lyon St Exupéry		
0.0	La Verpillière station	Come out of the station and turn L, then immediately R – D126 (Frontonas)
0.4	D126/N6	Turn L, then R – D126 [Frontonas]
0.7	Start of cycleway	Follow cycleway to roundabout
1.3	Roundabout	Go straight on – D126 (Frontonas)
5.4	D126/D163	Turn L – D163*

* Junction with route from Bourgoin-Jallieu – see below (reset odometer to zero)

Distance	Location	Directions
From D163/D126 junction to Lyon St Exupéry		
1.9	Gonas: D163/D163A	Bear L – D163A (Lyon)
3.4	D163A/D75	Turn L – D75
4.1	Le Chaffard: traffic lights	Turn R – Chemin de Rollinière
5.1	Roundabout	Turn R – D124-D155 (Satolas et Bonce)
10.7	D155/D26	Go straight on – D155 (Saugnieu)
12.2	Saugnieu	Turn R – Route de Planaise, then L – D155–D124 (Janneyrias)
15.5	Janneyrias: D124/D517	Turn L – D517 (Lyon)
17.3	Roundabout: D517/D517E	Turn L (St Exupéry)
21.7	T-junction: opposite Parc P6	Go into Parc P6 and head towards TGV station
22.2	TGV station	Entrance is in front of you

4A: FROM GRENOBLE AIRPORT TO GRENOBLE

Distance	Location	Directions
0.0	Grenoble airport terminal	Come out of the arrivals area and turn R
0.7	Roundabout	Go straight on along D154D
1.7	Roundabout: D154D/D519	Turn L – D519 (Sillans)
5.6	Sillans: roundabout	Go straight on along Ave Ambroise Carrier
8.6	Roundabout	Turn R (Col de Parménie)
9.4	Izeaux: jtn	Go straight on (Tullins)
10.5	D73B/D73E	Turn L – D73E (Tullins)
13.6	Col de Parménie	Go straight on
18.1	D73E/D153	Turn L – D153 (Tullins)
18.8	Tullins	Go straight on
18.9	Traffic lights	Turn R, and then L (Funerarium). Go under railway
19.4		Where road curves L, go straight on (Au Bon Gite)
19.5	Jtn	Turn L (Les Murailles)
21.3	Jtn	Turn L (Les Massons)
22.5	Les Massons	Turn L: no sign
22.8	Jtn	Turn L – do not go under motorway
23.1	Roundabout	Turn R – D45 (Grenoble)
23.6	Jtn before bridge over Isère	Turn L onto cycleway. (The cycling sign to Grenoble on the R points the wrong way)
47.3	Steps on L leading up from cycleway	Turn L to leave cycleway (just before going under a third bridge). At top of steps turn R and go over river. Cross major jtn (Place Hubert Dubedout) to go down Rue Casimir Brenier (no entry signs)
47.9	Grenoble station	The station is in front of you at the end of Rue Casimir Brenier

4B: GRENOBLE TO GRENOBLE AIRPORT

Distance	Location	Directions
0.0	Grenoble: railway station	Leave station via 'Centre Ville' exit. Go straight across street in front of station to Rue Casimir Brenier, which you follow to Place Hubert Dubedout
0.4	Place Hubert Dubedout	Go across square (easiest on foot). Cross River Isère and then turn L to go to gap in fence that leads down to cycleway
0.6	Cycleway	Turn R onto cycleway and follow it to the end (bear L after 2.9km to stay beside river)
24.3	End of cycleway	Turn R (Tullins)
24.7	Roundabout	Turn L (Les Massons)
25.5	Les Massons	Turn R (Manguely)
26.6	Jtn	Turn R – no sign
28.5	Jtn	Turn R – no sign
28.6	Jtn	Go straight on – no sign: 5.8km at 4.3%
29.1	Tullins: traffic lights	Turn R then L (Col de Parménie)
29.2	Jtn	Go straight on (Morette)
29.8	D153/D73E	Turn R – D73E (Izeaux)
34.4	Col de Parménie	Go straight on
37.5	D73E/D73B	Turn R – D73B and go straight through Izeaux
39.4	Roundabout: D73B/D519	Turn L – D519 (St Geoirs)
42.4	Sillans: roundabout	Go straight on
46.3	Roundabout: D519/D154D	Turn R (St Geoirs)
47.2	Roundabout	Go straight on (St Geoirs). Follow signs to Aérogare
47.9	Grenoble airport	Arrivals area is on your R

5A: FROM CHAMBÉRY AIRPORT TO YENNE (ACCESS FOR TOUR OF THE AIN)

Distance	Location	Directions
0.0	Chambéry airport terminal	Come out of the arrivals building. Turn L at roundabout and follow road to jtn with N202
0.7	Roundabout: N202	Turn L – N202 (Savoie Technolac)
1.8	Roundabout: N202/N211	Turn L – N211 (Savoie Technolac). Bear R onto cycleway [Chambéry]
4.5	Bridge over stream	Go over bridge and turn L
4.9	Le Bourget-du-Lac: Le Port	Go through the gate at the end of the cycleway and turn L to go through car park.
5.1	Jtn at end of car park	Turn R – D14 (Bourdeau): flat for 1.7km, then 2.4km at 4%
8.4	Bourdeau: D14/D13	Turn L – D13 (Abbaye de Hautecombe)
8.7	D13/D14A	Bear R – D14A (Abbaye de Hautecombe)
9.1	Jtn	Turn L (Abbaye de Hautecombe)
9.2	D14A/N504	Go straight on (Col du Chat): 4.1km at 7.5%
13.3	Col du Chat	Go straight on
17.8	Chevelu: D914A/N504	Turn L – N504 (Yenne)
18.2	N504/D921C	Turn L – D921C (St Paul-sur-Yenne)
20.7	D921C/D41	Turn R – D41 (Yenne): 2.5km at 3.5%
24.6	Jtn	Turn R
25.4	D41/D9241	Turn R – D921 (Yenne)
25.7	Jtn	Go straight on (no entry for cars)
26.0	Yenne	Turn R and *mairie* is on the L

5B: YENNE TO CHAMBÉRY AIRPORT

Distance	Location	Directions
0.0	Yenne: mairie	Come out of the *mairie*. Turn L and then immediately L (Novalaise).
0.1	Jtn	Go straight on
0.5	D921/D41	Turn L – D41 (St Paul-sur-Yenne)
1.4	Jtn	Turn L (St Paul-sur-Yenne)
5.1	D41/D921C	Turn L (St Jean-de-Chevelu)
7.7	D921C/N504	Turn R – N504 (Le Bourget-du-Lac)
8.0	Jtn	Turn R (Col du Chat) 4.5km at 7%
12.5	Col du Chat	Go straight on
12.9	D914A/D914	Go straight on (Le Bourget-du-Lac)
16.6	D914/N504	Go straight on (Bourdeau)
16.7	Jtn	Turn R [Chambéry]
17.1	Jtn	Bear L. **Do not follow (Le Bourget-du-Lac).**
17.4	D13/D14	Turn R – D14
20.7	Le Bourget-du-Lac: Le Port	Turn L into car park then turn R in front of Ecole Française de Voile to join start of cycleway [Aix -les-Bains]
21.3	Bridge	Turn L and go over river [Aix-les-Bains]
24.0	Roundabout: N211/N202	Turn R – N202 (Chambéry-Aix)
25.1	Roundabout	Turn R (Chambéry-Aix)
25.8	Chambéry airport	The terminal is in front of you.

6A: FROM CHAMBÉRY AIRPORT TO CHAMBÉRY STATION

Distance	Location	Directions
0.0	Chambéry airport terminal	Come out of the arrivals building. Turn L at roundabout and follow road to jtn with N202.
0.7	Roundabout: N202	Turn L – N202 (Savoie Technolac)
1.8	Roundabout: N202/N211	Turn L – N211 (Savoie Technolac). Bear R onto cycleway [Chambéry].
3.3	Roundabout	Turn L to leave cycleway and go straight on at roundabout (Savoie Technolac). Go straight on at next two roundabouts.
4.1	Cycleway crosses road	Turn L onto cycleway [Chambéry]
12.9	End of cycleway	Go straight on [Chambéry centre]
13.2	End of road	Go up to traffic lights and turn L onto cycle lane – Ave Général Cartier-Ave du Comte Vert
13.6	Roundabout	Take third exit – Ave du Comte Vert
14.1	Traffic lights	Turn L – Ave Maréchal Leclerc (Gares – SNCF and Routière)
14.3	Roundabout	Go straight on– Ave Maréchal Leclerc (Gare SNCF)
14.4	Chambéry station	The station is in front of you

6B: FROM CHAMBÉRY STATION TO CHAMBÉRY AIRPORT

Distance	Location	Directions
0.0	Chambéry station	Come out of the station and go straight on – Ave Maréchal Leclerc (Centre Ville)
0.1	Roundabout	Go straight on (Centre Ville Sud)
0.3	Traffic lights	Turn R – Ave du Comte Vert
0.8	Roundabout	Go straight on – Ave du Comte Vert
1.3	Traffic lights	Turn R (Ave Verte Nord)
1.5	Jtn: start of cycleway	Go straight on along cycleway
10.1	Jtn: University of Savoie	Go straight on
10.3	Jtn: cycleway crosses road	Turn R and leave cycleway. Go straight on at next two roundabouts (Aix-les-Bains).
11.1	Roundabout	Go straight across to cycleway and turn R to follow it [Aix-les-Bains]
12.6	Leave cycleway to fol-	low N211 to roundabout
12.7	Roundabout: N211/N202	Turn R – N202 (Chambéry–Aix)
13.8	Roundabout	Turn R (Chambéry–Aix)
14.5	Chambéry airport	The terminal is in front of you

APPENDIX 2
CLIMATE STATISTICS

The following tables give average climate data for five towns at different latitudes and altitudes. Note: the average adiabatic lapse rate is 6.5°C per 1000 metres of height gain. So, the average July temperature in Briançon (24°C) can be expected to be approximately 8.5°C higher than the temperature at the Col du Galibier (15.5°C).

GENEVA (400m)

	Jan	Feb	Mar	Apr	May	Jun	Jul	Aug	Sep	Oct	Nov	Dec
T max °C	4	6	10	14	18	22	26	25	22	15	8	5
T min °C	-1	-1	2	4	8	11	14	13	11	7	2	0
Rain mm	87	77	82	55	73	94	63	56	66	88	65	88

CHAMONIX (1000m)

	Jan	Feb	Mar	Apr	May	Jun	Jul	Aug	Sep	Oct	Nov	Dec
T max °C	2	5	8	11	17	20	23	24	20	14	7	3
T min °C	-7	-6	-3	0	5	7	9	9	6	3	-2	-5
Rain mm	87	92	80	82	112	130	112	110	105	120	117	105

GRENOBLE (210m)

	Jan	Feb	Mar	Apr	May	Jun	Jul	Aug	Sep	Oct	Nov	Dec
T max °C	7	8	14	17	22	25	28	29	23	18	13	7
T min °C	-1	0	2	5	10	12	15	15	12	8	3	0
Rain mm	82	80	79	80	82	84	72	80	100	92	90	82

BRIANÇON (1300m)

	Jan	Feb	Mar	Apr	May	Jun	Jul	Aug	Sep	Oct	Nov	Dec
T max °C	4	5	7	11	16	20	24	23	20	15	8	5
T min °C	-6	-5	-3	0	4	8	10	9	7	3	-1	-4
Rain mm	67	67	56	66	65	56	39	54	58	74	76	68

NICE (0m)

	Jan	Feb	Mar	Apr	May	Jun	Jul	Aug	Sep	Oct	Nov	Dec
T max °C	13	14	15	17	21	23	27	28	25	22	17	15
T min °C	5	6	8	10	14	17	20	20	17	14	10	6
Rain mm	83	60	61	67	48	39	16	23	77	142	94	89

(Information sourced from Météo France website)

APPENDIX 3

GLOSSARY OF
ENGLISH–FRENCH WORDS AND PHRASES

The following glossary of cycling terms is followed by a short list of phrases that may come in useful if you have a problem with your bike.

A

adjust	régler
adjuster	tendeur (m)
adjusting barrel	tendeur (m) (de gaine)
adjusting screw	vis d'ajustement (f)
Allen bolt	vis à 6 pans (f)
Allen key	clé BTR (f)/ clé mâle (f)
axle (bottom bracket)	axe de pédalier (m)
axle (hub)	axe (m)

B

saddle or handle-bar bag	sacoche (f)
bag for transporting a bike	housse (f)
ball bearing	roulement à billes (m)
battery	pile (f)
bell	sonnette (f)
bent	tordu(e), plié(e)
bicycle	vélo
bike lock	antivol (m)
bike box	valise de transport
body (freewheel)	corps (m) (roue libre)
bolt	boulon (m)
bottle	bidon (m)
bottle cage	porte-bidon (m)
bottom bracket	boitier de pédalier (m)
brake	frein (m)
brake lever	levier de frein (m)
brake pad/shoe	patin (m)

C

cable	câble (m)
cable housing	gaine (f)
caliper (brake)	étrier de frein (m)
chain	chaîne (f)
chain adjuster	tendeur (m)
chain tool, chain breaker	dérive chaîne (m)

chainring(s)	plateau(x) (m)
clipless pedals	pedales automatiques (f)
crank	manivelle (f)
crankset	pédalier (m)
cycle lane	bande cyclable (f)
cycle path/cycleway	piste cyclable (f)
cycling shorts	cuissard (m)

D

derailer	dérailleur (m)

F

fork	fourche (f)
freewheel	roue libre (f)

G

grease	graisse (f)

H

handlebar	guidon (m)
handlebar grip	poignée (f)
headset	jeu de direction (m)
helmet	casque (m)
hub, hubs	moyeu, moyeux (m)

I

inner tube	chambre à air (f)

J

jersey	maillot (m)

L

lubricate	lubrifier (v)
luggage rack	porte-baggages (m)

M

mountain bike	VTT (vélo tout terrain)
mudguard	garde boue (m)

N

nut	écrou (m)

O

oil	huile (f)

P

pannier	sacoche (f)
patch (for repairing an inner tube)	rustine (f) (R)
pump	pompe (f)
pump clip	porte-pompe (m)
puncture (GB)	crevaison (f)

Q

quick release (hub, seatpost)	blocage rapide (m)

R

rack (on car for carrying bikes)	porte-vélo (m)
rack (to carry bagage on bicycle)	porte-baggages (m)
rear	arrière
repair kit	trousse de réparation (f)
rim	jante (f)
rim tape, rim strip	fond de jante (m)

S

saddle	selle (f)
screw	vis (f)
screwdriver	tournevis (m)
seat post	tige de selle (f)
size	taille (f)
spanner	clé (f)
spoke	rayon (m)
spoke key	clé à rayons (f)
spoke nipple	écrou de rayon (m)
spring	ressort (m)
sprocket, cog (rear)	pignon (m)
stem (handlebar)	potence (f)
suspension fork	fourche telescopique (f)

T

tape (handlebar)	ruban (de guidon) (m)
tights	collant (m)
toe clip	cale-pied (m)
tooth, teeth	dent, dents (f)
tyre	pneu (m)
tyre-lever	démonte-pneu (m)

W

washer	rondelle (f)
wind jacket	coupe-vent (m)
worn (out)	usé(e)

USEFUL PHRASES

English	French
Hello. Do you do repairs?	Bonjour. Faites-vous des réparations ?

Problems	Les problèmes
I have a problem with my bike	J'ai un problème avec mon vélo
The front/back derailleur needs adjusting	Le dérailleur avant/arrière a besoin d'être réglé
I'm having problems changing gears	J'ai du mal à changer les vitesses
The front/back wheel is buckled	La roue avant/arrière est voilée
The front/back brakes are rubbing against the rim	Les freins avant/arrière touchent la jante
The chain slips from time to time	La chaîne saute de temps en temps
The chain slips all the time	La chaîne saute tout le temps
The brake/derailleur cable is broken	La câble de frein/dérailleur s'est cassé
The bottom bracket has come loose	Le boîtier de pédalier s'est devissé
There is a clicking noise when I turn the pedals	Il y a un claquement quand je tourne les pédales
The front/back wheel does not turn freely.	La roue avant/arrière ne tourne pas librement

I have lost one of the screws from the luggage rack — J'ai perdu une des vis du porte-bagage
The brake pads are worn out — Les patins de frein sont usés
The chain is dry — La chaîne est sèche
The chain is broken — La chaîne s'est cassée

Useful questions / Questions utiles

Could you adjust the front derailleur? — Pourriez-vous régler le derailleur avant ?
Could you adjust the brakes? — Pourriez-vous régler les freins ?
Could you straighten the wheel? — Pourriez-vous dévoiler la roue ?
Could you check the gears? — Pourriez-vous contrôler les dérailleurs ?
Could you change the brake cable? — Pourriez-vous changer le câble de frein ?
Could you fit a new chain? — Pourriez-vous mettre une nouvelle chaîne ?
Could you oil the chain? — Pourriez-vous mettre un peu d'huile sur la chaîne ?

Could you tighten the bottom bracket? — Pourriez-vous serrer le boîtier de pédalier ?
Could you service the bike – brakes, gears, and bearings? — Pourriez-vous faire une révision complète – freins, vitesses et roulements ?
Do you have Shimano 105 brake pads? — Avez-vous des patins (de frein) Shimano cent-cinq ?

Can you do it now? — Pouvez-vous le faire tout-de-suite ?
When can you do it? — Vous pouvez le faire quand ?
How long will it take? — Il vous faut combien de temps pour le faire ?
What time can I collect the bike? — Je peux venir chercher le vélo vers quelle heure ?

What time do you open/close? — Vous ouvrez/fermez à quelle heure ?
How much will it cost? — Combien ça va coûter ?
How much will it cost to grease the bearings? — Le graissage des roulements me coûtera combien ?

Are there any other bike shops near here? — Y-a t'il d'autres magasins de vélo dans le coin ?

Possible answers / Réponses possibles

Of course, no problem. — Bien sûr. Sans problème
Yes, but not until this afternoon — Oui, mais pas avant cet après-midi
I'm sorry. I can't do it. — Je suis desolé. Je ne peux rien faire
The workshop is fully booked — L'atelier est surchargé
I'm sorry, I don't have the right parts — Je suis désolé, je n'ai pas les pièces qu'il faut
The middle chain ring is worn out. You will have to replace it — Le plateau intermédiaire est usé. Il faudrait le remplacer.
Leave it with me and I'll have a look — Laissez-moi le vélo, et je regarderai
Come back in about two hours — Revenez dans deux heures
We close at 7 pm — Le magasin ferme à dix-neuf heures
It will be about 27 euros — Ça coûtera environ 27 euros

NOTES

NOTES

LISTING OF CICERONE GUIDES

NORTHERN ENGLAND
LONG-DISTANCE TRAILS
The Dales Way
The Reiver's Way
The Alternative Coast to Coast
The Coast to Coast Walk
The Pennine Way
Hadrian's Wall Path
The Teesdale Way

FOR COLLECTORS OF SUMMITS
The Relative Hills of Britain
Mts England & Wales Vol 2 –
England
Mts England & Wales Vol 1 –
Wales

BRITISH CYCLE GUIDES
The Cumbria Cycle Way
Lands End to John O'Groats –
Cycle Guide
On the Ruffstuff: 84 Bike Rides in
North England
Rural Rides No.1 – West Surrey
Rural Rides No.2 – East Surrey
South Lakeland Cycle Rides
Border Country Cycle Routes
Lancashire Cycle Way

CANOE GUIDES
Canoeist's Guide to the North-East

LAKE DISTRICT AND
MORECAMBE BAY
Coniston Copper Mines
Scrambles in the Lake District
More Scrambles in the Lake
District
Walks in Silverdale and
Arnside AONB
Short Walks in Lakeland 1 – South
Short Walks in Lakeland 2 – North
Short Walks in Lakeland 3 – West
The Tarns of Lakeland Vol 1 –
West
The Tarns of Lakeland Vol 2 – East
The Cumbria Way &
Allerdale Ramble
Winter Climbs in the Lake District
Roads and Tracks of the Lake
District
The Lake District Angler's Guide
Rain or Shine – Walking in the
Lake District
Rocky Rambler's Wild Walks
An Atlas of the English Lakes

NORTH-WEST ENGLAND
Walker's Guide to the
Lancaster Canal
Walking in Cheshire
Family Walks in the
Forest Of Bowland
Walks in Ribble Country
Historic Walks in Cheshire
Walking in Lancashire
Walks in Lancashire Witch
Country
The Ribble Way

THE ISLE OF MAN
Walking on the Isle of Man
The Isle of Man Coastal Path

PENNINES AND
NORTH-EAST ENGLAND
Walks in the Yorkshire Dales –
Vol 1
Walking in the South Pennines
Walking in the North Pennines
The Yorkshire Dales
Walks in the North York Moors –
Vol 1
Walks in the North York Moors –
Vol 2
Walking in the Wolds
Waterfall Walks – Teesdale and
High Pennines
Walking in County Durham
Yorkshire Dales Angler's Guide
Backpacker's Britain – Northern
England
Walks in Dales Country
Historic Walks in North Yorkshire
South Pennine Walks
Walking in Northumberland

DERBYSHIRE, PEAK DISTRICT,
EAST MIDLANDS
High Peak Walks
White Peak Walks Northern Dales
White Peak Walks Southern Dales
White Peak Way
The Viking Way
Star Family Walks Peak District &
South Yorkshire
Walking In Peakland
Historic Walks in Derbyshire

WALES AND WELSH BORDERS
Ascent of Snowdon
Welsh Winter Climbs
Hillwalking in Wales – Vol 1
Hillwalking in Wales – Vol 2
Scrambles in Snowdonia
Hillwalking in Snowdonia
The Ridges of Snowdonia
Hereford & the Wye Valley
Walking Offa's Dyke Path
The Brecon Beacons
Lleyn Peninsula Coastal Path
Anglesey Coast Walks
The Shropshire Way
Spirit Paths of Wales
Glyndwr's Way
The Pembrokeshire Coastal Path
Walking in Pembrokeshire
The Shropshire Hills – A Walker's
Guide
Backpacker's Britain Vol 2 –
Wales

MIDLANDS
The Cotswold Way
West Midlands Rock
The Grand Union Canal Walk
Walking in Oxfordshire
Walking in Warwickshire
Walking in Worcestershire
Walking in Staffordshire
Heart of England Walks

SOUTHERN ENGLAND
The Wealdway & the Vanguard
Way
Exmoor & the Quantocks
Walking in the Chilterns
Walks in Kent Book 2
Two Moors Way
Walking in Dorset
Walking in Cornwall
A Walker's Guide to the Isle of
Wight
Walking in Devon
Walking in Somerset
The Thames Path
Channel Island Walks
Walking in Buckinghamshire
The Isles of Scilly
Walking in Hampshire
Walking in Bedfordshire
The Lea Valley Walk
Walking in Berkshire
The Definitive Guide to
Walking in London
The Greater Ridgeway
Walking on Dartmoor
The South West Coast Path
Walking in Sussex
The North Downs Way
The South Downs Way

SCOTLAND
Scottish Glens 1 – Cairngorm
Glens
Scottish Glens 2 – Atholl Glens
Scottish Glens 3 – Glens of
Rannoch
Scottish Glens 4 – Glens of
Trossach
Scottish Glens 5 – Glens of Argyll
Scottish Glens 6 – The Great Glen
Scottish Glens 7 – The Angus
Glens
Scottish Glens 8 – Knoydart
to Morvern
Scottish Glens 9 – The Glens
of Ross-shire
Scrambles in Skye
The Island of Rhum
Torridon – A Walker's Guide
Ski Touring in Scotland
Walking the Galloway Hills
Walks from the West Highland
Railway
Border Pubs & Inns –
A Walkers' Guide
Walks in the Lammermuirs
Scrambles in Lochaber
Walking in the Hebrides
Central Highlands: 6 Long
Distance Walks
Walking in the Isle Of Arran
Walking in the Lowther Hills
North to the Cape
The Border Country –
A Walker's Guide
Winter Climbs – Cairngorms
The Speyside Way
Winter Climbs – Ben Nevis &
Glencoe

The Isle of Skye, A Walker's Guide
The West Highland Way
Scotland's Far North
Walking the Munros Vol 1 –
  Southern, Central
Walking the Munros Vol 2 –
  Northern & Cairngorms
Scotland's Far West
Walking in the Cairngorms

IRELAND
The Mountains of Ireland
Irish Coastal Walks
The Irish Coast to Coast

INTERNATIONAL CYCLE GUIDES
The Way of St James – Le Puy to
  Santiago cyclist's guide
The Danube Cycle Way
Cycle Tours in Spain
Cycling the River Loire – The Way
  of St Martin

WALKING AND TREKKING
IN THE ALPS
Grand Tour of Monte Rosa Vol 1
Grand Tour of Monte Rosa Vol 2
Walking in the Alps (all Alpine
  areas)
100 Hut Walks in the Alps
Chamonix to Zermatt
Tour of Mont Blanc
Alpine Ski Mountaineering
  Vol 1 Western Alps
Alpine Ski Mountaineering
  Vol 2 Eastern Alps
Snowshoeing: Techniques and
  Routes in the Western Alps
Alpine Points of View

FRANCE, BELGIUM AND
LUXEMBOURG
The Tour of the Queyras
Rock Climbs in the Verdon
RLS (Robert Louis Stevenson) Trail
Walks in Volcano Country
French Rock
Walking the French Gorges
Rock Climbs Belgium &
  Luxembourg
Tour of the Oisans: GR54
Walking in the Tarentaise and
  Beaufortain Alps
The Brittany Coastal Path
Walking in the Haute Savoie
Walking in the Ardennes
Tour of the Vanoise
Walking in the Languedoc
GR20 Corsica – The High Level
  Route
The Ecrins National Park
Walking the French Alps: GR5
Walking in the Cevennes
Vanoise Ski Touring
Walking in Provence
Walking on Corsica
Mont Blanc Walks
Walking in the Cathar region
  of south west France
Walking in the Dordogne

PYRENEES AND FRANCE / SPAIN
Rock Climbs in the Pyrenees
Walks & Climbs in the Pyrenees

The GR10 Trail: Through the
  French Pyrenees
The Way of St James –
  Le Puy to the Pyrenees
The Way of St James –
  Pyrenees-Santiago-Finisterre
Through the Spanish Pyrenees
  GR11
The Pyrenees – World's Mountain
  Range Guide
The Pyrenean Haute Route
Walking in Andorra

SPAIN AND PORTUGAL
Picos de Europa – Walks & Climbs
Andalusian Rock Climbs
The Mountains of Central Spain
Costa Blanca Rock
Walking in Mallorca
Rock Climbs in Majorca,
  Ibiza & Tenerife
Costa Blanca Walks Vol 1
Costa Blanca Walks Vol 2
Walking in Madeira
Via de la Plata (Seville To
  Santiago)
Walking in the Cordillera
  Cantabrica
Walking in the Canary Islands 1
  West
Walking in the Canary Islands 2
  East
Walking in the Sierra Nevada

SWITZERLAND
The Jura: Walking the High Route
  & Ski Traverses
Walking in Ticino, Switzerland
Central Switzerland –
  A Walker's Guide
The Bernese Alps
Walking in the Valais
Alpine Pass Route
Walks in the Engadine,
  Switzerland

GERMANY AND AUSTRIA
Klettersteig Scrambles in
  Northern Limestone Alps
King Ludwig Way
Walking in the Salzkammergut
Walking in the Black Forest
Walking in the Harz Mountains
Walking in the Bavarian Alps
Germany's Romantic Road
Mountain Walking in Austria
Walking the River Rhine Trail
Trekking in the Stubai Alps
Trekking in the Zillertal Alps

SCANDINAVIA
Walking In Norway
The Pilgrim Road to Nidaros
  (St Olav's Way)

EASTERN EUROPE
Trekking in the Caucausus
The High Tatras
The Mountains of Romania
Walking in Hungary

CROATIA AND SLOVENIA
Walks in the Julian Alps
Walking in Croatia

ITALY
Italian Rock
Walking in the Central Italian Alps
Central Apennines of Italy
Walking in Italy's Gran Paradiso
Long Distance Walks in Italy's
  Gran Paradiso
Walking in Sicily
Shorter Walks in the Dolomites
Treks in the Dolomites
Via Ferratas of the Italian
  Dolomites Vol 1
Via Ferratas of the Italian
  Dolomites Vol 2
Walking in the Dolomites
Walking in Tuscany
Trekking in the Apennines

OTHER MEDITERRANEAN
COUNTRIES
The Mountains of Greece
Climbs & Treks in the Ala Dag
  (Turkey)
The Mountains of Turkey
Treks & Climbs Wadi Rum, Jordan
Jordan – Walks, Treks, Caves etc.
Crete – The White Mountains
Walking in Palestine
Walking in Malta

AFRICA
Climbing in the Moroccan Anti-
  Atlas
Trekking in the Atlas Mountains
Kilimanjaro - A Trekker's Guide

NORTH AMERICA
The Grand Canyon &
  American South West
Walking in British Columbia
The John Muir Trail

SOUTH AMERICA
Aconcagua

HIMALAYAS – NEPAL, INDIA
Langtang, Gosainkund &
  Helambu: A Trekkers' Guide
Garhwal & Kumaon –
  A Trekkers' Guide
Kangchenjunga – A Trekkers'
  Guide
Manaslu – A Trekkers' Guide
Everest – A Trekkers' Guide
Annapurna – A Trekker's Guide
Bhutan – A Trekker's Guide

AUSTRALIA AND NEW
ZEALAND
Classic Tramps in New Zealand

TECHNIQUES AND EDUCATION
The Adventure Alternative
Rope Techniques
Snow & Ice Techniques
Mountain Weather
Beyond Adventure
The Hillwalker's Manual
The Book of the Bivvy
Outdoor Photography
The Hillwalker's Guide to
  Mountaineering
Map and Compass

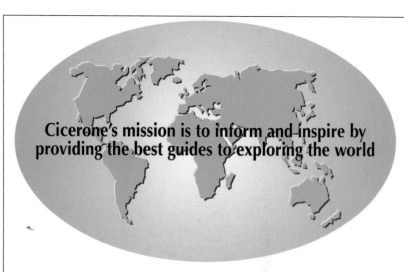

Cicerone's mission is to inform and inspire by providing the best guides to exploring the world

Since its foundation over 30 years ago, Cicerone has specialised in publishing guidebooks and has built a reputation for quality and reliability. It now publishes nearly 300 guides to the major destinations for outdoor enthusiasts, including Europe, UK and the rest of the world.

Written by leading and committed specialists, Cicerone guides are recognised as the most authoritative. They are full of information, maps and illustrations so that the user can plan and complete a successful and safe trip or expedition – be it a long face climb, a walk over Lakeland fells, an alpine traverse, a Himalayan trek or a ramble in the countryside.

With a thorough introduction to assist planning, clear diagrams, maps and colour photographs to illustrate the terrain and route, and accurate and detailed text, Cicerone guides are designed for ease of use and access to the information.

If the facts on the ground change, or there is any aspect of a guide that you think we can improve, we are always delighted to hear from you.

Cicerone Press
2 Police Square Milnthorpe Cumbria LA7 7PY
Tel:01539 562 069   Fax:01539 563 417
e-mail:info@cicerone.co.uk   web:www.cicerone.co.uk

CICERONE